OUT OF OFFICE

ESCAPING THE NINE-TO-FIVE

by

JOHN GREGG

Grosvenor House
Publishing Limited

This book is published by
Grosvenor House Publishing Ltd
28-30 High Street, Guildford, Surrey, GU1 3EL.
www.grosvenorhousepublishing.co.uk

A CIP record for this book
is available from the British Library

ISBN 978-1-78148-990-1

In memory of my father, Ronald Gregg,
and my brother, Joseph William Gregg.

Contents

Acknowledgements

Many thanks are due to the staff and the facilities of the numerous cafés, bars and other public spaces where I sat to write this book. These include:

Café Piola, Seville
Café Bib-Rambla, Granada
Café Louvre, Havana
Bar Los Campeónes, Playa Ancón, Cuba
Café Efsane, Schöneberg, Berlin
Barcomi Café, Kreuzberg, Berlin
The Crazy Bar, Venice
Café Zamboni, Bologna
Café Sova, Sarajevo
L'Equitable Café, Cours Julien, Marseille
The London Bar, El Raval, Barcelona
Café Libreria, Lavapiés, Madrid
Palacio de Cristal, Madrid
Royal Festival Hall Café-Bar, London

Thanks also to the many like-minded travellers I bumped into on my out-of-office journeys, for their company and inspiring stories.

Finally, thanks are due to 'The Office' itself and its many quirks, for giving me a reason for writing this book in the first place.

Office stationery - way too *stationary.*

'For the past 33 years, I have looked in the mirror every morning and asked myself: "If today were the last day of my life, would I want to do what I am about to do today?" And whenever the answer has been 'No' for too many days in a row, I know I need to change something'.

Steve Jobs

PROLOGUE

Blue Tuesdays

I don't know about you, but when I get out of bed on a dank autumnal morning, I like to feel that the reward might offer something more than just routine. But as I woke on one particularly grey November Tuesday, a tremor of intuition around the midriff alerted me to the uninspiring prospect of the hours to come behind a desk in my place of work. That's not to say that I actively disliked my job. I didn't. And although I won't pretend to have especially enjoyed it either, the job was one worth doing and I aimed to do it well. An ever reliable employee, I was never late, rarely absent and I had, I think, a reputation for just getting on with it. On the face of it at least, I had little cause for complaint. I lived within walking distance of the shiny new office block on the campus of the south London university where I worked, my colleagues were all highly likeable and in some cases good friends, and the regular monthly salary was comfortably enough to get *by* in life, if not quite comfortably enough to get *ahead*. What's more, on a good day at the office I could even draw a fair degree of job satisfaction in the worthwhile task of providing an emotional and financial leg-up to struggling students. So if you're thinking that in most respects my set up was enviable, you would probably be right.

Yet as my innards sank at the rather blank promise of the day ahead, I knew that this was no stuck-in-a-rut, passing moment. After all, days like this had the habit of turning into weeks, months and then into years, stretching ahead, relentless in their progress. Add to the mix the ingredient of this day being a Tuesday, and there you have a recipe for some much needed change. In fact, when you stop to think about it, in the context of the five-day working week there is something particularly lacklustre about the routine of a Tuesday. With memories of weekend sporting and social highs quietly fading and that 'Friday feeling' still a distant prospect, the second day of the five-day cycle seems to me to have little to recommend it. Tuesday was also the day of our weekly departmental team meeting – or 'team huddle' as some liked to call it. So at 08.59 for the nine-on-the-dot start, I joined a crocodile of similarly lukewarm workmates, each clutching an institutional notepad and pen, plodding dutifully along the artificially lit corridor. For this gnawing malaise, who was to blame? Was it me, or was it them? It can be difficult to admit to the end of a relationship, particularly one that has endured for so long. Three decades and counting is an awfully long time, but my yearning to escape had to be more than simply an impotent dream. Walking vacantly into that room, it was high time to look in the face the reality that me and 'the office' were finally through.

Given that we all were presented with a printed agenda lacking a single item of any real significance for this Tuesday morning meeting, it seemed to me that the act of simply being in the room, our *presenteeism,* was the ultimate point of the exercise – an arbitrary act of control consistent with the recently beefed-up regime of our department. It was Woody Allen who once said that eighty-percent of success in life was just showing up, but I am not so sure. I was – at least in body – certainly there in that meeting room, yet I still felt rather less than twenty-percent short of successful for being so. Non-attendance, by the way, was not an option. So I exercised what control I could by taking great care in positioning myself several seats down on the same side of the table as our 'Team Leader and Chair' – an individual of many a professional and personal merit but who, to the collective embarrassment of the team, evidently relished the wielding of power from her place in the middle rungs of the organisation's management ladder. Incidentally, I owed this seating ingenuity to the unlikely figure of Edward Heath who, when Prime Minister in the early 1970s, positioned his nemesis – one Margaret Thatcher – at the far end of his Cabinet table, thus avoiding eye contact and helping him ignore her interventions. In our own more modest, less febrile gathering, I didn't share the Iron Lady's desire for wild-eyed interjection, but hoped that my position out of eye-line would at least also place me out of mind. It didn't feel quite right to stay altogether silent as the meeting unfurled – I couldn't have my colleagues thinking me rude. On the other hand I certainly wasn't a ranter, raver or moaner – far too much energy expended there. Neither was I a 'mood hoover', intent on spreading negativity by sucking the life out of others. So all I could really manage were routine Tuesday morning responses to agenda items about which my pulse resolutely refused to race.

In truth, among the collection of glum colleagues gathered around that highly-polished corporate work-top, few appeared to have much interest in the business of the day. And in all fairness, the items on the less-than-aspirational agenda hardly suggested that much was about to be added to the value of the work of the team. Nor even did our agenda seem to have anything in common with the broader aims of the university – in short to 'educate, motivate and inspire'. As a result, challenge was a conspicuous, unapologetic absentee. As far as meeting highlights went that day, the minute-taker may have been moved to record the outcome of a discussion on the merits of providing lockable filing cabinets in the student interview rooms – a topic that prompted a surprisingly lively discussion, with one red-faced participant all but reduced to tears by the prospect of improving information security. With that issue done, dusted and filed away until next it raised its inconsequential head, we listened intently to another team member's heartfelt 'concerns' about what he felt were unhygienic hand-drying arrangements recently installed in the staff toilets. A jolly good point well made, we all agreed, amid much earnest head-nodding, awkward throat-clearing and flicking of hair.

I hadn't yet spotted prayer beads in the room, but as the meeting wore on each agenda item seemed to provide more slapstick value than the last – a dream Ricky Gervais script to fill an entire excruciating episode of *The Office*. All a bit awkward, really. But at last the earth moved infinitesimally for me courtesy of the sole item introduced in the 'Any Other Business' (AOB) slot, heralding a new and tougher reporting system for sickness. It was decreed that henceforth, any incapacitated member of staff must report their ailment in all its phlegmy detail to a designated twenty-four hour answer machine before 8.00am on the first day of sickness. By two in the afternoon a second call was to be made, this time to a human being in the form of the line manager – in my case the happily out-of-eye-line chairperson sitting three down on my right – detailing further the progress of the condition, its prognosis and the likely earliest date of return to work. I pictured myself lying in a hospital bed in the aftermath of some unfortunate accident, with my mind not so much concerned with my injured body, but with the urgency of making the two o'clock reporting deadline. I exaggerate, of course. But for an organisation whose mission statement enshrined just about every conceivable notion of equality, personal liberty and political correctness, this petty diktat revealed much to the team about the lack of trust existing between chiefs and Indians. Properly thought through the policy most definitely was not, but implemented it would be.

I have never dealt altogether comfortably with aspects of life that involve too much in the way of rhythm and obedience – one for my epitaph, someone please. So as a relative minnow operating in the regulation-driven world of nine-to-five, for my sanity's sake I always kept in mind the glorious option of the 'trap door'. Yet while I continued to conform, the forum of the team meeting came to represent much of what I had grown averse to in 'the office': the finger-wagging of over-promoted mediocrities presiding over confused departments – part totalitarian, part nanny-state – each of them generating a level of gibberish seemingly without frontiers. Oddly though, considering how manifestly non-threatening our little gathering in that meeting room was, on this particular Tuesday I was gripped by a palpable fear. If this had been a scene in a film, for dramatic effect the screen may have turned white, with the director artfully suggesting a moment of epiphany by cutting to a vista of blue sky yielding shafts of dazzling sunlight. But this low-key, workaday meeting (or indeed any other single event in my thirty-odd years in the workplace) was not the ultimate alarm-clock-moment that changed my world forever. Yet how slow I had been in accepting that I had no real business even *being* in those meeting rooms, let alone there as a pretending participant. Nevertheless, during this latest instalment of corporate claptrap, I was dragged over a red line and would take no more, marking the day as the 'Transformational Tuesday' I had been headed towards for so long.

I removed myself – in mind if not body – to retreat momentarily into a world of private contemplation, and then paused. A member of the catering team, resplendent in her dinner-lady hair-restraining white cap and net, was pushing a trolley of hot drinks and vacuum packed snacks past the glass wall of our goldfish-bowl room. My gaze fell on a slice of Battenberg cake in its cellophane wrapper, doubtless on its way to be consumed at some-or-other organisational talk-show. For a moment I envied the freedom of this calorie-laden treat and longed to join it on its odyssey down the corridor, far away from the containment of that room. Liberated by my thoughts, if not quite yet by my actions, I was driven by a tingle of raw intuition and a tremor of change that felt – without wishing to sound at all hyperbolic – like electricity.

Calming down a little, I spent much of the remainder of the meeting recalling other white-screen moments from my long and sometimes testy relationship with the world of work. I can only just bring myself to use the 'C' word here. It never really felt like a genuine *career* to me, more that my working life had thus far consisted of a series of random vocational stumbles – mere salaried interludes, with most of the entries on my varied curriculum vitae coming about more by accident than design. However, it might also rank as a small achievement that I had managed to chalk-off thirty-plus years in worthwhile, responsible positions despite sometimes carrying with me the restless instincts of a schoolboy. I had spent a fair wodge of that time ploughing a fractious furrow as a Careers Adviser – a feat of some irony, perhaps, for someone with such modest vocational drive. Yet I had been in good company, and most of the other career-choice 'experts' I worked alongside would probably also own up to not having any real idea of what line of vocation to follow themselves. In fact, looking back, I could hardly have wished to share a chunk of my working life with a motlier, more fun-loving and career-disoriented crew. As for my latest role, I had fallen into it – as you might inadvertently into a lift shaft – by writing the job application leaning on a *Times World Atlas* balanced between my knees as an improvised table, with the dual distraction of an early episode of *Big Brother* flickering on a TV screen in the corner of the room, and my one-handed attempt to eat a micro-waved dinner. With a pen in one hand, a fork in the other and one eye on the 'House' miscreants, I scrawled hackneyed responses to a long list of routine questions, delving for answers into my dusty archive of work-based achievements and competencies.

Much earlier, my first real venture into the world of work had been as a lowly government administrator, handing out welfare payments at about the point punk rock was usurping the Bay City Rollers in my genera-tion's musical affections. The experience sticks in my mind as an early indicator of my resistance to the kind of rhythm and obedience that most office-bound jobs demand. Each day as I made my way to the office by bus I hoped, in vain, that perchance some overnight misfortune had befallen the building where I worked, rendering it unfit for the purpose of keeping me in its control for the day. A small localised earthquake would have done me just fine – although I should add that as a decent youth, I wished for such a mishap only on the proviso that the building be unoccupied at the time. Needless to say, my civil service career was hardly mete-oric, but in its modest life span I was rewarded with lifelong friendships and the raucous enjoyment of the best office parties I have ever over-indulged at. But in its early days, just as I was getting the hang of the bizarre notion of having to be somewhere I would rather not be for five of the seven days of the week, this embryonic career hit the buffers following a departmental reorgan-isation. Had I played ball, the 'reorg' would have con-signed me to a daily seven-hour stint taking social security applications from behind a spit-proof glass screen, put in place to protect me from the physical and verbal vitriol of the benefit claimants of Thatcher's Britain. Although logic told me that handing out benefits would be more rewarding than receiving them, the lure of freedom was irresistible and so I left, taking up the department's incentive-to-leave offer of cashing in the modest value of my fledgling public sector pension scheme. To give you some idea of the cash value of this rashly-done deal, with the proceeds I was just about able to purchase a beaten-up fifth-hand Datsun in bright yellow. Carrying the look of a motorised banana, the car's principal appeal was its bold go-faster stripes (0-60mph in roughly forty-five seconds, so it's safe to say they didn't work) and smoked-glass sunroof (that leaked). Tragically for both myself and the hapless vehicle, a short time later I was forced to give it up to a scrapyard following a creeping rust problem that saw bits of the bodywork fall away in a car wash. The pittance I received from the grubby deal was fully exhausted by an evening out at the Kilburn branch of *Pizza Hut* – a lamentable return you might agree for the investment of my accrued superannuation on a clapped-out Japanese car. Yet despite the disappointment of my hitherto underwhelming career and poor financial husbandry, at the time I did take some quiet satisfaction in the knowledge that I was possibly the first person ever to have eaten their pension scheme.

With a favourable tail wind, life really can be as much as you make it. Treated with care and a little imagination, its possibilities are endless. So back in the meeting room and with this in mind, I sought inspiration by at last making an entry on my redundant note pad. If I struggle out of bed on a gloomy Tuesday, I wrote, with the good fortune of an able body and mind, with my street, my city and the world all mine to enjoy and explore, only then to choose a destination as meaningless to me as this drab meeting room, then I myself am the chief architect of my disappointment. It is often said that time is our most precious resource and that procrastination is its thief. Time, indeed, belongs to all of us, and here I was being mugged of mine. But procrastination wasn't the only culprit. The real time-thief in the room was my employer, with my near-silent contribution to a fruitless team discussion the scant evidence of my timid fight. 'Okay', I was saying to my paymaster, 'you can take as much of my time as you like as long as you compensate me with enough to allow me to pay my humble way in the world'. A miserable compromise indeed! So there was really only one course to follow, and a faint-hearted acceptance of my long stint in the social jail of nine-to-five as the *continuing* reality of my life, was as impossible as it was absurd.

I wasn't at all surprised one day to come across the statistic that the average UK worker spends around 100,000 hours of their entire life at work and another 10,000 hours just getting there and back. So that's 110,000 hours. 4,583 days. Twelve-and-a-half years. Less for murder, I hear you cry! My attention was also grabbed by some eye-widening revelations on the topic of time-erosion in the workplace that I read in a copy of the magazine *Management Today* I found discarded on a train. Under an irresistible banner evidently written for me and you – *'It's Official: You are wasting your life away in pointless meetings'* – this corporate comic revealed that during a routine week an office worker can easily while-away four of their precious hours on pointless posturing in team meetings. That, by the way, is roughly the equivalent to a full screening of *Gone With The Wind,* and if you're anything like me, you probably wouldn't want to sit through that once a week either. Expanding the figures over the lifetime of an average career, this sees the typical office-based worker sitting through around 9,000 hours of needless meetings, amounting to a terrifying *year and ten days* spent doodling on scraps of paper in-between stifled yawns over vacuous agendas. As Rhett Butler from that epic movie might have said, 'frankly, dear reader, I rest my case'.

With the meeting room's thin walls closing further in, I scribbled on, sketching a hasty audit of my life. I enjoyed the benefits of good health, the warmth of a close family and a clutch of valued friends. The good fortune of long-term employment had at times given me a measure of vocational purpose, the resurrected membership of a solvent public sector pension scheme (though not for long enough yet to be counting the days towards a gilt-edged payout), a more than decent place to live, a photo-album bursting with memorable holiday moments and a healthy amount of self-esteem. In return, I had kept my side of the bargain in my long list of roles helping to improve the lot of the inner-city vulnerable and disadvantaged – a worthwhile pursuit in which I continued to believe. Yet my instinct now was to cut and run, and to leave behind the risk-averse environment of that meeting room, where even the refreshments laid out on a plate in front of the team were offered free of wheat, dairy, sugar and thus of interest, pleasure and surprise. Life is not a dress rehearsal goes the mantra – and let's face it, every so often you just have to re-invent yourself. What's more, I was a man with a plan. I had been telling them all for months. Hang on, make that years. This was a plan of long gestation, saved to a memory stick hanging from the corporate chain around my neck like a medallion for change, to be unhooked daily and tinkered with furtively on my screen between meetings, appraisals and line management one-to-ones. Saved unambiguously as my 'Post-Work Plan', the document contained the mapping of a new reality of travel and self-discovery.

I was jolted back to the dull regime of the meeting by a colleague's well-meaning offer of an organic wholegrain rice cake. Politely, I declined. I needed more to sustain me, not least the full and uncontested, sugar-encrusted custody of my life – a life newly off the market and no longer for sale. But how could I reinvent and maintain value while continuing to grow as human being, without the status and crutch of a steady job? And there, I suppose, is the rub. So if you have picked up this book in search of some self-help, self-starting quick-fix guide to career change, early retirement on a plump pension scheme or to follow a new and inspired twelve-step programme to achieving a life you can truly love – while in the process amassing a stash of cash – then carefully replace it on the shelf. If, on the other hand, you too feel disconnected – perhaps even a little lost – in the routines of your workplace and may be open to inspiration for making changes of your own, then wish me well and do read on. My simple aim is that you may enjoy following the meandering and free-spirited out-of-office exploits of an ordinary working man, who dared to take a chance and walked away.

Not that this transition to a life of spontaneity proved to be a walk in the park. After all, I had always been one of those mildly obsessive types who take comfort in laying out work clothes in the evening to wear the following morning. Nevertheless, I had grown into the belief that too much time-management (another pre-occupation of the modern workplace – I had been on all the courses and was 'role-played' out) can lead to life becoming ultra-functional, making it easy to forget that drifting around (a much underrated pleasure in my view) making mood-compatible decisions as you go is key to a happy existence. I was encouraged in this train of thought by Rosie Millard, who writing in the *Independent* argued that spontaneity – even time-*wasting* – could be important elements in a contented and free-spirited life. So, embracing that and unimpeded by work-based obligations, I planned to travel, experiencing the heady thrill of movement and new destinations as I went, while immersing myself in some of the language, passion, history – and sometimes the irresistible frippery – of the countries I crossed. Wandering both on and off well beaten tracks, I looked to bond with other adventurers and like-minded souls as I went. My movements would be liberated from constraint and conformity, would be sometimes planned and at other times spontaneous – but always intrepid and determinedly never dull.

This was my own, very personal, agenda for change I took away from that spirit-sapping meeting room, in excited thought as my pulse raced just that little bit faster than before. Yet as the day wore on, with my mind now set on a purpose and my shoulders lighter for the decision I had made, I began to consider the dull defeatism of that team meeting to have been not such a waste after all. In fact, had I been tasked with taking the meeting's minutes, I would happily have recorded as a resounding outcome, that at least one member of the team had, quite irreversibly, just reclaimed his Tuesdays.

Granada's Moorish masterpiece, the
Alhambra – a sight to make grown men weep

*Out of Office Reply...Thank you for your email. I am unable
to reply as I am currently away from my desk pursuing
other interests far away from the routines of the department.
Please do not wait for a response as this arrangement
is permanent and I will not be returning. Do remember
though, it is in your gift to consider for yourself the option
of doing the same.*

– 1 –

Aventura Andalucía

So...options. Well, I was spared prolonged agonies of
indecision by a hastily implemented, mealy-mouthed
departmental reorganisation that made the decision to
quit the arena of office politics an easy one. There was
nobody holding an arm up my back and I could have
played it safe, plodding a risk-averse path in the newly
dumbed-down department. Yet my role would be dimi-
nished, my position untenable, with not the faintest
chance of being my own man, on my own terms. While
they wanted more of me for less, I just wanted something *different*. A faint voice in my head murmured a
cautionary 'stay-put', but a far louder cry implored me
to go. Cue – for a short while – sleepless nights. But to
wither on the corporate vine was not an option and raw
intuition ensured I walked away of my own accord, to
activate my carefully-crafted plan and begin that freer
life. So once I had completed the satisfyingly cathartic

task of disposing in recycling bags the paper detritus from years of pen-pushing service, I was ready to move on, spread my wings and travel. Every middle-aged mortgaged-man's dream, maybe. Yet this was no jetting off to 'a place in the sun' moment off the back of a lucky lottery win or the proceeds of an unexpected inheritance. I had made a few sacrifices along my own slow 'Road to Damascus', putting aside what I could, not so much for the onset of a rainy day, but more the torrential downpour of my inevitable exit from the workplace. And once I had committed to investing in my future well-being by turning my post-work plan into a reality, it really wasn't so difficult. If I could do it, then just about anyone could.

I chose as a starting point to exercise my freedom the southern Spanish city of Seville, for no other reason than the soft landing its familiarity would provide for me. Besides that, I could be sure of good weather and after the drawn-out shenanigans of the office reorganisation process, I felt like a holiday. It was also a chance to renew my efforts to learn Spanish, having already made various aborted attempts at a variety of adult education venues in London. For my failure to advance much beyond the '*dos cervezas, por favor*' stage, I had often blamed the workplace and my inability to rise to any sort of meaningful challenge after a day hunched over a desk under the glare of strip lights. But those days of abdicating responsibility were over. As for Seville, personally I have always preferred its Spanish inflection to the flattened English version – surely the more exotic vowel sounds of *Seveeeyaaa* do better justice to this sensual place. As any guidebook will tell you, Seville is a place where all the stereotypes and extremes of Spain come together in a riot of noise, passion and fiestas. The adventurous aesthete Lord Byron probably would have agreed, but was still a little underwhelming in his appraisal of Seville as 'a pleasant city famous for oranges and women'. All perfectly true perhaps, although the young Byron may also have added to his list of Seville's charms the infectious spirit and click-clacking shoes of flamenco, its warren of cute white-washed alleys, its verdant sunny plazas, the brilliant year-round blue skies and punishing summer sun, its abundant tapas taken over extravagantly long lunches on sweltering terraces, lazy *siestas* followed by late, late nights and – love it or loathe it – the blood and drama of the *corrida* – the bullfight. Phew! Extraordinarily justified in the name of art, this latter aspect of Seville's fiery spirit was not for me. Yet a heart of the hardest stone could not resist the charms of this sultry city, and mine was wide open to seduction.

So high were my spirits as the adventure began I even enjoyed the cramped budget airline flight I took due south towards the sunshine. As the plane neared landing I peered at the ground from my window seat at the sun-dried Seville *tierra,* my nose pressed up against the plexi-glass like a kid outside a sweet shop. Even though in the heat-haze the runway tarmac looked like it had turned to treacle, the plane hit the ground with a solid enough bump, just ahead of schedule heralding the airline's signature on-time trumpet fanfare, which in my over-excited imagination seemed embellished with a flamenco refrain. I stepped out of the plane to be met by the hot draught of the early evening air, feeling like I had opened an oven door to check on a baking cake.

Forget the bullfighting, this was one aspect of Seville most definitely for me. Nevertheless, with the temperature hovering around gas mark seven, I was glad of the air-conditioning on the airport bus which took me to the city centre stop on Avenida de Carlos V. Aware that in the fierce heat my pace was already slowing from its relentless London rush, I ambled through Los Jardines de Murillo to the heart of tourist Seville to find an old favourite of mine and a decidedly acquired taste – the queen of naff accommodation, the Pensión Bienvenido. At check-in, I was met by the on-duty octogenarian *señor,* an old *amigo* of mine who had helped me with bits and pieces of Spanish on previous visits, including on one occasion the simple word for towel – *toalla* – which he enlivened with a throaty Andalucian rasp betraying his habit of twenty-a-day. His distinct *Sevillano* pronunciation, characteristic of a city where the locals omit the ends of words for fun and speak impossibly quickly, reminded me that learning Spanish in Seville was something like choosing Newcastle as a destination for learning English. A later attempt to mimic his pronunciation of the word when I asked for a towel in a *hostal* in Madrid – where people often look down their noses at the impurity of Andalucian Spanish – was met with a *Castellano* snort. Incidentally, the towel I was issued with at the Bienvenido was less colourful than my friend's accentuation, and did not benefit much either from having the texture of a well-used brillo pad. The old *señor* smiled sympathetically as I attempted some small talk in his language about the oppressive heat and declining standards of hotel towelling, but gave not the slightest indication that he had the faintest idea what I was attempting to bang on about. But I really didn't mind. Fluency in Spanish could wait. Upbeat and purposeful, I had arrived.

I had one night only to enjoy the Bienvenido's recent modest investment in air- conditioning, in the form of a creaking free-standing fan that circulated the hot air rather than noticeably cooling it. There was no real point in unpacking (this became a regular feature of my 'out-of office' life), as the following day I was due to move in with my host family, found for me by the language school I was enrolled at to provide me with, as they marketed it, 'a fully-immersed Spanish experience'. Despite the clawing heat, the sparse facilities and general air of austerity, I was happy as a sand boy in that tiny room. I looked around the hot cramped space I occupied and mused at the multitude of health and safety issues it might generate for discussion at a departmental team meeting. I imagined a flippant agenda: the quality of air conditioning, suspect linen (the cigarette burn in the bed cover was a particularly nice touch), hazardous plug sockets hanging out of leaning walls, the likelihood of picking up an itchy ailment from some mattress infestation or other (now that one will get the team going), and the impossibility of escape in the event of fire aside from the option of plunging two floors from my window onto the cobbled surface of Calle Archeros below. But risk aversion had been left behind in the workplace, and I sat on the edge of my spring-less bed bent double in laughter for a full unabated minute, thinking of my newly stripped down circumstances and the hilarious irony of the establishment's moniker, Bienvenido – welcome!

It was after nine and already dark when I left the pensión to take a walk through the maze of alleyways and tiny streets of Seville's atmospheric Barrio Santa Cruz, past groups of chattering locals and tourists seated at tables scattered randomly on the terraces of the area's countless tapas bars and *bodegas*. This former Jewish quarter is the embodiment of picture-postcard Seville, each street and back-alley lined with tall terraced houses, whitewashed to protect their occupants from the ferocity of the summer sun. Trust me on this one, Seville in summer is a seriously hot place to be – an August choice meant only for mad dogs and absconding Englishmen. Thoroughly enjoying my new role of absconder, I walked through streets narrow enough to reach out and touch both sides simultaneously, before taking a seat at a rickety table on a sloping section of pavement outside Bar Teresa, a few sweltering steps away from the magnificent bulk of Seville's cathedral. Like everyone else around me, I ordered tapas and a tall jug of fruity *tinto de verano*. When it finally arrived, in the sultry heat and in my high mood of celebration, I could hardly decide whether to drink the icy nectar or pour it over my head. Having so recently exchanged my modest salary for no salary at all, the thirst was quenched. Rather too quickly, I became overwhelmed by the concoction's mellowing effect and the truly sensational, uplifting feeling of having achieved something I had been daydreaming about for years. Finally, I was truly free.

Everybody it seems these days, from former Prime Ministers to reality TV 'personalities' and celebrity sports stars, love to talk up with a cringing intensity, their own very personal *Journey* – aka the selected events of their life. If I may follow suit for a moment without risk of embarrassment, I regarded my current journey as one made up of two distinct legs – the emotional and the physical. Freed emotionally from the social conditioning that had kept me grounded in the routine of nine-to-five for so long, I had at last set-out on my physical journey. That, at least, is how I was content to see it. In fact, sitting in the evening warmth of a beautiful Spanish city represented for me nothing less than a conquered mini-Everest, which I had been stood at the foothills of for way too long. The ascent completed and summit reached, I had planted my triumphant flag – or at least it felt something like that. Perhaps the heady mix of heat, fruity wine and the serenity of a freed spirit carried me away a little on that first night in Seville. Whatever it was had taken a soporific toll and I was back in the stuffy charm of my Bienvenido room within an hour, wondering how on earth I would sleep through the heat. The low hum of high spirited *Sevillanos* revelling in the sultry streets wafted in through my partially opened window. Despite the stifling temperature, the buzz of a hungry mosquito and relentless creak of the ineffectual fan, the night passed wholly undisturbed. In fact, I neither saw nor heard another guest, another curious feature of my many stays at the Bienvenido. On that first night in Seville, that first night of my new-found freedom, I slept for England.

Before leaving London, I had tasked the Don Quijote language school with finding me a room with a host family in the Barrio Santa Cruz, so my homestay in the quaint cobbled Calle Vidrio was about spot on. Staying with a family was to be part of my immersion in all things Spanish, although as it turned out my 'family' consisted of a single woman who was rarely at home, with the occasional appearance of Paco, her fully grown son and his constant canine companion called China. Despite the lack of numbers, Ana's exuberant greeting on her doorstep approximated that of an entire family, and I was overwhelmed by her hugs, kisses and *encantadas,* feeling as if I had been thrown into an emotive scene from *Long Lost Family.* The sixty-something *Sevillana* laughed (understandably), first at my nervous Spanish and then (less charitably) at my gift to her of a souvenir tea-towel of London scenes I had picked up in haste as I passed through Gatwick. She scanned the images of Tower Bridge, Buckingham Palace, a Beefeater and a couple of token ravens before placing the evidently unwanted item well to the bottom of her kitchen drawer. I doubt it has seen the light of day since. Speaking of Spanish kitchens, according to the marketing blurb of the school, Spanish cuisine was to play as big a part of my immersion experience as Spanish grammar, so Ana duly quizzed me about my dietary preferences. Given her complete lack of English and my eminently improvable Spanish, this was not straightforward. During the guided tour of Ana's flat I gathered from the near-empty fridge and kitchen cupboards that she catered frugally. This suited me fine as I planned to do a bit of solo al-fresco dining on the outdoor terraces of bars, where I hoped to engage in spontaneous conversation with any number of *camareros* as keen as I was to advance my level of Spanish. Despite the lack of ingredients on show, Ana insisted on drawing up a plan of *menus del dia,* but something told me that my request for a choice based around the Mediterranean simplicities of bread, cheese, fruit and the odd salty helping of *mariscos* had failed to get through. So it proved to be. Anyway, once I was unpacked I spent the rest of the day wandering around the picturesque lanes of Santa Cruz, idling my time among the tourist tack of souvenir shops, stopping occasionally to admire the extravagant floral arrangement of a pretty patio or a tantalising cathedral glimpse. Yet as the day wore on I felt a creeping disquiet at the prospect of long air-conditioned hours in the classroom. Mood-compatibility appeared already to be under threat.

Early the following morning I arrived at the Don Quijote school, located favourably in a wide and sunny street adjacent to the Plaza de Toros de la Maestranza – Seville's famous eighteenth-century bullring and one of Spain's best known 'sporting' arenas. Taking the compulsory level test, I was comfortable enough with the first twenty of its forty questions but stumbled through the ordeal of the oral section, conducted informally standing up in an airless corridor. Once confirmation came through from my test results that indeed I was not fluent in Spanish (but that hope sprang eternal), I joined a brisk walking tour of the immediate area along with twenty-five other inductees. Conducted by the energetic Marga, the highlight of the tour was a steep climb to the summit of the rotund thirteenth-century Moorish Torre del Oro (Gold Tower), one of Seville's mustdo tourist attractions. A twelve-sided construction (a dodecagon no less, we were briefed by a know-all German member of the party), the Torre del Oro was built to order by the Almohad Governor of Seville as part of the city's walled defence of the Moorish royal palace, the Alcazar, and later put to use as a medieval prison following Spain's Christian comeback in

1492 – the *Reconquista* – an event that saw the nation reclaim its sovereignty from the Muslim occupiers. During our breakneck tour, Marga made no noticeable effort to slow her Andalucian commentary to a pace that could be understood. Racing through a flashcard of what I could only guess must be interesting histories and anecdotes about the buildings we passed, she barely drew breath. '*Muy interesante*' and '*que bonito*', we all concurred as we were rushed past one arresting sight or stunning monument after another, with little idea of their identity or the content of Marga's commentary. In the end I stopped trying to catch what she was saying and focused instead on the absolute clarity of what I could see. This was, I guessed, the total immersion in all things Spanish I was promised.

The tour of the school building was more straightforward. With its badly lit corridors, echoing staircases and hum of student activity, the institution reminded me of a place I had recently left. In fact, once I entered the first classroom my gut feeling – an involuntary tremor evidently a first cousin of the 'fight-or-flight' response – implored me to switch from regular classes to one-to-one tuition. When faced with the reality of hours of daily confinement sat in a hard chair in front of a whiteboard, this aspect of the plan I had hatched so carefully back in London seemed no longer for me, so I tested the school's flexibility by requesting they draw up a new timetable to consist of a class of one hour at ten each morning over a period of five weeks. Surely even I could deal with the level of obedience that would entail! Once the changes were ironed-out to everyone's satisfaction, I was mightily relieved that the best part of each day would now belong to me, leaving me free to explore and immerse in Seville's delights, wholly at my leisure.

Though friendly and charismatic, my teacher for those one hour sessions, Rosa, lacked most of the other key attributes a tutor of a foreign language ought to possess. Sound grammatical knowledge, the ability to plan a lesson and above all the exercise of patience had all been drummed into me during my own training to become an English teacher on an arduous course I had taken in Barcelona several years before – a course, by the way, that I was motivated to complete on the basis that the qualification would provide me with a lifelong passport to working in the sun. How I then ended up working in a grimy suburb of south London is still beyond me. Anyway, I knew a thing or two about the lot of a language teacher, so in fairness to Rosa I too wouldn't much relish being stuck for an hour in the same room with a student as easily distractible as me. Still, her lack of patience and focus was startling, and during the two weeks in Rosa's charge, I hardly learned a thing about her mother tongue. In fact, the only memorable moment from our short time together was her unnervingly brutal slaying of a bloated cockroach that met its end under her weighty flip-flopped foot as it scuttled grotesquely across the wooden floor from its home beneath a skirting board. I can't tell you how grateful I felt to the unfortunate insect for its timely intervention that brought to a crunchy end a laboured, space-padding exercise presented by Rosa to practise the maddeningly multifarious uses of Spanish prepositions.

Feeling a tad sluggish from the stupefying hours in the rather dull company of my Spanish text books and a few too many lazy, carb-laden lunches, I set about a fitness regime by joining the Cuesta Sport gym. I joined as a student – a perk I hadn't enjoyed for some time – and midway through my first pink-cheeked work-out bumped into the mop-wielding Marie, the gym's cleaner who also doubled up as a fitness instructor. An exuberant native of Buenos Aires with the gift of cheering up all those in her company with a permanent toothy grin, the versatile Marie became both my first pal in Seville and first ever partner in *intercambio* – a method of language learning so effective that if it were more widely practised it might well render just about every teacher of a foreign language redundant. For the uninitiated, *intercambio* involves meeting up with a native speaker of the language you are learning and chatting with them over a coffee or beer for an entertaining hour or so in their language, followed by the same in yours. *Intercambio* is completely free (not counting the bar tab), guarantees you a social life in a foreign country and provides precious moments of belly-aching laughter. The method is effective for the simple reason that it involves actually *speaking* to a real person, rather than sitting in a classroom filling in blank spaces on photocopied exercise sheets. However, if after reading this you are of a mind to try out *intercambio* yourself, please do tread carefully. For all your effort and enterprise you could well end up with more than a widened foreign vocabulary. As a subscriber to the lively online learning tool, *NotesinSpanish,* I was engrossed by the linguistic-and-love-story-combined of its two co-founders, an Englishman called Ben and his Spanish partner Marina. Having met in a Madrid bar for a bit of innocent *intercambio* over a glass of the local Mahou beer and a plate of tapas, a blink-of-an-eye later the industrious duo found themselves, as well as being near-fluent in their respective languages, stood gazing at each other at the altar. As far as I know Ben and Marina continue to live happily and bilingually in a groovy apartment in the centre of Madrid, which is no doubt an appealing way to live. Yet when I heard that their *intercambio* sessions had progressed well beyond the mere rudiments of language, I couldn't be certain whether the matrimonial outcome was a huge reward for their linguistic endeavour, or an absurdly heavy price to pay.

I abandoned my workout, and Marie her dripping mop, for an impromptu *intercambio* session on the building's scorching outside terrace. Avoiding the banalities of our favourite food and music (but steering well clear of the topic of marriage), bizarrely we opted for the more random, highly challenging theme of household cleaning implements. In an engaging anecdote, Marie told me in slow and deliberate Spanish for my benefit that sounded like a 45rpm vinyl record being played at 33rpm, a little of the history of her favoured instrument of cleanliness – the humble mop. Spain of course boasts an enviable list of poets, writers, painters and explorers, but in fairness is a little low on A-list inventors. However, as Marie enlightened me, one inventive Spaniard who undeniably has made a shining mark on the world is Emilio Bellvis Montesano. Born in Zaragoza in 1914, Emilio's considerable claim to fame is as the undisputed 'Father of the Mop'. Fine-tuning a technique of floor cleaning already squelching its way across the linoleum floors of suburban America, the *Mopfather's* life-changing Eureka moment came with the realisation that the future of kitchen floor hygiene lay in the ease of squeezing a mop head through a slatted funnel built into the side of a bucket. If you have ever spent an extended period of time in Spain, or have even just popped over there for a weekend of sunshine and R&R, you might have noticed that floor mopping is a national sport. In flat-shares, hotels and pensiónes wherever I have stayed in Spain, I have never once seen a Spaniard pass up the opportunity of a good old run around the floor space with a soapy mop head.

Knowing a little more of the country in which I was immersed – not unlike, dare I say, a mop in a bucket – my aversion to the containment of the classroom led me in search of more Spanish speakers willing to trade their rapid-fire southern adaptation of the pure *Castellano* for my English. Hopeful that as a native speaker of the world's foremost language I would be in high demand, I placed an online advert for *intercambio* buddies which yielded around a dozen responses from willing *Sevillanos*. After a careful selection process steering well clear of marital risks or the deranged, I came up with a shortlist of names that included Jesús, Pilar, Magdalena, Silvina, two Josés and a Manuel Jesús Martínez Romero, who caught my attention as I searched through my inbox for having the most Spanish-sounding name that I had possibly ever come across. Within a few days of arriving in Seville, *intercambio* became my favoured, unscripted, self-generated mode of learning – a formula entirely compatible with my general holiday mood and absolute lack of interest in the constraints of a college timetable. My theory went like this – that no more on the receiving end of dull grammatical exercises and prescriptive lesson plans,

I would learn of my own accord on sunny terraces with real and exciting *Sevillanos,* who I hoped would become friends as well as language mentors.

Back in the immersion of my host family, meal times were challenging affairs for all concerned. Ana tried out a selection of her recipes on me, none of which included any of the ingredients I had suggested might work when I first arrived. Instead she encouraged me to no avail with a series of seaweed-based preparations, each of them doubtless packed with any number of vitamins and other benefits to my health and well-being, but also terminally flawed by being wholly inedible. On one fraught Friday evening, devastated by my lukewarm response to yet another shrek-coloured creation, Ana gave up the culinary ghost and sent me out to the street to fill up on anything palatable I could find. By the way, I have nothing at all against Spanish food – very far from it. Sit me at a table in any bar or restaurant in any Spanish town or city outside of Ana's serving range, holding a cold *cerveza* as I try and translate a tapas menu, and you will find a very contented man. Nevertheless, despite the struggles at meal times (including often waiting until as late as 11.00pm for it to be served, as is the custom in Seville), within a few days Ana and I were more or less good friends – or at least I hoped we were.

My working life has by no means been entirely wasted, and chief among the attributes I have picked up in the workplace is the ability to empathise with virtual strangers. As I got to know Ana better, I sensed in her a craving for a different quality of life to the one she led, totally reliant as it was on the income she pulled in from faddy-eating foreign students. Her son, Paco, was naturally the centre of her world, and his absence left a void that surely wasn't filled by itinerant Spanish learners. On one particularly sultry *Sevillan* afternoon, I returned unexpectedly to Ana's flat to find her in tears (not, I hasten to add, over the quality of the daytime Spanish TV on in the background, the awfulness of which has to be seen to be believed), but worse still hunched over an ironing-board. In the semi-darkness of her shuttered front room, which at the time was running a temperature in excess of forty degrees celsius, Ana had taken on the herculean task of ironing out the creases of a small mountain of towels and bed sheets – an exhausting effort that to me seemed hardly worth it. With streams of sweat and inconsolable tears pouring down her burning cheeks in a single salty stream, Ana cut a sorry figure, a woman utterly worn out by the sheer drudgery of it all. I persuaded her to put down the hot iron and pull up a chair so we could set about finding a solution, which we attempted through our unique, surprisingly effective, interpretation of that popular English/Spanish hybrid language, *Spanglish*. The result was her disclosure that all she really wanted in life was to retreat somewhere far away from the city, where she could escape her responsibilities as cook, housemaid and domestic goddess-come-dogsbody. Given half a chance, this overworked *mujer* would be a certain absconder too.

But just as I thought we had bonded as friends for life (or at least for the month I would be living with her), Ana took me by surprise one sticky evening with an outburst of unrestrained anger after catching me in the act of taking my *second* (admittedly uneconomic) shower of the day. Over what seemed to me a trifle,

Ana completely lost it, banging on the *baño* door and screaming Hispanic grievances as I stood under a weak trickle of tepid water. To give you an idea of just how much I needed that second shower, at the time the street temperature was so fierce you could have fried a full English breakfast on the pavement outside Ana's home – a home I was paying a decent amount of money to be immersed in. After our low-level *Watergate*, the whole 'host family' set-up suddenly felt quite mercenary, which of course is exactly what it was. Why else would Ana put up with catering for clammy foreign strangers in her home for weeks on end if it wasn't for the incentive of their moolah? As for me, I was no more than another sweaty punter in desperate need of a leg-up with my Spanish, not to mention a shower when I felt I needed one. An innocuous, hand-baggy kind of row ensued, and both of us were taken aback at how much more fluent and indeed forceful my grasp of Ana's language became when I had things I *really* needed to say. The fraught little role-play beat by a country mile anything I could have found in a classroom, and Ana never queried my personal hygiene habits again. As my hostess scuttled away from the scene of the row to live up to the national stereotype and take it all out on her kitchen floor with a mop and bucket, I thought how much better a gift to Ana than that discarded London tea-towel it would be to send her away for therapy and deep relaxation at some far flung mountain retreat. After playing chief cook and bottle washer to me for more than a fortnight, she looked like she needed it.

Slowed down by the heat and welcome lack of deadlines, I soon fell into the sort of unhurried routine for which I had long yearned. I worked breakfast off with a gym session of variable intensity (I had no problem with Ana's breakfasts – they were always sugary affairs that fell out of packets with not a trace of seaweed), and rewarded myself for the exertions with a lazy lunch sometimes accompanied by an *intercambio,* which in turn might lead to the indulgence of that most Spanish of pleasures – the *siesta.* It is of course a myth that *all* Spanish people drop what they are doing, kick off their shoes and take a nap in the middle of the day. For one thing the demands of the modern workplace simply don't allow for it. But where it can, the tradition endures. The word *siesta* derives from the Latin *hora sexta* – in this context meaning midday, literally the sixth hour from dawn. The Spanish custom of the midday nap dates back to a time when agricultural workers were allowed respite from the heat of the day to rest a while, enabling them to resume work refreshed and productive until late in the evening. Although the *siesta* is a Spanish tradition in gradual decline due to the economic pressures of the nation's ongoing financial crisis (many people feel that they simply cannot afford to sleep during the day), here in the hot south the afternoon nap is still commonplace. There are two reasons for this and Seville illustrates both of them perfectly. Shops and businesses in the city, particularly the smaller ones, tend to close (often frustratingly!) between 2.00pm and 5.00pm each day creating a moribund period when the streets are practically deserted. This allows time for a long, slow and often heavy lunch, requiring some sleeping off before resuming work. The second reason for the continuing popularity of the southern *siesta* is that many *Sevillanos* like to stay up and play late. At midnight on any day of the week during the warmer months (and in Seville that accounts for much of the year), it is quite usual for the city's streets to be packed with people, including small children and the elderly. So in Seville and other parts of Andalucia, the concept of 'getting an early night' barely exists, thanks in part to the tradition of the *siesta*. Mind you, even if opportunities for daytime napping disappear for good, I still can't imagine the good people of Seville – a city where summer night-time temperatures of thirty-five degrees are quite common – tucking themselves up in bed at ten-thirty with a good book and a mug of horlicks.

One Spanish institution that takes no part in the sleepy traditions of the *siesta* is the nation's ubiquitous, always open for business department store *El Corte Inglés* (The English Cut). This *John Lewis* in the sun is a Spanish retail institution, founded in 1934 by a group of enterprising Madrid tailors who had the commercial sense to name their brand 'The English Cut' to piggyback the reputation of British tailoring – although these days of course, as Spain's last remaining department store chain, *El Corte Inglés* sells rather more than just suits. To escape the ravages of Seville's afternoon heat, I often retreated to the basement of the store's branch on Plaza de la Magdalena to walk up and down its expensively stocked, air-conditioned aisles, wondering for instance why anyone in this city of a thousand tempting *pastelerías* might wish to spend their hard-earned euros on packets of imported, tartan-emblazoned Walker's shortbread fingers. Speaking of imports, on one of my trawls of the *El Corte Inglés* shelves I came across a display of that staple of the British breakfast table, orange marmalade. Randomly, I picked up a jar bearing the brand name *Mackays* and read that the contents included, '*the highest quality bitter Seville oranges*' – a fruit whose thick dimpled skin makes it ideal for marmalade. So in an example of global consumerism gone completely bonkers, the oranges contained in the jar I held had been plucked from a Seville tree – quite possibly one of those flourishing outside in the small square in front of this very *El Corte Inglés* store – to then be sent on a flight northwards away from the sun to some bleak factory in rainy Dundee. On arrival in the eastern central lowlands, the oranges had been shredded and pulverised into a tangy pulp, before then being squeezed into the glass jar for export to – among many other marmalade-loving destinations – Seville. So returning home after an ozone-busting round-trip of almost 4,000 miles as a rather bitter, love-it-or-loathe-it preserve, the well-travelled oranges met their fate on knives by being scraped across the crunchy *tostada* of *Sevillano* breakfasts, more than likely enjoyed on café terraces surrounded by the orange trees whence they originally fell. As for marmalade, personally I am not a big fan. Those dimpled, thick-peeled Seville oranges look so much more appealing left hanging from a sunlit tree.

Meanwhile, responses to my online *intercambio* advert continued apace, although barely twenty-percent of responses resulted in an actual meeting. A number of times I stood on street corners or sat on café terraces (no great hardship in Seville, I know) waiting in vain for faceless names to materialise to transform me into a fluent speaker of their colourful language. Great fun as it invariably was, *intercambio* in Seville was also the epitome of Iberian insouciance, a learning experience that at times felt very much a case of hit, miss and *mañana*. So if you're reading this Antonio and Esther, Javier, Raúl and Raquel – where were you when I needed you? However, I was impressed by one response from a lively-sounding *chico* named Pablo, who describing himself as being 'Anglo-Saxon' in his habits, promised to arrive for our *intercambio* session on time on the fascinating basis of wanting 'to do things the English way'. I couldn't be certain, but this most un-Spanish-sounding Spaniard may even have owned a wristwatch. As was the custom, we agreed a meeting place, in this case outside the Puerta de Jerez metro station at eight o'clock one Monday evening. Like the good Englishman I was attempting to be, I arrived at five minutes to, and pretending to myself that I was waiting for a bus hung around for a good twenty minutes more. But wouldn't you know it, Pablo – that self-appointed Anglo-Saxon *Sevillano* of religious time-keeping – was a no-show. Whereas this level of informality, even unreliability, may have irritated me back in Blighty, here in the unhurried ambience of southern Spain I rather enjoyed its novelty. So taken did Pablo seem to be with doing things 'the English way' – apart from falling at the very first hurdle by not showing up for his free lesson in the English language – I wondered how he might fare with the increasing British workplace obsession with Key Performance Indicators and the like. Given the early signs, if I had ever got to meet Pablo I might just have given him some friendly advice to stay put in the sun.

I quickly grew fond of the reliable band of *Sevillanos* who did bother to turn up now and again – a select group of *amigos* and mentors who, during many warm afternoons and sticky evenings, helped inch forward my level of Spanish. All for different reasons, Jesús, Silvina, Pilar and José Miguel were those I most relished language sharing with. Jesús Muñoz Fernández, a studious, intelligent and ultra-reliable *Sevillano* brought up in the vibrant northern barrio of La Macarena, carried with him into adulthood a love of the English language and a fascination for the comic detective, Tintin. After just a few meetings, Jesús became a good and lasting friend. To begin with at least, our language levels were roughly equally matched, and we sat many times on sunny terraces talking in occasionally fatuous, often faltering – but slowly improving – tones about the big topics of the Andalucian weather, sport, our families or any old nonsense we could think of. At our most ambitious – this would usually be with loosened tongues after a drink or two – we might even have a stab at some aspect of the rich and sunny history of Seville, or the inexhaustible topic of life and love in the London metropolis. Jesús invited me into his home to spend time with his partner, Carmen, to swim in his communal pool, to eat his delicious *salmorejo* and *tortilla* and to drink his *sangria*. I was immersed briefly in the life of his family and taken out to eat with them on warm terraces, where during one particularly lengthy lunch I spent an enjoyable half-hour chatting to Jesus's Catalan brother-in-law, Oriel, who regaled me with stories of his Barcelona youth, his devotion to the cause of Catalan independence and of his current free-spirited adventures working as a professional globe-trotting clown. My fleeting membership of Jesús's family was the dream *intercambio* ticket – a rich experience bolstered by friendship, wonderful indigenous food and plentiful booze. And for all their generosity, for restraining their laughter at my Spanish howlers, and for treating me as one of their own, I hope one day I can find a way to repay those open-armed, open-minded, naturally hospitable people.

Another regular *intercambio* pal in Seville was the larger than life José Miguel – a man far less interested in the mutual benefits of language exchange than having a new beer buddy and someone on who he could offload his angst about twenty-first century Spain. José Miguel had contacted me through an online ad I had placed before I left London, and often brightened dreary office days with the bizarre content of his emails. Using impossible grammar structures and words made up of fragments of both English and Spanish to form an entertaining variant of *Spanglish* – a lingo at which we both excelled – I made neither head nor tail of much of what José Miguel wrote. My replies to him in a tortured Spanish doubtless had a similar effect. When I could understand anything through the grammatical catastrophes, his unique take on the English language was peppered with youthful vernacular like *cool, bruv'* and *dude,* words I guessed he had picked up from American TV. Once I was resident in José Miguel's home city, we set up a blind *intercambio* date and met in searing heat outside a crowded *cervecería* on the shadeless Calle Fernando. Looking around for the funky young thing I was expecting to see bounding towards me, I was approached instead by a portly sixty-year old dressed in ill-fitting baggy shorts, a New York Yankees baseball cap and a garish t-shirt polka-dotted with multi-coloured stains of indeterminate origin. All but knocking me over with his robustly tactile greeting,

I decided immediately that I was going to like José Miguel. He took one look at me and played his *guiri* card – a playfully derogatory term that he evidently kept up his sleeve for such occasions, and one used generally by the Spanish to describe a foreigner with the good sense to want to spend time working or studying in their wonderfully clement country. He gently mocked my touristy garb of printed t-shirt (washed, unstained), denim shorts, baseball boots and wrap around (categorically not designer) shades. José Miguel assumed full control of the evening, frog-marching me along the tram lines of Avenida de la Constitución to Calle de José de Velilla, where I was deposited (quite willingly) at the bar of the Bodega Los Cerillo. It was here in this rowdy room of nonsense that I was introduced to the local practice of *camareros* chalking a running total of drinks consumed onto the wooden surface of the bar at the exact point you are standing – you then pay as you leave. Based on informality and centuries of tradition, I came across this rather charming system of payment at several other bars in and around Seville, and often wondered how such a system of trust involving the consumption of alcohol might work in Britain. I was thinking of, let's say, Nottingham, Manchester or Newcastle on a Friday night.

In our handful of evenings together José Miguel never quite got the hang of *intercambio*. He just wasn't the sharing type. I did, however, learn a thing or two about where he stood on the Franco era. Evidently a devotee of the paunchy *El Generalissimo,* and a man unburdened by the merest shred of self-doubt, José Miguel was effusive in his view that divine providence had sent Franco to rescue Spain from the lily-livered, left-leaning Republic of the early 1930s. Bristling with an alarming pride that Franco's forces led the victory march on Madrid from his home city of Seville, José Miguel held forth on his topic long and loud enough to be heard on all sides of the bar, railing against what he saw as the ineptitude of the diminutive dictator's successors. In a bid to keep me on-side, he threw in the occasional English invective that he thought he understood the appropriate use of, jabbing his right hand in my direction like a post-match José Mourinho ranting against a referee, his eyes misty behind rose-tinted spectacles as he recalled his youth of political commitment and relative economic certainty. Looking back on his younger days in Seville as something of a 'Golden Age' both for himself and his city, he had evidently been a much happier *Sevillano* back in the day when it was Franco's Civil Guard parading the streets in their shiny hats, rather than today's homogenous groups of backpack-wearing *guiris*.

Although Seville and the rest of Spain endured an unsplendid isolation from most of the outside world during the dictatorship years of 1939 to 1975, José Miguel left me in no doubt that if he could, he would have Franco disinterred and reinstated to power in a heartbeat. This fervent, unreconstructed Andalucian Falangist wasn't in the least bit interested in my attempt to argue the Republican case through my patchy knowledge of George Orwell's anti-fascist contribution in Catalonia, dismissing the writer's activities with an Andalucian snort of derision and shrug of indifference. Despite his views, José Miguel was generally great fun to be with, although my unlikely new friend had not of course been around himself to see Seville's bloody and short-lived resistance to Franco. On 18th July 1936, a Nationalist military uprising of 4,000 troops led by General Queipo de Llano succeeded in Córdoba, Granada, Cádiz and then here in Seville. But the city did not go down without a fight, and once the Nationalist coup was underway, Seville's trade unions called a general strike. Workers built barricades in solidly working class districts of the city such as La Macarena and across the wide expanse of the River Guadalquivir in Triana, but achieved little aside from temporarily stalling the Nationalist advance. This resistance ensured a violent backlash, and once the coup had succeeded and insurgent forces occupied the entire city (bolstered by reinforcements flown in from Morocco in German planes), all those of a Republican or leftist persuasion were rounded up, imprisoned and in most cases assassinated without ceremony. Galvanised by their success in the feisty south, in August 1936 Franco's troops left Seville to begin their long slow march on Madrid. I have no idea how José Miguel might feel now about Seville's bloodiest hour had he endured it himself, but this little back street *bodega* was his home turf and centre stage. I disagreed with much of what he had to say, particularly some fairly dismal comments he made about minority groups who I had seen for myself currently down on their luck around and about the city's streets. Never mind, as even with his tendency to rant rather than chat, I found it impossible to dislike José Miguel. As crude and reactionary as much of what he had to say was, at least he attempted (and in a second language to boot – third if you count his impressive command of *Spanglish*), to present his arguments unambiguously and without gibberish. There's a lesson there, perhaps, for the corporate meeting room. I also suspected as I looked around at the other punters of a certain age in that crowded bar, that José Miguel was among friends, most of whom probably felt the same way as him about life in the modern, *guiri*-packed city of Seville, reinvented for the twenty-first century as a haven of the office escapee.

The day after that first evening of entertaining verbosity I spent with José Miguel (it wouldn't be the last), in a vain effort to escape the blast furnace of *Sevillan* heat I took a day trip by train to Cádiz, the ancient Atlantic coastal city that lays a credible claim to being Europe's oldest. Once described by Hispanophile Laurie Lee as a city 'sparkling with African light', Cádiz was a place I had long wanted to visit, partly I think because the city had once, albeit briefly, been Spain's capital after the nation's very first constitution was signed there in 1812. I was also attracted to Cádiz by its enviable topography on a peninsular jutting out into a glistening bay, and so almost entirely surrounded by water. Full of good intentions as the day began, I crammed into my small rucksack various materials associated with the learning of the lingo, and during the journey south from Seville I did make a half-hearted attempt at completing an exercise on the perplexing and multifarious uses of subjunctive verb forms. Needless to say, with the impressive distraction from the train window of the Cádiz Sierra presenting a major barrier to learning, the grammatical puzzle remained unsolved. In place of serious study, my solitary away-day in Cádiz allowed for plenty of soul searching, which revealed my pretence at having made the break from paid employment to pursue a serious educational challenge.

After years of office confinement, at long last I had the space, time and momentum to really lick the Spanish, but as I was now operating well outside the comfort zone of paid holidays and annual increments (well-earned or otherwise), I experienced disconcerting moments of anxiety at my hitherto modest progress. After quitting work, I still needed clear objectives and achieving fluency in Spanish was one of them. However, simply *being* in Spain revelling in the sultry ambience of cities like Seville and Cádiz, while relying for my language learning on a lazy process of osmosis, was evidently not enough. I had become, with little effort, far more a contented tourist than a committed student, not to mention a keen exponent of the hugely under-rated pursuit of time *wasting* – but wasted, I think, with a purpose.

Anyway, deciding on a foot-off-the-gas approach seemed an easy act of compromise to make as I wandered lazily around Cádiz, first through the narrow atmospheric lanes of the old town, and then along its sunlit promenade. Suspended above the golden sands of the Caleta beach, what a wonderful vantage point this was to take in the dazzling Costa de la Luz, and for peering southeast along the coastline towards the Strait of Gibraltar, which separates the Spanish mainland and the northern tip of the African continent by a tantalisingly short fourteen kilometres of ocean. Eventually I came to rest in the serenity of the city's cathedral square, where I succumbed to the soporific heat of the Andalucian high-noon, chatting idly about the joys of spontaneous travel to my transient new friends, Peter and Dagmar, a colourfully hair-braided, adventurous young couple from Dortmund. I paused between sips from my *jarra* of cold beer, gazed up at the brilliant blue sky and wondered why on earth I hadn't thought of spending my weekday afternoons like this before.

Back in the high-summer inferno of Seville, I resumed my efforts in Spanish at the Don Quijote school with a series of one-hour lessons with my new teacher, Xavi. Hoping I might fare a little better with Rosa's replacement, the early signs were unpromising. At our first meeting Xavi wore the downcast look of a man who wished desperately he could be somewhere else. I knew well the territory he inhabited, and all became clear when he told me that far from being a rabidly motivated language teacher (just as if), he was in reality a budding anthropologist dreaming of a lectureship at the University of Seville. Having no more desire to be in that stuffy little classroom than I had, Xavi admitted that teaching his mother tongue was no more than a fill-in while he waited for his life to start for real – a revelation that explained much about his languid classroom style. Not the most inspirational of tutors perhaps, but unlike his predecessor Xavi did at least prepare the odd engaging exercise to challenge me. One afternoon I was sent away like a year-nine student on a summer term project to research the legend of the fourteenth-century *Rey Pedro de Castilla* – Peter the Cruel – whose incognito nocturnal escapades around Seville led on one unfortunate occasion to a street altercation and his murder of a stranger. Protesting his innocence, the errant king vowed to place the head of the perpetrator at the exact spot where the murder took place. Unluckily for Pedro, he was rumbled by an elderly local curtain-twitcher – an *anciana* – who had seen the murderous drama unfold from her window and exposed him for the scoundrel he evidently was. Mortified and guilt-ridden by his unmasking and public humiliation, Pedro sought atonement by bequeathing to the city an effigy of himself to be placed on his death in a niche on the narrow Seville street that still bears his name. All fascinating stuff, made more so for me by the challenge of presenting my findings in Spanish. To pad-out the hour, enabling Xavi to sit back, merely listen and fill the room with his laughter, I was also tasked with choosing a legend from English history with which to do the same. Thanks to a bit of shortcutting via an online translator (innocent as I was at that stage of the perils and often painful inaccuracies of those devices), I made a decent fist of the murderous antics of the old Spanish king, but rather less so with my choice of Jack the Ripper as a legend of English notoriety, who specially for the occasion I re-christened in Spanish, *Jack El Destripador.* In what I kidded myself might be a plucky attempt at adding a Hispanic twist to the antics of the Whitechapel murderer, all I achieved was to gift my tutor with possibly the most entertaining hour of his soon-to-be-aborted career in language teaching. More to the point, thanks to my stumbles over grammar and pronunciation, the ultimate 'whodunnit' remained unsolved. The elusive Jack was off the hook once more.

In hindsight, swapping one set of daily rhythms and obediences (aka the workplace) for another in the form of a college timetable was perhaps always doomed to fail. As far as organised classes went, my unconvincing account in Spanish of a murderous king and a Victorian madman was the final straw, so I unburdened myself for now of the demands of the classroom to enjoy the happy state of being commitment free and left entirely to my own devices – apart of course from the far looser demands of *intercambio*.

To celebrate my release I took a series of short day trips – to the former Roman stronghold of nearby Italica, to the vertiginous whitewashed town of Arcos de la Frontera in the Cádiz Sierra, and finally to the tiny city of Carmona, built spectacularly on a high plain above the eastern suburbs of Seville. Away from the language school – and much further away than I had ever been in my adult life from the routines of the workplace – I became acutely aware of the yawning chasm that had opened between the former disaffection of my previous life of nine-to-five and its liberated replacement. One blisteringly hot Wednesday, I sat in Carmona's gargantuan Plaza de San Fernando picking over a salad and rolls of soft, newly-baked bread helped down by a rough and tasty *fino*. Relishing the buzz of everyday small-town Spanish activity – accompanied by a characteristically Spanish soundtrack of yapping dogs and the high pitched squeals of excited, free-to-roam children – my thoughts turned to my life back at the office. I mused that at this precise mid-week point I would so often feel jaded by the grinding dullness of the routine. I took out my notebook, shielded my eyes from the sun, and sketched an assortment of plans, ideas, hopes and possibilities. Aside from what I could see immediately before me, nothing was certain as I kicked-back in that sunny square high-up on an Andalucian plain. Yet rather stirringly, almost *anything* now seemed possible.

Leaving the Don Quijote language school also meant departing the bosom of Ana's small family. In search of a new home I ventured into Seville's private rental market and took a room on a side street close to the lively Plaza Alfalfa, which I found through an accommodation agency run by an enterprising band of young chancers from Germany. Leaving their office clutching a piece of paper containing my new address, recalled the excitement I felt when as a bit of a young chancer myself I arrived in big bad London from the leafy lanes of Cheshire to take up a junior post in the Civil Service – a lucky reinstatement following my earlier public service resignation and modest pension 'cash-in'. I rolled up in the capital with a suitcase (to add here 'and guitar in hand' could sound too much of a Paul Simon cliché, but actually was true) and the address of my lodgings arranged for me by the long defunct, rather maternal, Civil Service and Post Office accommodation service. The elitist W2 Hyde Park postcode didn't then necessarily suggest the affluence it does today, and meant very little to me as I made my way south to take up my duties as an unwitting agent of Thatcherism in that old spirit-crusher of a government department – the DHSS. Looking back at the raw excitement of those salad-days, it is difficult to believe that my octogenarian landlady, Miss Rixon (thank you Nancy for the memories), felt able to charge per week for a decently appointed bedsit room at her opulent address, as little as the cost today of a day return train ticket from London to Brighton. Now, half a lifetime later as I climbed the dingy staircase to check-in with my latest Spanish landlady, the formidable Fatima, I experienced a similar thrill of adventure and a frisson born of not knowing quite what was coming next. Under the circumstance that I was about to place a wad of used notes in her plump outstretched claw, Fatima's greeting fell only just the right side of friendly to be acceptable. Throughout our transaction I was distracted from Fatima's brusqueness by the extraordinary oral dexterity she displayed in keeping her lit cigarette in the corner of her mouth as she spoke, while simultaneously inhaling and exhaling the smoke. Fortunately her jollier, non-smoking taxi-driving husband Fernando had enough generosity of spirit about him for both of them, and I sensed he might be glad to have another man-about-the-house for a bit of sporting talk. The pity was that neither he nor Fatima spoke a word of English. With the lady of the house lacking the will – and her husband the patience – to sit and listen to my laboured Spanish, not very much of any significance between us was said. Although the level of conversation in the house was minimal, there was also something quite appealing to me about this air of anonymity, and Fatima's place quickly became a home from home.

But not so fast...After a peaceful couple of weeks, another euro-laden English-speaking guest called Emily arrived to fill the remaining space in Fatima's home and wallet – an arrival that succeeded in fracturing Anglo-Spanish relations to an extent rarely seen since Sir Francis Drake's skirmish with the Armada in 1588. With two queens now occupying the same smoky hive, hostilities broke out the minute Emily had unpacked. The Yorkshire firebrand got off on entirely the wrong foot with our hostess by lodging a complaint to the German lads at the agency about a number of the flat's advertised appliances that were either out of order or in fact non-existent. These included the TV in her room, the TV in the communal area (a depressing, grubby internal room I avoided as it enjoyed no natural light), the oven, the iron and kettle (both the latter were non-existent – evidently Fatima and Fernando weren't tea drinkers in the Yorkshire tradition, or cared much about walking around with creases up their shirts), the internet connection and the complete lack of any form of heating in the said communal seating area – a criticism I thought a little unnecessary in Seville's late-summer heat.

Unsurprisingly, once Emily's litany of complaint was fed back to Fatima from the agency, it went down like the proverbial lead-balloon and unleashed the bully in her. Returning home the same evening, Emily was greeted with an astonishing onslaught of abuse spewing from Fatima's mouth as it belched smoke like the filthy funnel of a steam train. All highly entertaining for me as a neutral, until the bi-lingual slanging match made its angry way down the hallway towards my door, which Emily banged upon in a state of hyperactive distress. Thus I was thrust into the unenviable position of umpire and peacemaker, the consolation being the gift of about as good an *intercambio* opportunity as they get. Spending way too long pondering over choices of adjectives and verb conjugations, I attempted nonetheless to plead Emily's case. Here she was, our Emily, nobbut a lass, an innocent abroad, fresh from the bosom of her family, as green as the rolling Dales whence she hailed, and forced to fend for herself in the austere surroundings of a semi-derelict building down a back street of a strange city of absurdly high temperatures. Unmoved by my stuttering, linguistically inept representation of my compatriot, Fatima was reduced – unfathomably it has to be said – to hysterical tears.

Emily responded in kind, leaving me with a feeling that recalled a thousand team meeting moments of what-on-earth-am-I-doing-here? With conflict resolution apparently not among her key attributes, Fatima retreated to the kitchen shouting goodness-knows-what anti-English sentiments. Alarmingly, she grabbed a sharpened knife, but thankfully with no more flesh-wounding intent than to hack a couple of slices from the leg of *jamón ibérico* that had lain for the best part of a fortnight in an advancing stage of decomposition on the draining board, dripping its bacteria-rich juices onto drying plates. Emily, meanwhile, had decided on a quick getaway and an early end to her tenancy, and so was busy in her room stuffing her belongings into a suitcase. I have never been much good with tears, but as a fellow Brit abroad I did feel a little responsible for Emily's immediate well-being and persuaded her not to leave that night. I, on the other hand, led by gut-feeling – an instinct never to be mistrusted in my book – knew it was time to move on.

Clawing back as much self-contained independence as my budget allowed, I swapped the nicotine-coated chaos of Fatima's home for a perfect little place around the corner I found through the online international accommodation kings, *Airbnb* – a place so fitting that I could quite easily have seen out the rest of my days there. Admittedly my new crash-pad didn't look much from the outside, but the tiny studio flat on a narrow cobbled street between the Alameda de Hércules and the River Guadalquivir was bang on the money. I had the luxury of my own front door, a kitchenette, a compact bathroom in a novel semi-open plan arrangement, and to top it all a private terrace with views over the rooftops of Seville, where I began and ended each day soothed by the dulcet bells of the nearby Iglesia de San Vicente. The studio was a clever conversion from a former rooftop potting shed into a fully-functional, self-contained living space, suitable for anyone not interested in hosting dinner parties or inviting sleepovers. My new landlady, Magdalena, a gregarious fifty-something divorcee who lived in a much larger flat in the same house, and whose mortgage I suspected I was paying, left me entirely to my own devices. She did contact me occasionally, but only through text messages to check that a) I was still alive and b) if the answer was yes, did I have all that I needed to ensure a comfortable stay? Answers in the affirmative were encouraged and well-received. A curious feature of this small-scale living arrangement was that I was able to see, touch and hear every item and appliance wherever I stood, sat or lay in the room. After a couple of sleepless nights listening to the hum of the small fridge, which stood less than a metre from my bed, I decided to switch it off last thing at night with the reward of a small pool of water to step into as I left my bed each morning to switch it back on. All said and done, it's as well I have always enjoyed camping. Nevertheless, the minor privations of my materially reduced circumstances were soon forgotten once I reminded myself of my fresh purpose. 'Hey, today is Tuesday', I might mutter to myself as I mopped the water away from the foot of my bed. 'Remember what used to happen on a Tuesday'? – an unsettling thought that would spur me to a more vigorous mop action and a sing-a-long to some cheesy Spanish pop tune blaring out from the radio.

To make myself feel really at home, I bought for a song a battered old grey and orange bicycle, which for no reason at all I gave the name Billy. Heartbreakingly, after Billy and I had bonded over some weeks up and down Seville's gratifyingly smooth bike lanes that provide a virtually unbroken 360 degree circuit of the city, Billy was stolen. After long afternoon hours in his company pedalling the hot tarmac through the city's atmospheric barrios of La Macarena, Los Remedios, Nervión and Triana, Billy's loss came as quite a blow. Secured – or so I thought – to a lamppost near the Alameda de Hércules, my trusty steed was taken, I imagined, to be desecrated with new paintwork before being whisked away to some dusty out-of-town market and sold into the slavery of a new unappreciative rider. But the criminal tale has a curious footnote. On another visit to Seville a few months later to immerse myself in the city's extravagant Easter jamboree, *Semana Santa,* divine intervention brought Billy and I back together for a few precious final moments. On the Wednesday evening of the week-long parades of gaudy figures of Christ tailed by a multitude of papier-mâché virgins, I was following a float of the Brotherhood of Monte-Sión towards the cathedral (as you do) when I had an apparition of my own, not of a wobbly virgin, but of another icon of Seville worthy in my view of some veneration – bicycle Billy, no less. Tethered shoddily to the trunk of a tree, there was no doubt it was him. Those unmistakable tangerine forks, chipped grey alloy tubes, torn saddle and the hanging parts of a long-defunct dynamo light system – all remained unadulterated since the theft. I considered waiting for Billy's illegal custodian to appear and confront him with a little piece of Spanish invective I was composing for the moment. I even thought about involving a small huddle of police gathered nearby, but with close to a million people lining the narrow streets of Seville for the free Catholic theatre show, they possibly had bigger fish to fry than a stolen bicycle. Instead, knowing it was our last, I spent a little quality time with my old friend, took a few photographs and then, with a knot in my stomach and without looking back, I walked away. In the end I didn't much care to stand and wait for Billy's new owner to appear, but did take a little satisfaction from leaving a note attached to the torn saddle making it perfectly clear in the very best, most assertive Spanish I could muster that Billy, in actual fact, still very much belonged to me. I think you might call that closure.

I had been in Seville for close on two months, when on one intensely warm evening as I walked through the crowded Plaza Alfalfa and could take the enervating heat no more, I stopped on a shaded terrace, ordered a cold drink and set about a casual stock take of my post-work life. My recently discarded employment had involved helping international students to progress through the various stages of culture shock. Here in Seville I was now myself, in a manner of speaking, an international student – a neat train of thought and role reversal that I must admit rather pleased me. I had rushed through those culture shock stages of acclimatisation, from the initial excitement of everything being new (take the Andalucian convention of eating at 11.00pm for starters – I had tried restaurants at seven in the evening and they were always either closed or completely empty), through the frustrations and annoyances of everyday differences (in Seville this was marked by the daily frustration of finding shops and services that I needed being closed for three hours during the afternoon), before ending, two short months later, in acceptance and assimilation. Admittedly, I was living in another EU country where life was not *so* different to home. But with its unrelenting heat, its exotic vegetation, its towering palm trees and late-night culture, Seville felt different enough, and at this early stage of my piecing together of a rewarding post-work lifestyle, I felt pleased with the ease of the transition. The flip side to all of this was that having negotiated acceptance and assimilation, I found myself now parked-up in yet another comfort zone – albeit a rather sunnier zone than the one I had left behind. In fact, if it hadn't been so hot, I might well have pulled up an armchair, donned a pair of slippers and lit a pipe.

One aspect of the *Sevillan* lifestyle that I had no acceptance problems with was its bar culture. In fact, I can think of hardly anything more pleasant than sitting on the lively outdoor terrace of one of the city's 4,000 tapas bars at ten o'clock at night wallowing in a temperature still comfortably north of thirty degrees. Fresh from my office resignation, in those first heady days and weeks in Seville my drink of choice was usually a *jarra* – a little under a pint-sized measure of beer available in many of the city's bars for as little as €1. In my mood of post-work celebration and general abandonment of responsibility, the habit of taking an enlivener or two at the end of the day became ingrained all too quickly. Just as my Seville routine took me to the same *fruterias* and *supermercados* on the lively Feria and Sierpes streets, so my regular *intercambio* and bar haunts tended to be around Plaza Alfalfa, the Alameda de Hércules and the tiny, wonderfully ambient Plaza de los Terceros. On my way to the terraces of Los Terceros,

I would often stop to enjoy the shade of the Metropol Parasol, better known locally as Las Setas (the mushrooms) – an extraordinary German-designed wooden structure dominating Plaza Encarnación. Completed in 2011 after a four-year build and reputed to be the world's largest wooden edifice, Las Setas consists of six giant irregular-shaped parasols arranged over four levels, rising at their highest above the square to twenty-six metres. Thanks to spiralling costs exceeding €50 million (to date the final cost has been withheld from public scrutiny), long delays caused by miscalculations around the suitability of the birchwood chosen for the project, and the fact that the structure looks, well frankly a little odd amid the splendid antiquity of this old part of Seville, Las Setas has divided opinion in the city. When I first set eyes on the strange airborne wooden canopies (that do indeed resemble giant wild mushrooms, even in their beige colour), admittedly I wasn't too sure. Yet once I had taken the lift to its panoramic terrace to survey the vista of the Giralda – the late twelfth-century Moorish bell tower of Seville's cathedral – and then over a sea of ramshackle rooftops and church spires stretching far and wide in any direction, I was a Las Setas convert.

As for the low-key hedonism of my *Sevillan* lifestyle, for the first time in my life the possibility of developing a real drink habit crossed my mind – a dangerous risk to which Seville lends itself all too beautifully. During those first carefree weeks in the city, on the dodgy pretext that it would be good for the progress of my Spanish, I was often tempted into gatecrashing a street *bottellón,* one of those impromptu gatherings of boozy *Sevillanos* draped over street furniture (underneath Las

Setas is a popular venue for the activity) drinking cold beer from *litronas* – litre bottles of the golden fizzy stuff available from the *Dia* supermarket chain for around the price of sparkling mineral water. Beware! Luckily though, I don't have an addictive personality but to avoid compromising the fun of bar-hopping too much by turning to soft drinks, I took the when-in-Rome – er, Seville – approach by switching to *cañas*. Now, to your average British beer drinker a *caña* might seem to be a derisory offering – a measure so modest that if it were green and minty would just about suffice as a mouthwash. However, with a bit of practice and even more restraint, I learned to make a *caña* last as if it were a glass of wine, replacing the northern European swig with the sip of the *Sevillano* (those that preferred not to drink from litre bottles, that is) – a drinking style that offers one explanation in this city of abundant bars for the noticeable absence of boorish outdoor drunkenness. Not that the nocturnal streets of Seville never get animated at night. They do, and largely because the majority of the city's 4,000 bars have at least half-a-dozen tables strewn on the pavement outside. During a *caña* break in the popular Bar Central on the Alameda de Hércules with my old fascist-sympathising buddy, José Miguel, he told me that the killjoy suits of Seville's conservative Local Authority (*El Ayuntamiento*) were in the process of enacting new laws to combat the problem of street noise – the inevitable by-product of a culture of street drinking until the early hours of the morning.

To be fair, the men in suits do have a point. For permanent residents of Seville's bar-dense areas, to have tables of excitable drinkers sat a few feet below their bedroom windows must be a nightmare – even if the

rowdiness is of a good nature. As I had added infinitesimally to the problem myself, I felt I should at least
investigate a little further, which is how I came across
the despair of Emilia de la Serna of the anti-noise action
group, *Plataforma Por El Descanso en Sevilla*. In a
determined pursuit of undisturbed sleep for herself and
her family, I read that Emilia had recently invested a
small fortune insulating her family home in the centre
of Seville from the noise pollution of adjacent bar terraces. As Emilia says, '*someone else has taken control
of your life, and in order to make money is telling
you when you can sleep. You are abused in your own
home*'. In fact, many of Seville's outdoor terrace
arrangements breach the city's existing environmental
laws, leading to a recent crackdown by the *Ayuntamiento*
that included the draconian, headline-grabbing measure
of prohibiting the playing of dominoes outside bars.
Action against the clack-clack of old mens' domino
pieces was one thing, but José Miguel was more animated about a recent raid on the very bar where we
were standing. In a purge that recalls the mean spirit of
Francoism and the *Guardia Civil* of the 1930s, local
police with council backing arrived in vans at the
Alameda de Hércules at 9.00pm to close down a dozen
of the noisiest bars. After a ticking off and small fine,
most were reopened within a fortnight. However, as
one of the noisiest perpetrators, Bar Central was again
the target of a recent heavy-handed police raid that
beggars belief in modern day Spain. The raid saw police
snatching glasses and bottles from punters, smashing
them to the ground and forcing people into the bar with
threats of €100 on-the-spot fines for public drinking.
A rather cunning policing ploy, this meant that the bar's

licence to hold forty people inside was immediately breached, allowing them to close the joint down completely. As José Miguel unfurled the story, an image of Nazi thugs raiding the Berlin cabaret clubs in the 1920s sprang to mind. Luckily, there wasn't a jackboot in sight or even a sniff of police action at Bar Central on the warm evening we stood outside drinking (breaking one bye-law), and talking on the bar's terrace at some volume immediately below private residences (probably in contravention of another bye-law). True to form, as he railed against the scourge of outdoor noise in his city, José Miguel revelled in the fascist connotation of the recent raids. Mind you, as each of those moreish little *cañas* begot another (sipping wasn't José Miguel's preferred style – he much preferred the Anglo-Saxon down-in-one approach), there was absolutely nobody in the vicinity making anything like the amount of noise he was. *La Policía* and the *Ayuntamiento* might occasionally wield a strong arm to curb Seville's noise pollution, but after a couple of months living in this spirited southern city, I came to the conclusion that there is no humane way of keeping a true *Sevillano* quiet – at least not while there is still breath in his body and a *caña* in his hand.

I read in the *Guardian* recently an article about travel writing opining how it should avoid involving the reader in too much of the minutiae of the writer. To this, please allow me a brief exception. For a week or so I had been hindered by a sizeable and painful blister on my right foot, the result of hours of walking in ill-fitting trainers along the hot pavements of Seville, made worse no doubt by standing around inadvertently breaking bye-laws on those noisy bar terraces. Having little previous experience of minor foot ailments, I became a little anxious once the blister ballooned to roughly the size of a golf ball. In search of a remedy I went online and read, quite unwisely, the disconcerting blog of a blistered Californian man who had intervened in the healing process by bursting his own 'balloon' with a pin, allowing the fluid it contained to enter his bloodstream, resulting in infection and the unfortunate blogger losing his foot and lower leg to amputation. Strongly averse to this particular risk – if not especially these days, you may have noticed, to others such as alcoholism and penury – I consulted various sources on the topic before concluding that self-administered surgery might end in catastrophe. So I left the protective balloon to its own devices and waited patiently for nature to take its course. Given the amputation scare, and the inconvenience of my EU medical card lying redundantly in an old shoebox at the back of a ward-robe in south London, the progress of this small disor-der had assumed in my mind a disproportionately high level of concern. Nature did eventually intervene one stifling evening as I lounged on the roof terrace of my studio flat. But the significance of this otherwise incon-sequential tale is that the blister's messy demise jolted me from the rhythm and routine into which I had lapsed. Now I was foot-loose once more, and free to move without impediment. With a lightness of step in my right foot to match the left, I found a pharmacy, stocked up on plasters and in the process picked up from the willing assistant the vocabulary for a blistered heel. So, for what it's worth, if you ever find yourself somewhere in the Spanish speaking world in a similar podiatric predicament to mine, direct the attention of the pharmacist to your throbbing foot and holler, '¡yo tengo una ampolla dolorosa'! Anyway, fully mobile once more, feeling a little over-cooked by the Sevillan heat and with an insatiable appetite to keep moving, I felt that for now my time in the sultry Andalucian capital was up. Thus I made a destination decision based partly on ease and practicality, but equally on the compatibility of my mood, a mood that had me reach for my timetable of eastbound trains from Seville, con destino the ancient Moorish stronghold of Granada.

In my old office-bound days, as I switched on my computer each morning, leaning across my desk from a madly-swivelling chair, the screen-saver image that greeted me was of Granada's sumptuous city jewel, the Moorish Alhambra Palace – in Arabic literally 'The Red'. This spectacular image of the Islamic Alhambra was one taken from the vantage point of the Mirador San Nicolás, across the narrow Rio Darro and a maze of tiled roofs – an image made more miraculous still by the towering backdrop of the Sierra Nevada. If ever there was a view to lift the sagging spirit on a routine workday, then this was it. Far better still than viewed on a computer screen is to enjoy the vista in the flesh, most spectacularly from the Mirador San Nicolás at sunset. When I have been in that blessed spot myself, seduced by the views, the infectious rhythms of fla-menco guitar and the passionate singing and handclap-ping of local gitano musicians, rarely have I seen groups of tourists so easily persuaded into the generous surren-dering of loose change into the open palms of buskers. Andrés Segovia once described Granada as 'a place of dreams, where the Lord put the seed of music in my soul'. I have no idea where the virtuoso guitarist

happened to be when he came up with this accolade
for the city, but I wouldn't be surprised to learn that at
the moment his soul was so infected he was taking
in that dreamy view towards the Alhambra Palace from
the Mirador San Nicolas. If you have been there yourself, you will know precisely what I mean. If you
haven't, you will have gathered from all of this that
Granada really is a very special place.

I arrived in the city by train on a scenic regional
service from Seville reminiscent of a Rocky Mountain
Railway theme park ride. Taking a little over three
hours to cover the 250 kilometre journey, the train
meandered along a single track through arid valleys,
rugged mountain terrain and stepped olive groves.
At one point, as the train lumbered around a sharp
bend I looked out of the window towards a section of
track that was so twisted and undulating it took me a
moment to realise that this was the track my train was
actually on. Laboured as my train journey from Seville
to Granada was, it still seems a pity that a high-speed
upgrade is due to open soon to connect these two great
cities of the Spanish south. Whatever route the new
line takes, let's hope it will still pass by the extraordinary sight of the 'Man of Antequera' – a curious lump
of rock shaped remarkably in an angle-perfect profile of
a man's face gazing majestically up at the sky. Whether
the newly modernised service will retain its original
staff is altogether another matter. If so, some hasty
retraining in the art of customer service may be required.
In an audition for the part of a gratuitously cruel female
warder in some low-budget prison soap opera, the
ticket inspector who patrols the coaches of the Seville
to Granada line would have no trouble landing the part.

When I joined my allotted section of the train at Seville I found a virtually empty carriage, with only a few of the hundred or so seats occupied. As my reserved seat was next to a panel between two windows and I was looking forward to a scenic ride, I took an unreserved seat with an unobstructed view. But in Spain, a reserved seat on a train means precisely that, and woe betide anyone – especially an uncooperative *guiri* like me – taking a bit of initiative by sitting in an unpopulated area of carriage. Sure enough, less than ten minutes into the journey as the train crawled through the dusty eastern suburbs of Seville, the on-board dominatrix, amid much cursing and arm-waving, hurried over to eject me from my seat. As the lady cracked her whip in my direction, a discernible smile danced across her thin scarlet lips – a smile of satisfaction at a job well done as another *guiri* was put in his place. Foolishly I protested, inviting a response from her that stopped just shy of physical violence, but promised expulsion from the train at the next stop (the drab-looking Osuna) should I persist with my mutiny. Tail firmly between my legs, I was sent to disturb the comfort of the man occupying the space adjacent to my booked seat, who until I arrived had been enjoying the advantage of being able to spread his considerable frame across two whole seats. For what it's worth, my preferred hand-picked seat, along with two-thirds of the rest of the carriage, remained unoccupied for the entire journey. The guardess had enjoyed her small public humiliation of me, yet I could feel no real angst towards this punitive employee of the Spanish railways and pitied her entrapment in the petty bureaucracy of a rail company. As I left the train at Granada I thanked her – trying not to betray sarcasm – for a worthwhile job very well done. Looking back, I can even feel grateful to her for reminding me of the capacity of the workplace to flatten the human spirit – although let's face it, we all need a good reason for getting out of bed on a Tuesday morning. The lady evidently has hers.

Meanwhile the progress of my Spanish language learning had stalled. To get back on track I signed up for classes at the Don Quijote college in Granada, which I also knew would give me a decent chance of meeting a bunch of interesting people. For my accommodation I plumped once more for the 'host family immersion' option, but as I had a few days to find my feet in the city before the course began, I booked into an old Granada haunt of mine, the Hostal Landazuri on Cuesta de Gomerez, a long steep street that climbs from the city centre Plaza Nueva up towards the glorious Alhambra Palace. As a fairly regular former guest, I was greeted at the Landazuri door like an old friend by the venerable owner, Matilde, and her rather lugubrious son Manolo. Decorated in a colourfully-Moorish style, the Landazuri's highlight is its superb roof terrace – a little oasis of greenery and calm high above the buzzy streets below, offering the considerable bonus of a fortuitous side view of the Alhambra. It was while I was sat on the terrace gazing up at the sheer burnt orange walls of the Moorish masterpiece, that I encountered fellow Landazuri resident, Candy Black of South Carolina. With a style of speech reminiscent of machine-gun fire, Candy won me over with her tales of corporate disillusionment while working for the US Government machine in Washington D.C. One spring afternoon, Candy told me gleefully, in a fit of pique following a series of interfering management emails (which, by definition, can be hardly anything but interfering), she stood up from her desk, put on her coat and calmly walked out of the building, never to return. But America, as Candy testified, is 'not a country that loves you back', and her decision to walk away resulted in near financial meltdown, threats of house repossession and refusals by the state – despite years of paying contributions – of any kind of help from welfare. Still, for everything Candy had lost materially, she had at least preserved her sanity. Ever resourceful, she assumed full control of her life, sold her car and other unwanted items, rented out her property and then embarked on an open-ended sojourn around Europe. Only a couple of months earlier, Candy had been marooned in a Washington D.C. tower block – salaried and pensionable, maybe, but desk-bound and bored out of her disinterested skull. Now she was sat with a fellow nine-to-five runaway sipping a cup of herbal infusion on an Andalucian terrace in awesome gaze of the Alhambra Palace – overall a happy transformation for her, we both agreed.

As well as revelling in her freedom of spirit, Candy also enjoyed a keen sense of humour, put to the acid test the following morning when she joined me and several other Landazuri guests at an outside ground-floor breakfast table. As we sat munching our way through the Spanish breakfast staple of tomato puree on toast (with the option of marmalade, quite possibly arriving at our Granada table via a tree in some sunny plaza of Seville and a factory in Dundee), a street cleaning truck lurched towards us, and despite his clear view the driver decided to brighten his working day a little by spraying our table and lower halves with cold water – a reviving reminder of the often devil-may-care approach of Spanish public services. The result was a sparklingly clean street, cups of watered down tea and a few sodden and bedraggled tourists – mere trifles quickly forgotten following Candy's sudden and winning declaration that having spent a little time in Granada, she felt so ecstatically happy with the progress of her life that she planned to move permanently to southern Spain. As we queued to hug her in congratulation, I think the term I was searching for was kindred spirit.

After effusive farewells to Candy, in preparation for the resumption of my Spanish classes at Don Quijote I moved into my Granada homestay in the care of the inestimable Encarnación Cazorla Álvarez. A keen and brilliant cook, Encarni welcomed me into her home with the early observation that I looked badly in need of a decent meal. Once we had got through the list of foodie dos and don'ts, she proceeded to feed me up on platefuls of home cooking backed up by enormous slabs of her speciality *bizcocho* – a delicious Andalucian cake very like madeira. As well as benefitting from this riot of cholesterol, I had a comfortable room in Encarni's third floor apartment benefitting from a partial view of the peaks of the Sierra Nevada, the complete run of her home and unrestricted access to the well-stocked fridge. Family Encarni also included a plump, somewhat neurotic housecat whose name I never quite got to the bottom of, as Encarni seemed only to refer to her as *Gato* – yes, that's the Spanish word for cat. Catchily named or not, the feline's unpredictable mood swings would transform her from contentedly-purring ball of fur one moment, to eye-gouging monster the next,

behavioural issues I put down to a lifetime of house-
bound indolence – a reminder no less that similar personality traits might also emerge should a human being
spend half a sedentary lifetime confined behind a
desk gazing at a computer screen.

Once I was ensconced in Casa-Encarni, I set about
reviving my efforts to learn her language at Don Quijote,
which happily for me turned out to be pretty much
everything its Seville counterpart was not. By the end
of my fortnight as a student there, not only had my
Spanish jumped a noticeable level (words fail me for
how satisfying this felt), I could list a couple of engaging
new friends, and had knocked a decade or two off with
a series of energetic nights out on the town. Before all
of that, following the ordeal of the written and oral tests
I imagined an administrative error had been made when
I was placed in a class bearing the legend, *Avanzado*.
Given that the previous evening I had initially mistaken
a Spanish-speaker's question to me in the street about
directions to the Alhambra, for a question about what
time of day it was, my promotion to such a lofty class
seemed undeserved to say the least. The level of this new
class certainly proved a challenge, with the use of the
'subjunctive mood' in everyday Spanish chatter (an old
grammatical chestnut to be avoided in life if at all possible) leaving me flummoxed for half of the first week,
before a penny dropped from goodness knows where
and I caught up with the rest of the group. Or perhaps
they had all been winging-it too – it was hard to tell.

Whatever the difficulties posed by the vagaries of
Spanish grammar, the class was a whole heap of fun,
thanks partly to the excellence of the teachers, two of
which stood out. The first, Manuela, gifted with a smile

to light up any room on a Tuesday morning, went above and beyond her normal call of duty by offering the class what amounted to an open invitation to pop round to her place to join her and the family for dinner. '*Mi casa es tu casa*' – my house is your house – she would often say to lighten the mood amid a tricky grammatical explanation, coining a phrase I heard many times during my travels in Spain. I have no idea how Manuela would have responded if her entire class had rocked up at 10.00pm one evening hungry at her door, but my guess is that she would have poured us all a drink, made us a feast fit for kings and invited us all to share our life stories – in Spanish, of course. The second teacher worthy of a mention is Santiago, who on the face of it was a less hospitable soul than Manuela, and had a manner about him bordering on the brusque. There wasn't the slightest danger of a dinner invitation from Santiago, but his no-prisoner-taken approach to sharing his language paid dividends for all of us. Perhaps not a teacher for the faint-hearted student, with Santiago there was little elbow room for error. '*Sí o sí*', – yes or yes – he would say after his demonstration of some or other awkward grammar item. On one occasion, failing to grasp a tricky verb conjugation in the handful of seconds allowed by Santiago to think through an answer (a daily occurrence for me), I asked him if perchance answering '*no*' could ever be an option in his class. '*Absolutamente no*', he shot back at me, just a tad ironically.

It was during those lively and instructive classroom hours in Granada that I got to know a lady called Gisela – a smart German septuagenarian adventurer who had made the trip to Granada to hone her Spanish skills, and in doing so shunning convention and defying the expectations of many of her family and peers. That she didn't appear in the slightest out of place in a group that included students just about young enough to be her great grand-children (I was more of the youngest son bracket), is testament to her outgoing, can-do approach to life. Gisela wore every one of her years extremely lightly, which to her really were but a number. By the time I met up with Gisela again in a later, cherished encounter in her native Berlin, we had become firm and lasting friends. At the other end of the age scale of the class was Olivier, a diligent, bespectacled Parisian, who appeared to take events seriously enough in the classroom, but flourished in an otherwise non-conformist approach to life. Over a lunchtime drink he told me that he could never fit comfortably into the corporate world and wanted to spend his life travelling and immersing in diverse experiences. The last I heard of Olivier, he was filling his intrepid boots in the Laos capital, Luang Prabang, brushing up his social and language skills for a career in the hospitality industry that he planned would take him around the world. Also in the class were two Chinese girls who sat together in a corner of the room in virtual silence until one or the other was asked a question, prompting furious finger-tapping into their smartphone translators – their responses then often skewed by their reliance on a two-way translation, first from Spanish to English, then to Chinese or vice versa. Completing our group was an elegant well-polished sixty-year old from the South of France with the suspiciously Hispanic-sounding name of Marie-José (no wonder she got the hang of the subjunctive so quickly), and finally Béatrice, another

French student of a certain age, who curiously made several attempts during lesson breaks to pin me down on what she saw as Britain's failure to prevent France's Nazi occupation during the Second World War. Yet despite the odd lingering grievance of modern history and the considerable age, cultural and linguistic differences within the group, we all rubbed along pretty well, enjoying the comfort of our shared ground of simply being *somewhere else* than we probably ought to have been, doing *something different* to what the rest of the world quite possibly expected us to do. It really was no more complicated than that.

There is an old Spanish adage that says, '*si mueres sin ver La Alhambra, no has vivido*' – 'if you die without seeing the Alhambra, you haven't lived'. A sizeable book could be compiled of places with grounds for a similar claim, but it really would be a serious oversight to spend any time in Granada without visiting the grand Moorish edifice. A lavish complex of royal palaces, gardens and fortifications, the Alhambra was constructed as a representation of 'paradise on earth' by a succession of tyrannical rulers of waning power during the Nasrid period. This last remaining Muslim dynasty in Spain lasted until January 1492, the landmark date in Spanish history on which the 'Catholic Monarchs' (the compliment awarded them by Pope Innocent VIII), King Ferdinand of Aragon and Queen Isabella of Castile, rode into town to claim Granada for Christendom, a triumph that earned them a permanent burial site in the Royal Chapel of the city's cathedral. The Alhambra is of course the outstanding, quite beautiful, reminder that Granada was once part of Spain's Islamic caliphate – the only country in western Europe ever to have had this status. Despite the use of modest materials in parts of the Alhambra's original construction (principally wood and stucco rather than marble and stone), after much restoration the exquisite carvings on display for the modern visitor to the palace are an absolute sight to behold. I spent the best part of a day at this old Moorish stronghold, taking my time as I ambled through the Patio de Los Leónes with its magnificent centrepiece of a fountain resting on twelve marble lions, then passing through the throne room of the Salon de Embajadores and the later sixteenth-century addition of the bagel-shaped Renaissance palace of Carlos V.

I ended the day in the calm of the nearby Generalife Gardens, the country estate of the Nasrid kings, built as a place of refuge from the politics and drama of the Alhambra court – and there was always plenty of that worth escaping from. As I walked around the lush Patio de los Cipreses, I cast my mind back to a small internal courtyard garden at the university where I had until quite recently worked – another popular workplace refuge where I would often see harassed members of staff sitting in quiet contemplation, quite possibly – like me – dreaming up some scheme or other to leave the building behind forever. That little oasis of south London greenery could not of course quite boast the serenity of the Generalife. Indeed, as I wandered through those splendid Alhambra gardens in the early autumn sunshine, I felt wholly light of both body and mind – the result, I had no doubt, of recently shedding my own burden of the relatively lame dramas and politics of life in 'the office'. When I eventually prised myself away from the Alhambra, I found plentiful reminders beyond its walls of Granada's rich Moorish heritage and last vestiges of Islamic Spain. As I walked along the old city's ancient cobbled lanes, I spotted the embellishment of Granada's symbol – the pomegranate fruit – on street furniture, on countless manhole and service covers in the ground and on a thousand varieties of souvenir tea towels and key rings. Thus the city's rich historic diversity lives on through its name – Granada is, no less, the Arabic word for pomegranate.

Once the Spanish course ended, aside from the enlivening company of Encarni and her ferocious feline, I found myself quite alone in Granada. Gisela returned to Germany to continue her life of eclectic interests and continual self-development, the French female contingent returned home to continue being French and Olivier, true to his word, wasted no time in getting on with his adventures in the Far East. Once more with abundant free time on my hands, I took to the hills that surround Granada, beginning in the tourist honeycomb of the Albayzín. This enchanting district – formed of a steep outcrop of little white houses clinging to the hill opposite the Alhambra – was the last remaining Moorish quarter of the city after the *Reconquista* of 1492. In the spirit of the writer, Ray Bradbury, who opined so imaginatively that half the fun of travel was 'the aesthetic of lostness', I ditched my street map in favour of wantonly losing myself in the Albayzín's disorienting jumble of steep cobbled alleyways. Yet despite the confusion of its labyrinthine street plan, I seemed to be never more than a few steps away from a teashop or café, where middle-aged men sat in huddles dealing cards or shuffling dominoes as they inhaled the calming vapours of shisha pipes. I browsed the Albayzín's multitude of outdoor market stalls, each one crammed with Islamic-themed tat, and snatched brief conversations in Spanish with Moroccan stall-holders – at least when I could hear them above the din of the wailing of piped Arabic music. I surrendered fully to the charms of this surviving Moorish corner of Granada, which with its allure of scents and haunting sounds felt like the meeting, in miniature, of Istanbul's Grand Bazaar and a Marrakech souk.

In a bid to escape the mounds of Taiwan-made Alhambra souvenir trinkets, I stretched my legs beyond the centre of Granada and the Albayzín to become a regular walker around the narrow hilly lanes of Sacromonte. Apart from the magnificent lofty views the area offers of the city, the real draw of Sacromonte was its colourful and unique collection of tile-decorated, stone-carved houses. Once the exclusive domain of Granada's *Gitanos* – or Romas – who settled here after the Moorish expulsion, Sacromonte retains much of its indigenous spirit with many of the little cave houses that cling to the barrio's hillsides still fully occupied and kitted-out for the twenty-first century with electricity, TVs and running water. Although the *Gitano* community is well used to nosey visitors like me pointing camera lenses at their homes (the area is, after all, plugged heavily as a tourist attraction), I still felt the unease of an intruder as I trod my way along the steep Sacromonte paths, cracked and baked to a crust by months of intense sunlight. Trying not to appear intrusive, but doubtless failing, I peered over makeshift fences of mattresses and coloured plastic beer crates into the extraordinary cave dwellings, deterred from lingering for too long outside many of them by the bared teeth and salivating of fearsome guard dogs.

Women stood on front porches wringing-out washing by hand, their biceps rippling from years of physical labour and covered in chestnut brown skin leathered by unshaded decades of the fierce Andalucian sun. I watched as men tended small arid vegetable plots in ramshackle gardens strewn with stripped motorcycle parts, rusted agricultural implements and mounds of old car tyres. The chimes of a medieval bell sounding in the city below the Sacromonte hills would tell me if it was twelve, two, or four. But among these ancient terraces of cave dwellings, aside from the nods to modernity revealed by the TV aerials and mobile phone masts, time in Sacromonte seemed to be stood quite still.

Seeing for myself Granada's cave dwelling community put to bed my notion that a home in a cave would, by definition, be dark, dangerous and undesirable. This is evidently not so. Included in the scope of the UNESCO World Heritage Site established in and around the Alhambra, many of the Sacromonte cave dwellings offer substantial square footage and a decent level of comfort. Although I wasn't so taken by an overflowing communal lavatory that I passed, the insulation of solid rock ensures that the cave houses benefit from impressive energy efficiency, making them cosy in winter and bearable in summer – a handy combination in a region where temperatures throughout the year can range from well below freezing to approaching fifty-degrees celsius. Construction costs and timescales also compare favourably with those of conventional homes, and once completed the cave dwellings are largely immune from the risks of earthquake and fire. Imaginative use of paint and light ducting can also overcome the obvious problem of providing natural light, and because houses are carved out of irregular rock formations, no two homes are identical in layout, creating an estate agent's utopia of 'unique opportunities'.

One afternoon, as I made my way down a recently constructed stone staircase linking the upper reaches of Sacromonte with the centre of Granada, I got chatting to a young Senegalese man named Eric. Clad in the blue of a replica Chelsea FC shirt, Eric told me that he had lived in a cave house since the age of seven, had no real desire to move away for good, but wouldn't half mind spending some time in London principally to take in a game at Stamford Bridge and, as he put it, 'to meet some nice English girls'. I encouraged him in his belief that those nice English girls may also be on the lookout for someone just like him, but added that on my next visit to his fascinating hillside community I might well bring him the gift of a football shirt of an alternative English football club, which would still be in a dark shade of blue, but of a more northern vintage. In the event, I bumped into Eric several more times during my daily walks around Sacromonte. After one of our chats as I made my way down the steep calf-toning Carril de San Miguel towards the city centre, I sat at a small table outside a ramshackle cottage carved out of the rock at Mirador de Mario Maya. The owner of the house, a deeply-tanned, rather stern lady of indeterminate age called Marisa, had set up a makeshift café for leg-weary passers-by where she served up simple *bocadillos* and tall glasses of deliciously-chilled, salmon-pink *gazpacho*. Scruffy feral cats meowed plaintively as they brushed themselves around my legs, their engines purring as I befriended them with scraps of tuna and cheese. I looked across at the imposing walls of the

Alhambra standing on the verdant wooded slopes of the opposite hill. In an attempt to capture and preserve this most perfect image, I closed my eyes as if they were shutters on a camera, wishing that my afternoon adventure in the Sacromonte hills could last forever.

Savouring this precious moment, I made no attempt to restrain the discernible quiver I felt in my bottom lip, an involuntary response to just *being* so close to the great Moorish Palace. In fact, the spectacle of the Alhambra has been known to reduce even the most powerful of men to tears. In 1492, after the Spanish had kicked the Moors out of Granada and the last Arabic King, Boabdil, was fleeing the city after handing over the keys to the Alhambra, he is reputed to have sobbed as he looked back at the imposing stone walls of his beloved former home. Boabdil's mother, not displaying the sort of maternal tenderness you might expect in such circumstances, as legend has it turned to her vanquished son as he dried his tears and chided, '*do not weep like a woman for what you could not defend like a man.*' Oh, the pressures of fifteenth-century manhood! And far more recently, during a family holiday in Granada another world leader not averse to a bit of public blubbering – one Bill Clinton – also wept as he caught sight of the great Moorish citadel. As I wiped away a small tear of my own attempting to escape the corner of my eye – not for one moment believing my own pretence of it being down to facing the gusty breeze – I was content to join the doubtless long list of Granada visitors who, faced with the same extraordinary Alhambra views, have been reduced to emotional, sobbing wrecks.

As the Granada days turned effortlessly to weeks, I was content to drift along doing just what my budget allowed. There was the daily physical exertion of the hill-walking in Sacromonte and the rather shorter visits to Granada's university library where, for as long as I could stand, I poured over the confusion of Spanish verb tables. Now a man of considerable leisure, I sailed calmly through each day, making decisions about my movements as the mood took me – an impossible indulgence in my previous life of salaried compliance. I often rewarded the effort of it all by some café and bar-hopping around the atmospheric El Realejo district, which along with Sacromonte became the focal point of my loose Granada routine. I spent afternoons in Casa Lopez Correa, an eclectic hangout where I tried out my Spanish in small talk with locals, often from the comfort of a huge corner sofa scattered incongruously with Union Jack cushions. It was during these uncluttered daytime hours that I would occasionally feel the sensation of a warm glow – not the result of the climate I was in, but little rushes of euphoria to remind me that I was about as free as any man could be. Freedom of choice, I concluded, was everything. In fact, so at home did I feel in Granada, this captivating, transient centre of my world, I even toyed with the idea of disbanding ideas of travelling further in favour of finding a room to rent longer-term in one of the steep winding streets of El Realejo. In the event, for a month or so a single day trip was about as far afield as I got as I immersed in the magical qualities of Granada, the perfectly formed city jewel that had become, without any effort at all, a home from home.

The destination of my day trip was Monachil, the principal ski resort of the Sierra Nevada. I reached the town in less than an hour by a spectacular bus journey along twisting mountain roads, most of which I spent gasping at the heart-in-the-mouth drops on either side. In truth, all I found in Monachil's compact town centre was a fairly charmless pastiche of an alpine village, blighted by gratuitously loud music piped from speakers outside cafés, lending the town a somewhat downmarket feel. Nevertheless, it seemed a contented place to be at the onset of the ski season, with rosy-cheeked visitors clad in heavy boots congregating in the brilliant, very early winter sunshine, boasting animatedly about their latest on-piste derring-dos. There was a crop of distinctive regional British accents to eavesdrop on, including from a large party of Brummies intent on consuming as much of the local 'Alhambra' brew as they could from oversize plastic cups. But I discovered the best of Monachil by following a steep road north from the main square. Eventually I reached a series of precariously swaying iron staircases, taking me up to the town's highest point where I was rewarded for the nervy climb by wonderful views of the snow-covered peaks of the Sierra, the hanging gondolas ferrying skiers up and down the slopes and then the spectacle of their descent on the virginal snow. I paid an inflated, snow-premium price for a modest lunch at a small café, and took my money's worth by basking for over an hour on its elevated sunlit terrace. With a bird's eye view of the skiers, I sat transfixed for a while by the absurdity of an activity that in most cases seemed to climax in no more than a face-first plunge into snow – at the same time taking great vicarious pleasure from the evidently wonderful time they were all having.

Back in Granada, I stayed on with Encarni as a paying, well-fed guest beyond my time as a Don Quijote student. This arrangement between the two of us (strictly forbidden by the school as they missed out on their cut of my rent), became *nuestro secreto* – an insignificant little conspiracy that somehow bonded our friendship. I added to my daily routine of walking, panorama-gazing, verb-checking and bar-hopping some light training at a small, scenic and completely gratis open-air gym situated improbably at the foot of the Alhambra Hill. Never before had I been spurred on to such effort on a treadmill as I was by that view of the extraordinary Nasrid Palace. Less energetically, I read Spanish and English newspapers as I dipped deep-fried *churros* into thick hot chocolate in Café Bib-Rambla, a city institution that has been busy fattening up its clientele since first opening its doors in 1907.

But there is only so much chocolate and deep-fried dough a man can take, and once the darker evenings and night chills set in, I began to feel that my time in Granada was drawing to a close. On one rather grey and chilly Friday afternoon during my regular walk towards the Mirador San Cristobal and the hills of Sacromonte, I passed along the touristy tapas bar strip of Calle Elvira. In truth not the prettiest of Granada's historic lanes, every inch of reachable wall and street furniture was plastered with the bright colours of graffiti art and posters large and small advertising everything from massage services, rooms for rent, bicycles for sale and the mobile numbers of prostitutes. Ever open to ideas and inspiration, two items on this bright urban patchwork caught my eye. The first carried the catchy, no-nonsense slogan, '*NAZIS FUCK OFF*!!' The second had more artistic merit – a fine charcoal sketch of Cuba's Revolution demi-god, Che Guevara, depicted in his instantly recognisable, beret-wearing revolutionary pose. As it happened, scribbled on a multitude of versions of my 'post-work plan' was the intriguing option of visiting a Spanish speaking country that wasn't Spain, and into the bargain one that was far out of the range of the overpriced drinks trollies of a budget airline. I paused outside La Tortuga tapas bar, picked up a menu from a terrace table and looked down the long list of exotic drinks, working my way quickly past the Manhattan, the Tequila Sunrise and the Singapore Sling before pausing at the Mojito, that rum-infused cocktail that brought to mind a destination I had often dreamt of visiting. Sublime city as Granada is – and I would surely be back – it didn't feel quite the optimum place to be mixing Mojitos. So with that in mind, and the image of Che Guevara eyeballing me wistfully from the adjacent wall, there was really only one thing for it. My next stop would be Marxism in paradise, on the Caribbean island of Cuba.

Under Che Guevara's wistful gaze in
Havana - *Until the victory, always*.

*'I'm suffocating...I think I would rather go somewhere
where I don't know what's going to happen.'*

Andrew Motion

– 2 –

Cuba Libre

After ten hours of breathing the second-hand tinned
air of Virgin Transatlantic, it was a relief to land at
Havana's José Martí Airport, albeit as the tourist fodder
of a hundred Cuban cabbies. The welcoming party in
the arrivals lounge had eyes, not for me, but only for
the wad of convertible pesos stuffed inside the money
belt wrapped around my waist. Quite why I bought the
money belt in the first place, I'll never know. Perhaps
it was a response to the angst of an online travel blog
issuing dire warnings about Cuba's notoriety for street
crime – warnings that in my experience over the coming
month proved to be unwarranted. Even so, a money
belt is the sort of safety-first item I often feel an aversion
towards. Not an aversion as strong as I have to, let's
say, the nonsense of a Tuesday morning team meeting.
But for me, it is one travel accessory too many – far less
a deterrent to crime than an invitation. Other than a roll
of bank notes, travellers' cheques or a credit card, what
else would a potential petty-thief think might lie within

the dead-giveaway bulge of the midriff pouch? A puncture repair kit? Anyway, I hadn't travelled close-to five-thousand miles to this exotic strip of Caribbean communism to fret about the what-ifs of life. That was the sort of energy-sapping neuroses I had hopefully consigned to the past within the four short lines of my office resignation letter. So with my relationship with risk transformed by my exit from the workplace, less than twenty-four hours after its hasty purchase, the money belt was deposited in an airport bin.

It is probably fair to say that taxi drivers aren't often of a shy, retiring nature when it comes to drumming up trade, and the group that met me in Havana was by far the most eager, most opportunistic I had ever come across. The only other cabbies I could think of that came anywhere close to their pushiness were a heavy-handed, money-grubbing mob I bumped into in the arrivals hall at Moscow airport several years earlier. Perhaps it is communism, or its remnants, that drives a man to such monetary fervour. Anyway, the drivers at Havana airport seemed to sense that I was over-burdened with pesos and could use a bit of their help in getting them spent. As it was, throughout the month-long trip me and my fellow traveller, Amigo, were offered stacks of support and encouragement by the many determinedly go-getting acquaintances who came our way – each one of them far more creative in the art of local cash disposal then we were. Amigo, by the way, was tagging along for this Cuban leg of my odyssey as a kind of curious holidaying observer, and was intrigued by my – as he saw it – 'audacious flight from the world of nine-to-five'. By joining me in the Caribbean he had made quite a commitment of his own by using up the bulk of his hard-earned corporate allowance of annual leave, leaving him with barely enough throughout the rest of the year to enjoy a long weekend. For Amigo then, as well as for me, there was much at stake.

Before leaving London, we had followed some odd advice from the *Rough Guide* that not only branded Cuba an expensive place to visit, but warned that it could take several hours of queuing at the airport to obtain a supply of pesos. Neither proved to be the case, but it was handy to know in advance of the trip that there are two currencies in circulation in Cuba – one for Cubans (the peso), the other for tourists who must buy on arrival in the country a stock of convertible pesos (known locally as CUCs), valid only in Cuba and not exportable. In other words, every note and coin we had just bought with our sterling had to be spent before we left the island. Feeling for a few moments like X-Factor judges, we went through the charade of a selection process before picking our driver. The selection criteria was quite simple – any cabbie who didn't insult the Queen or mention Manchester United was in with a shout. Of the gaggle of contestants vying for our atten-tions and tips, the winner – chosen for no better reason than his polite persistence and winning smile – led us away from the rabble of his disappointed colleagues, eyes wide in anticipation of the windfall to come. We paid the fare to our man, Javier, in advance with a roll of banknotes we discovered later was possibly enough to have put a decent deposit down on buying his car, disappointingly though not one of the 1950s classic American numbers we soon became so familiar with. In the event, Javier's company was worth every convert-ible peso he lifted from us, and as we bumped along the pot-holed road away from the airport towards the centre of his flamboyant capital city, he enlivened the ride with a pacey commentary in a mesmerising form of Caribbean Spanish, making the Andalucian variety I had recently been grappling with seem pure by comparison. With the help of some frantic arm waving and the odd resort to *Spanglish*, we made the most of our short time with Javier, whose sunny demeanour was that of a man recently come into money – our money.

Javier bristled with pride as he showed off some of the achievements of the 1959 Cuban Revolution. Passing one of these, the white bowl of the Sports City complex, gave Javier an early opportunity to wax lyrical about the benevolence and success of the regime, particularly in the field of sports. With a discernible catch in his voice, the avid baseball fan recalled his early childhood when participation in sport was the preserve of a wealthy elite, like much else in his country before Fidel Castro and Che Guevara came ashore in a leaky boat to seize power. Later I discovered that before the Revolution, organised sport in Cuba had been limited to four professional baseball teams, with virtually no provision in schools. In a shrewd post-Revolution gift to his people, Castro developed Cuba's sports infrastructure and encouraged the culture of participation as a right of the people – an act of benevolence that doubled up nicely as a cheap and convenient means of control. It isn't clear whether Castro took his lead on this from the Roman poet Juvenal, who said famously of keeping the masses quiet, *'give them bread and circuses'*. Nevertheless, looking at the tally of medals gained by Cuban Olympic athletes before and after the Revolution, it is impossible to rate Castro's sporting bequest to his nation as anything less than a resounding success. In the sixty years of Olympic competition between 1896 and 1956, Cuba won a meagre five gold medals. Since 1959, including at the London games of 2012, the best athletes of the communist island state of eleven million have thrown, jumped, ran and sprinted their way to a further sixty-seven, the two most famous being those won by national cult hero Alberto Juantorena – known fondly in Cuba as *El Caballo* (the horse) – who bust a gut for Castro at the Montreal Games of 1976 on his way to victory in both the 400m and 800m finals. Truly a Revolution for Gold!

Since the actual Revolution, the Cuban regime's commitment to sport has not been matched by its investment in buildings and infrastructure, much of which appeared from the back of Javier's cab to be in a state of terminal decline. Once past the impressive white drum of Sports City and a sprawling general hospital, much else that we saw as we approached the heart of the capital would do nicely as the movie set of a war zone, with lines of derelict buildings seemingly in imminent danger of collapse. As Javier steered a stomach-churning chicane around the wide pot-holes – full of murky rain water the colour of a hundred cups of tea – I listened hard through his heavy accent as he explained that most of Cuba's once grand relics were built by the Spanish sometime between their annexation of the island after Christopher Columbus's landing in 1492, and their expulsion following the Spanish-American War of 1898. Pock-marked by gunfire from the six years of revolutionary battles between 1953 and 1959, the crumbling colonial edifices we rumbled past on Avenida de México Cristina cry out plaintively for a little love, care and a great deal more money. We drove past overcrowded bus stops, no more than tin shacks dropped haphazardly onto pavements, and through countless more water-filled scars in the road, some of them wide and deep enough to be decent paddling pools. At last we met with grandeur in the imposing form of the domed neo-classical El Capitolio building, formerly the seat of the pre-Revolution government and recently restored to prominence as the home of the Cuban National Assembly. Javier brought us skidding to a noisy halt at the entrance of our hotel, the grand old Inglaterra – an iconic Havana institution since 1875 and the oldest hotel, not just in Havana, but in the entire country. But before my right leg was able to follow my left in leaving the car, I was pounced on by two young porters in a fierce competition for the tip they knew was coming their way. Hell bent on relieving us of our luggage and banknotes, both *chicos* stayed close on our tails as we walked towards the hotel's ostentatious entrance. Before we entered, the Inglaterra's external imported Alicante mosaics and *Sevillan* grilles caught my eye, causing a little pang akin to homesickness as I was taken back for a moment to those long sultry days I had recently spent in southern Spain acclimatising with modest effort to life beyond the workplace. The riot of decoration and flamboyance continued beyond the hotel frontage, its interior abundant with chandeliers, faux-rococo trompe l'oeil mirrors, ornate wrought iron work and marble floors. This kitsch throwback brought into sharp relief the inescapable truth that the hotel's halcyon days are possibly someway behind it, and the reviews I had read were decidedly mixed. But I had travelled to Cuba with a wide open mind, and if the elaborate décor was anything to go by, the very least the Hotel Inglaterra promised was nostalgia and a truly Cuban experience. A Marriott this most definitely was not.

As a reward I think for our undemanding approach at check-in and my determined effort to see the process through in Spanish, we were given a twin room with a small balcony offering a view of Parque Central, a popular spot we were told for all manner of Havana rendezvous. The drizzle had eased, prompting tourists to leave their hotels in droves to join locals in the park stood around in huddles, chatting animatedly in noisy competition with the boom of dance music from 1980s ghetto-blasters. For the benefit of visitors and the relief of their convertible currency, some performed conjuring tricks with multi-coloured balls, faked the swallowing of swords and flames or offered decent impersonations of Michael Jackson and Elvis. Feeling a miniscule of the nuisance of fame that either of those poor souls might have felt in their heydays, within a few seconds of reaching the square we were surrounded by a gang of boisterous youths, who in well-rehearsed English tendered rooms, taxis, cigars and unless I misheard, permission to marry their sisters. This was our first exposure to Cuba's famed hustlers and smiling swindlers – the *jineteros* or street jockeys – a constant, sometimes tiresome, but often quite entertaining feature of our stay on their socialist island. Once I had got the hang of warding them off, I grew to quite admire the *jineteros* for their entrepreneurial spirit, unthreatening opportunism and energetic determination to extract – mostly legally – as much of the tourist buck as they could manage. And in those first few hours in Cuba, high on the spirit of adventure and feeling as I might had I just arrived by a shuttle from Mars, I would have been offended if they had just ignored me. Not that there was the slightest chance of that. In fact, I may as well have been wearing a sign around my neck announcing, '*Buenos dias...newly arrived from a developed country with a bundle of CUCs in my pocket and no idea how to spend them. Please help. Muchas gracias'*.

After shaking off the *jineteros*, we began an exploration of Habana Vieja – old Havana – on the main entertainment thoroughfare, Calle Obispo – Bishop Street – named for its popularity as an eighteenth-century ecclesiastical hangout. After the rain, the evening had turned out fine and the Cuban world and his wife seemed to have joined us as we shuffled along the teeming street, notable among other things as the first Havana byway to be fully paved. Nowadays the bishops have given way to a less sober crowd, and once the lights went down the street was transformed into a catwalk of beauties both male and female (and the odd ambiguity in between) parading their perfect forms and outlandish garb. With not a whiff of high street homogeneity, Calle Obispo felt like stepping back in retail time, offering the kind of shops now missing and mourned in British town centres. Small shoe shops (albeit with no more than two or three clumpy styles to choose from) jostled with ironmongers, bakeries and shops selling party masks, balloons and cheap striped shirts in polythene wrappers. Less colourful were the many small groceries and supermarkets offering the window shopper only forlorn displays, including one making the best of a meagre stock of detergent by arranging the plastic bottles in the shape of the Eiffel

Tower. We reached the end of the street and entered the spacious Plaza de Armas, the oldest and most animated of Havana's squares dominated by a huge second-hand book market displaying what might possibly be the world's greatest collection of Che Guevara-themed material. The Argentinian's powerful image, the same one that had caught my eye in Granada inviting me to travel to Cuba, now carried even greater potency in this – if not his actual home – the absolute heart of his fame. Not surprisingly, throughout the month on Che's Revolution island we encountered his image everywhere we went. Even if we had tried, it would have been impossible to ignore Che, omnipresent as he was on every wall, billboard and peeling colonial façade.

The following morning we entered the fray of Havana's morning rush hour to an exhilarating cacophony of engine noise, blaring horns and competing car sound systems. This was also my first daylight glimpse of the ubiquitous 1950s classic American Studebakers and Oldsmobiles that have turned Cuba's streets into a living motor museum. I snapped away furiously as the colourfully nostalgic old beasts rumbled past, belching noxious lead fumes into the air for all to share. I had taken around thirty photographs of the cars before the absurdity of this dawned on me – virtually *every* car on the road was a beaten-up, pre-Revolution American stalwart. I guessed that there is nothing especially iconic about these old bangers to the people of Havana, beyond the marketing potential of their images on souvenir ash trays and t-shirts. Not surprisingly, new cars in Cuba are a rare and precious thing, and in a month on the island I didn't see a single one. In any case, new cars are really only available to purchase from abroad by senior party officials and a wealthy few. In this communist relic state, some people are evidently still more equal than others. Although unlikely to redress the imbalance, a recent 'freedom of import' initiative now allows the slightly easier import of new cars by ordinary Cubans, even if the cost of a standard model such as the Peugeot 508 still comes at a wholly prohibitive $250,000. So Havana's roads will continue for a good while at least to be bumper to bumper with these rather beautiful – but dirty and unreliable – symbols of Cuba's near six decades of post-Revolution austerity. I wouldn't mind wearing a t-shirt printed with an image of a big blue Studebaker. Yet would I swap my CO2-conscious, zippy little hatchback for one of those rusting, motorised emblems of political intransigence? Of course I would!

In a bid to escape the fumes, we headed in the direction of the El Malecón sea-front promenade, by way of the well-faded elegance of the Paseo de Martí. Laid out in the late eighteenth-century in a style resonant of a Parisian boulevard, the Paseo de Martí crumbled into disrepair after the Revolution, with many of its buildings now in an abject state, albeit benefiting inadvertently from the quirky feature of trees growing out of their ramshackle roofs, creating an unusual 'hanging-gardens' effect. With or without its rooftop foliage, the boulevard is a developers dream, with the recently constructed high-end Hotel Parque Central a confident sign of more lucrative times ahead. When we reached the sea wall, we walked along a section of the eight-kilometre promenade that snakes west along the coastline from the mouth of Havana Harbour to the city suburb of Vedado. We were taking in gulps of the salty air (to counter the pollution of the Studebakers) when we were approached by a solo *jinetero* named Jordi, whose rather lame opening gambit of 'where are you from?' was the one we had already heard a hundred times in less than twenty-four hours in his city. Aside from the usual cheap cigars, a *casa particular* (a room in his family house) and a subsidised table at his brother's restaurant, he had nothing novel to offer us. An engaging young hustler, Jordi would have made charming company had it not been for his sole motive of fleecing our cash. His cause wasn't helped much either by a sorry tale he told us of his 'seriously ill' grandmother, who he claimed to be raising funds for to buy 'miracle medicines'. Unfortunately, Jordi's charm was not matched by his sincerity, and so the young *jinetero* walked away empty handed, something about which I later felt a tad guilty. What if his story had been true? Although the type of low-key hassle we experienced with Jordi was a constant throughout the trip, it was nearly always unthreatening, and once a rebuff was repeated two or three times the *jinetero* generally backed off – in stark contrast to, say in Marrakech, where the *jineteros'* Moroccan counterparts think nothing of bringing you to the ground with a rugby tackle to prevent your escape and seal a deal. Part of the reason behind this fairly innocuous Cuban *jinetero* hustling are the steep penalties currently handed out for offences against tourists. Given the parlous state of its economy, the very last thing Cuba can afford is a reputation for crime and a dip in its tourist income.

Much of our time in Havana was spent wandering around the ramshackle, highly polluted streets of the old city. The area we explored was one largely constructed in the sixteenth-century by Spanish colonisers who used the city as a handy stopover for treasure galleons heading for the old world's entry ports of Cádiz and Seville. As far as restoration in Havana goes, the official line of the Cuban state is that it is 'striving to preserve and renovate' the city's precious collection of pastel-coloured colonial buildings. True to the regime's word, I did spot the odd renovation project already underway, but with so many buildings in such poor repair, significant restoration of Havana looks to be an aspiration for the considerable long-term. Passing the fortress of Castillo de la Real Fuerza – a Spanish colonial scheme completed in 1577 to ward off the threat of pirates – we entered the Plaza de la Catedral and found a perch in a sunny corner of a bar to admire the eighteenth-century Baroque Catedral de San Cristóbal. As we walked away from the square along San Juan de Dios, we were propositioned by a solidly proportioned, exuberantly attired lady called Marcia. There was nothing notably illicit about her simple scheme but had we bitten, it would have involved us placing her foot-long Havana cigar between our lips, while simultaneously being enveloped in her ample girth for a once-in-a-lifetime photo opportunity. I took one look at the soggy, well-chewed mouth-end of the torpedo cigar and declined to add to the saliva build up, but went for the photograph anyway, holding the unlit stogie ridiculously between my index and forefinger a couple of safe inches from my mouth. Where it had been before really was anyone's guess. Amigo took the requisite photo, and as we beat a hasty retreat after emptying our pockets of loose change into Marcia's broad palm, she followed us shouting incomprehensibly down the street offers of other services that may have proved even less hygienic than her cigar. In all honesty, when I looked at the photographic evidence of our encounter later, I felt grubby for having exploited Marcia for a cheap tourist snap. I could, after all, have simply given her the money without forcing her through the charade with the damp cigar. But then again, I had contributed to her earnings for the day, and this warm and smiling entertainer was most definitely not a beggar.

We hadn't travelled all this way to watch a movie, but when we came across the Teatro Payret picture house directly opposite the Capitolio building, we were weary of foot and it seemed just the place for a bit of a sit down. Quite unexpectedly, the first film we saw on the double bill transported me back to the exact south London location of my former paymasters. *The Block* documented the violent disaffection of gangs operating on the tough – now demolished – Heygate Estate at the Elephant and Castle. The film also showcased some impressive camera work around the rough and tumble Walworth Road, with one long-shot catching sight of the university building where until recently I had worked. My reaction to this curious juxtaposition of Cuban cinema and abandoned working life rather surprised me. Far from recoiling at the sight of the building from which I had plotted and then executed an escape, I felt a little knot of nostalgia. That's not to say I had much desire to be back amid the grind, chaos and confusion of my recently reorganised department – I was enjoying the chaos and confusion of Havana far too much for that. Yet the camerawork brought on the rather pleasing thought that the nine-to-five routine I had plodded through for so long had after all been a worthwhile exercise. What doesn't kill you probably does you good, or something like that. Anyway, the second film on the bill was less instructive and even less edifying. Starring Clive Owen in a dark tale of online child abuse in suburban America, *Trust* made for pretty grim viewing in that two-thirds empty flea pit – this most definitely was not a moment for popcorn (although it was on sale). As we left the cinema, I did wonder whether it was just a coincidence that both films on the double bill matinee had portrayed contrasting – but in both cases violent, abusive and overwhelmingly negative – aspects of our free, supposedly better, capitalist world.

After the sobriety of the film diversion some light relief was needed – so cometh the hour, cometh the Mojito! The venue for this landmark moment in our trip was the atmospheric pavement café at the front of the Hotel Inglaterra. Formerly *La Acerca del Louvre*, the café has an intriguing history. In the nineteenth-century it was a regular haunt of supporters of Cuban independence from Spain, and can also boast of being the site of conversion to the independence cause of a famous high ranking Spaniard. On 27th November 1871, dismayed by the arbitrary execution of eight Cuban medical students, Gran Canaria born Don Nicolás Estévanez broke his sword in two and renounced his military career with the attention grabbing declaration that, *'humanity and justice are more important than my fatherland'*. As we sat in much the same spot as Don Nicolás had, looking out at the incessant hustle of Parque Central, I read back his brave words and reflected on my own rather less emblematic recent conversion to independent living. *'Freedom and spontaneity are more important than a pay check'*, I blurted out in the spirit of Don Nicolás after a long slug of my Mojito. A roll of Amigo's eyes told me he had heard it all before. Incidentally, just as I had imagined when I first felt the thirst for one back in Granada, the Havana Mojitos were as good as their ingredients promised – a delicious blend of rum, cane sugar, sparkling water, lime juice and yerba buena, a locally produced variety of mint. With little thought to an alternative, the intoxicating mixture became the liquid staple of the trip.

And so to the Revolution – for all roads in Cuba will take you there. We began our trail at the windswept expanse of Plaza de la Revolución – apparently the world's thirty-first biggest square. Pretty much devoid of charm or conventional beauty, the concrete plaza with its collection of authoritarian government buildings and the landmark memorial to Che Guevara, is nonetheless an important focal point of the Revolution. More than just a shrine to the victory, the square has also hosted countless mass party rallies, and standing in front of the towering memorial to Jose Martí – hero of the nineteenth-century independence struggle against colonial Spain – it was easy to imagine Castro in the same spot, bellowing anti-American invective at an adoring crowd. Most striking in the square is the huge stylized steel-frieze replica of Alberto Korda's ubiquitous image of Che's enigmatic, distant Christ-like gaze, hair flowing from beneath his proletariat beret – truly *the* man of the people.

After Plaza de la Revolución it seemed logical to visit Havana's most popular museum, the Museo de la Revolución, housed pointedly in the former presidential palace of General Batista, the arch enemy of the 'People's Revolution'. As you might expect, absolutely no detail

is spared in proselytising the moral high ground of
Castro and his crew. In truth, attempting to absorb the
statistical minutiae of post-Revolution Cuba proved
heavy going – a success story told through exhaustive
lists of economic achievements, exceeded crop production targets and prolific industrial output. Fortunately
there was also plenty of less earnest material to keep
us interested, with the museum's general lack of entertainment value rescued by the considerable wall and
floor space dedicated to the lampooning of the United
States – with George W. Bush in particular coming in
for some harsh treatment. Under an unflattering carica-
ture offering the impression that the ex-President had
recently absconded from a city zoo, Dubya's rude tribute
declares, '*Gracias cretino por ayudarnos a hacer irrevocable el socialismo*' – '*Thank you cretin for helping
us to make socialism irrevocable*'. Hear hear, some
might say. The museum also has what is possibly the
highest ratio of staff to visitor of any public attraction
in the world – one of the many examples of communist
job creation schemes on view around Cuba. Outside
the entrances to each gallery stood huddles of smartly
dressed, yawning attendants, with no apparent function
other than to gaze suspiciously at visitors. I pulled out
a few well-rehearsed phrases from my patchy arsenal
of Spanish to try out on one bored young attendant,
and in the process committed a cardinal sin by asking a
few too many questions about plans for his country
post-Fidel Castro. Flustered by my gentle interrogation
about the future of the regime he was born into, the
junior attendant went away to consult an older, considerably more wizened colleague who stood close by, and
returned to relay in grave hushed tones the breaking

news that '*hay un plan*' – 'there's a plan'. Never one to pass up the chance of running through a well thought through plan, unwisely I pressed him for detail – 'who, what, why, when'? Rather like Premier League strikers do to celebrate a goal, the response was a firm forefinger to lips. Disappointed with his response, I thought about recommending the young man come up with a plan of his own, possibly involving leaving the country as soon as he could and by whatever means, but settled instead on studying a chart on the wall behind me listing a range of thrilling national achievements in the field of wheat harvests.

Away from the museum's stuffy interior and tight-lipped guides, far more inviting was its memorial to the *Granma* – the legendary little boat that played such a seminal role in kick-starting the Revolution. Boarded by Castro and eighty-one of his revolutionary pals in Mexico in November 1956, the *Granma* crash-landed at Los Cayuelos near Cuba's eastern city of Niquero. The mishap forced Castro and his men into the mountains, in the process establishing the bearded *comandante* not only as an icon of the Revolution, but also as an international celebrity and people's champion. We also found parked in the gardens a clutch of armoured vehicles used by both sides during the CIA sponsored Bay of Pigs invasion in 1961, a US attempt to defeat the Revolution that was beaten back within three days by Castro's army. Ensuring we left the museum without a shred of doubt about the rights and wrongs of the Revolution (the museum doesn't suggest that this may under any circumstances be up for debate), we stood transfixed in the gardens for several minutes in front of a flame rising high from a single Cuban star, encircled by the legend *Gloria eternal a los héroes de la patria nueva – Eternal glory to the heroes of the new country.*

This hardly needs spelling out, but aims and objectives in Havana were fairly light touch. Much of the time in the city was spent in a gratifyingly aimless fashion, wondering idly where the next Mojito might be coming from. But I did have a Havana bucket list of sorts, which included the Hotel Ambos Mundos back on Calle Obispo – the 1930s Cuban billet of Ernest Hemingway, where the writer is reputed to have penned the first lines of *For Whom the Bell Tolls*. Hemingway's former room – 511 – is now open as a tourist attraction where we viewed a display of his possessions, including a typewriter in a perspex case and other writing paraphernalia, his bed (surprisingly short for six-footer Hemingway), above which hangs an attractive Art Deco lampshade, copies of some of the political pamphlets he wrote in the room and – to show he was a man of wide interests – his fishing rod. Access to the room was by the odd arrangement of ringing a doorbell, answered by a rather stern hotel employee whose job was to stare at a watch and allow us precisely ten minutes to digest the room's frugal contents, before pointing at her wrist and ejecting us in favour of the next bell-ringing, paying guests. After poking around Hemingway's old Havana HQ, it seemed only good manners to continue the research with a drink at the writer's bar of choice, the legendary Bar El Floridita located further along the same street. As we entered we were a little surprised to see Hemingway himself waiting there for us, leaning nonchalantly against one corner of the bar as if he had never been away – or at least we met a life-size bronze of the man, in situ to celebrate the many hours he spent in that very same spot sating his various voracious appetites.

When Hemingway left Cuba in July 1960 it was in something of a hurry, forced out by the U.S. ambassador in Havana for reasons that remain unclear. Leaving behind him a fully-furnished finca, a clutch of possessions (fishing rods and a typewriter among them) and several unfinished manuscripts, the likelihood is that Hemingway fell out badly with the regime he initially supported. His death by suicide in Idaho exactly a year after his sudden flight from Cuba suggests all was not well with the man, although the absolute truth behind his demise will probably never be known. However, in the immediate aftermath of the Revolution Hemingway was a man of considerable repute in Cuba (his wealth and influence in America undoubtedly helped), a status illustrated perfectly by a photograph hanging behind his El Floridita statue of him handing over a prize to none other than Che Guevara for – somewhat bizarrely it seemed to me – the hero of the Revolution's victory in a fishing competition. I stood in a short queue to have the regulation photograph taken with El Floridita's most famous punter, aware that apart from the bar staff and waiters there wasn't a single Cuban in the room, an omission that does nothing for the bar's sense of authenticity. El Floridita's lack of local flavour is easily explained by the bar prices, which at several times the Havana average has turned Hemingway's old drinking den into an expensive preserve of tourists. We overlooked the obvious iniquities of this arrangement, agreed that it would have been very different in Hemingway's more licentious days, and got stuck into an ambitiously priced dish of scampi, washed down by wantonly overpriced Mojitos – mixed with great care and potency it must be said and then served by the most obliging, tip-keen *cantineros* I have ever come across.

Away from its smoky drinking haunts and monuments to the Revolution, the greatest pleasure in Havana was simply to walk the streets among its open and often quite beautiful people. In fact, sharing the city space with the *Haberneros* as they went about their daily business was an endlessly fascinating free attraction, and one that was occasionally jaw-dropping in its absurdity. One bright morning as Amigo and I dawdled along the Paseo de Martí towards the Malecón promenade, we joined an excited crowd gathered on the pavement in front of one of the many colonial houses crying out for a little investment, external rendering and general loving care. We followed the gaze of the crowd upwards to witness a scene as terrifying as it was hilarious. The spectacle was of two young men moving a Smeg-size fridge-freezer between two balconies (set around six feet apart) of two neighbouring fourth floor apartments, tottering precariously – to say the very least – on the crumbling ironwork of the balcony rails. Along with the rest of the crowd we held our breath, then gasped as the bulky appliance was passed awkwardly between the balconies, where one slip would have sent both the men and their appliance plunging to oblivion on the pavement below, killing them instantly and quite possibly anyone else unlucky enough to be caught in their way. At one alarming moment the door of the freezer section swung open (although its contents were not spilled, averting the risk to onlookers of being struck by falling fish fingers), a mishap that almost caused one of the foolhardy removal men to lose his footing. After a nimble recovery and several more tense minutes, the gymnastic manoeuvre was completed without injury to either man or appliance, earning a rapturous and relieved round of applause from the delighted crowd. A more fascinating, more spontaneous Havana attraction than any concrete memorial to victory in war, the photographs I took of this display of athletic nonsense were among the best of the trip – unforgettable images of an inspired piece of inadvertent street theatre.

Whatever loose plan we had for the day as we walked one muggy afternoon along Calle Obispo, getting a haircut was probably not part of it. But Amigo could not resist the allure of a dingy passageway leading off the street from under a red and white barber's pole sign. The passageway led us to the spartan premises of the cigar-smoking Carlos, whose 'salon' consisted of one squeaky revolving chair with a badly torn foam seat, a set of aged blunt clippers, a long-since seized-up pair of scissors hanging from a rusty nail, a cracked wash basin and a foully stained hand towel. The unhygienic hand-drying 'concern' that had made its way on to an agenda of a long-past office team meeting sprang to mind – the principal difference here in Havana being that this hygiene controversy really *was* one to get in a flap about. It would be unfair to compare a back-room in Havana shrouded in a fug of cigar smoke with the clinical environs of Nicky Clark of Mayfair. Yet for a price less than what might be paid by one of Nicky's stylists for a west-end cappuccino, Carlos set about Amigo's hair with gusto, attempting to plough through his thatch the blunt clippers held in his right hand and a cut-throat blade poised menacingly in his left in preparation for the quite possibly, very bloody finishing touches. As with most Cuban businesses, Carlos's salon was a family affair, so mid-styling cue the arrival of his brother José – a jovial man with the broadest grin in town. A born chancer he, José buttered me up for his inevitable business proposition with stories of the antics of his London-based nephew who had somehow drummed up the funds to travel to Britain to study English. Then, with a perfectly straight face, he expressed his surprise that I didn't actually know his nephew personally even though I lived in London myself – a city, I had to inform José, of more than eight million people. I knew it was coming, but it was a full *three minutes* before I was offered an opportunity to part with my cash in return for José's services as a tour guide, taxi driver or supplier of the 'finest and cheapest' Havana cigars, more than likely being rolled out by his wife on the kitchen table at home with some counterfeit 'baccy' as we spoke.

By the second week in Havana I was used to this gentle style of hustling, but was less prepared for the attentions of another member of Jose's family – the hot-pants-clad Chloe – who I assumed was his niece as she called him *Tio*. Chloe was also very much open for whatever business might come her way, and evidently not being the type of girl to waste time on ice-breakers offered both of us on-the-spot sex. I have no moral axe to grind here, but I did think that Chloe may have overstepped the mark in what was acceptable as part of the traditional barber shop offer of, 'something for the weekend, sir?' She didn't commit to a price for her services, but I speculated later that it would have come in at not much more than the price of Amigo's rather imperfect haircut. In all seriousness, Chloe was a pretty, bubbly girl and I felt sorry that she resorted so readily to the oldest trade for the sake of a few grubby tourist CUCs. I was less understanding, though, when I was forced to intercept her hand as she thrust it in the general direction of my midriff in a vain attempt to keep alive the possibility of a deal. Amigo, meanwhile, was enduring the final stages of his trim. With Carlos's cut-throat razor encircling his neck, he remained silent and perfectly still throughout the operation, restraining laughter at my expense as he watched Chloe's lewd entrepreneurial antics through the mirror. After declining Chloe's services as sensitively as I could, I offered her some friendly careers advice involving thinking through the option of doing something – *anything* – else for a living but sell her body to strangers. I beckoned Amigo to leave the barber's chair as soon as he safely could, which he did gingerly to avoid any sudden movements around the edges of Carlos's blade. We tipped handsomely – for what, I am not entirely sure – and left the salon hurriedly and a little shaken, looking back over our shoulders as we reached the relative safety of Calle Obispo, fully expecting the cut-throat wielding, multi-talented family to be pursuing us along the street. As we reached the café bar of the Hotel Inglaterra, we collapsed in laughter and ordered a couple of generously mixed enliveners to celebrate getting away from the clutches of *familia* Carlos, somewhat miraculously with no more than the scars of one bad haircut between us.

The novelty of on-tap cocktails, over-priced El Floridita lunches and the freedom to travel as we pleased in Cuba were all well and good. Witnessing the often harsh realities of the day-to-day lives of the average Cuban was less gratifying – at times even reducing the pleasure of being there. Take, for example, shopping. Aside from cigars and the endless lines of Che Guevara paraphernalia and assorted revolutionary tourist tat of no interest whatsoever to Cubans, there really wasn't very much to buy. Shops selling goods deemed to be beyond the basics are generally priced for tourists and the small island community of diplomats and foreign workers. The vast majority of ordinary Cuban families are still reliant for their food intake on the rationing system, introduced in March 1962 by the fledgling communist state to provide only for basic need. Scanning the shelves of the *Libreta* ration stores in Havana, there was precious little to choose from beyond staples like rice, baking powder and flour. Nevertheless, in a modest relaxation of food control in 2009, the humble pea and potato were taken off the list of rationed goods making it possible to purchase unlimited quantities of the two vegetables, albeit at around twenty-times their former cost. There are of course two well documented reasons for Cuba's continued relative poverty: the United States embargo on exports to Cuba imposed in 1960 (known in the country as *el bloque*), and the collapse of the Soviet Union in 1991 – an utter catastrophe for Cuba that pulled the rug from under the regime and consigned the country to a period of even greater economic hardship. Things, however, are set to change.

At the time of writing, President Barack Obama and Raúl Castro are on hand-shaking terms and engaged in genuine, well-meaning talks to bring an end to more than half a century of antipathy, mistrust and general skulduggery. What's more, in a game-changing move seen by many as the final chapter of the Cold War, the U.S. State Department has removed Cuba from its list of 'state sponsors of terrorism'. And in a moment of epic historical proportion, in August 2015 the Stars and Stripes flag was hoisted above its embassy in Havana for the first time in fifty-four years – by the very same U.S. marines who had lowered it back in 1961. Roberta Jackson, one of the state department's senior negotiators in the long process of restoring diplomatic ties between Cuba and the U.S., summed up the mood nicely on the day the embassy re-opened with some well-chosen words – *suddenly it feels like everything's in technicolour, like when Dorothy enters the land of Oz and the world becomes colourful*. Not to be outdone, the president also pitched in with some upbeat rhetoric of his own by declaring, *when something doesn't work for fifty years, you don't just keep on doing it. You try something different*. Well said, that man. But once the travel and trade restrictions are lifted as promised, how long will it be before Cuba's first Starbucks *barista* is pouring skinny lattes inside a renovated colonial mansion on the Paseo de Martí?

After the racket, pollution and constant *jinetero* attention of Havana, Amigo and I sensed our time in the capital was up, so moved on for a bit of respite to the beach resort of Varadero, two hours east of Havana aboard one of Cuba's ubiquitous *Viazul* buses – and as the name suggests, the vehicles are a vision in blue. Not perhaps most people's idea of an indigenous Cuban experience, there was plenty in Varadero to compensate, not least its famous twenty-five kilometres of beach – a tourist mecca of fine white sand of the sort that falls pleasingly between your toes as you walk

across it. Before the Revolution, Varadero had been the
playground of the Cuban elites and visiting Americans
who had the money and inclination to make the short
ninety-miles hop across the Florida Strait. After the
victory in 1959, Castro's government initially frowned
on this hedonistic surfer's paradise and the resort
fell into disrepair, until an economically-savvy 1990s
rethink allowed for a vast redevelopment and a prolif-
eration of all-inclusive four and five star resort hotels.
Incidentally, Castro may not have been much of a beach
bunny himself, but he certainly wasn't averse to a bit
of indulgent living of the variety that suited him. Indeed,
he didn't hold back in making the very most of the
opportunities presented by his veneration as globe-
trotting hero of the left. Take for example a state visit to
East Germany in 1972. Understandably finding the
routine of visits to the proletariat in their factories and
collective farms a little dull, in-between such obligations
and meetings with drab ministers of the German
Democratic Republic about the virtues of revolution
and central planning, the Cuban leader was known
to evade his Stasi bodyguards by slipping out of hotel
room windows to seek comradeship of rather less
gravity in local brothels. Oh, the dignity and sacrifice of
office! But before we judge the man, he should perhaps
be excused partaking in pretty much anything that
offered him relief from afternoons spent in the company
of the GDR Head of State, Erich Honecker.

We turned up in Varadero without a place to stay
(adding at least a small dash of intrepidness to the
experience), so were able to take advantage of a locally
advertised deal at the beachside Los Delfines – one
of those same Castro-built inclusive resort hotels.

Admittedly this was an unadventurous choice, but the food was far better than anything we had come across in Havana, not to mention the appealing novelty of the hotel's all-inclusive alcohol – a benefit ruined somewhat by the drinks being served in flimsy plastic cups, resulting in every drink tasting exactly the same – of plastic. After a couple of days of sun-worship around the hotel pool, we left our all-inclusive confinement to head out on a beach-bar crawl, an escapade we justified on the basis that it would both support local enterprise and allow us the enjoyment of a drink from a proper breakable glass. In truth, it's difficult to point to much else that happened in Varadero of any real consequence, save perhaps for the discovery of a small flood in our room and the dispiriting sight of my half-read copy of Deborah Devonshire's autobiography floating towards the open door of the balcony. Just in the nick of time, I rescued the last of the Mitford sisters from complete submersion and dried her off with a beach towel in the late afternoon sun. Another exertion of this five-day beach stopover was a thirty-minute muscle-mangling sports massage I received at the hands of the resident manipulator, Mateo, inside his Atlantic-facing beach hut. Just like other Cubans I spoke to during a month in their country, all Mateo could talk about was his desire to get as far away from his homeland as possible – in his case he said preferably to London. Sand, sea and sun were clearly not enough for this man.

With a decent amount of luck and even more finance, Mateo may soon get his wish. Under the recent relaxation of the regime – which among other things has allowed for the sale and purchase of property by private individuals, the ownership of mobile phones and access to hotels previously reserved for foreigners – Cubans can now consider realistically the possibility of overseas travel. Whereas travel outside Cuba before the relaxation was a pipedream for most (requiring an exit visa at a cost of around *fifteen* times the average monthly salary), now it is possible for ordinary Cubans to travel on a regular passport costing only $100. This may of course still prove to be prohibitive for many, quite apart from the obvious challenge of stretching a Cuban budget in, say, an American or European city. But the travel relaxation may at least reduce the risks taken by the thousands who have attempted crossing the shark-infested Florida Strait on dangerous illegal craft. In the half-century and more since the Revolution, more than a million Cubans have escaped the country to seek political refugee status overseas, mostly in the US although plenty of others have made it to Spain, Mexico and Canada. The ingenuity of those attempting the crossing to the 'Yankee Paradise' (as Castro once called the US), has known no bounds. Examples of makeshift craft filled with Cubans desperate for escape include a homemade kayak powered by a lawnmower engine and the conversions of a 1951 Chevy and 1959 Buick Sedan, famously pictured navigating the choppy waters of the Strait resembling an amphibious fantasy straight from an episode of *Thunderbirds*. Neither voyage made it to American shores, with both returned to Cuba to face the wrath of the regime.

Revitalised by Varadero, we continued our socialist odyssey southbound by *Viazul* coach to the city of Santa Clara in the Villa Clara region, a location famous as the burial place of Che Guevara. We drove towards Santa Clara on the Autopista Nacional A1, a diabolical stretch of pot-holed road that seemed unnervingly quiet given we were travelling between two of Cuba's tourist hotspots. We barely saw another vehicle during the entire journey, something that surprised me at the time but is easily explained by the high cost of fuel discouraging drivers from making anything but short essential journeys. As a result, outside the centre of Havana and other main cities, heavy traffic of the type taken for granted in the 'developed' world simply does not exist. However, the journey was not without distraction. Part way to Santa Clara we were deposited at a service station to discover that this, too, was all part of the on-going Cuban conspiracy to extract as much of the tourist buck as possible. Yet far from being a greasy spoon, this roadside café was a veritable mecca of entertainment. Right on cue as we stumbled from the bus, as if a coin had been dropped into a slot a resident five-piece band struck up a pulsating salsa beat. Wasting not a moment – time really is money in these parts – the maracas-waving lead singer approached our group of disgorged passengers with a wide toothy grin and the shameless intention of forcing hands deep into pockets. We all obliged of course – it really would have been rude not to – and during the fifteen minutes or so that we were allotted to jig around at the roadside gig and bolt down a drink from the small bar (quite possibly served by the maracas player's sister), the ten gallon hat used as a collection receptacle became full to the brim with the coveted notes and coins of the convertible peso. As we re-boarded our bus, I looked back at the band and each member had already laid down his instrument, the maracas-man's grin now switched off until the arrival of the next cash-cow tourist coach.

Before we had even reversed out of the parking bay, I saw our musical entrepreneur emptying the contents of his heavy hat onto a table, counting each CUC with undisguised glee. We had been thoroughly used and abused in that roadside café, but personally I felt all the better for it. After all, this had been by far the most rewarding motorway service station experience of my life. Watford Gap, eat your pricey heart out.

When we arrived at the bus station in downtown Santa Clara, we found it awash with local *jineteros* – groups of eager youths touting a predictable shopping list of rooms, cabs, cigars and dodgy haircuts. The hassle was intense and unrelenting, and when we finally accepted the offer of a cab from a particularly persuasive hustler, it was hailed for us by a chain of whistles from his co-conspirators along the street. Within less than a minute a horse and cart emerged from a dusty side street, onto which we and our belongings were bundled and then hauled towards the centre of town along the badly-rutted road. The driver used a light whip on his horse, something I didn't feel altogether comfortable with – my unease at being party to this low-level animal cruelty ruining what otherwise I might have claimed as an authentic Cuban experience. Never before had I regretted so much forgetting to slip a couple of carrots into my trouser pocket before setting out on a journey. We gave our driver (who for an unknown reason refused to share with us his name, and who remained silent and stony faced throughout the entire twenty-minute ride) a very healthy tip in the vain hope that some good would come the way of the wretched horse.

Our Santa Clara hotel, chosen from a short list of only two located in the centre, was the extraordinarily bad Santa Clara Libre – the tallest building in town and impossible to miss with its garish mint-green concrete façade. At a room rate of less than twenty pounds per night, little was expected of the hotel and, to be absolutely fair, far less even was delivered. We rejected the first cramped dimly-lit room we were offered by the wholly disinterested receptionist, once we realised it was blighted by a position directly above the hotel's ground floor discotheque. The second offer – a room on the eighth floor – seemed a little better, but came with the noise of rain water dripping onto an external air-conditioning unit, a problem Amigo circumvented by placing a spare pillow on top of the unit, no doubt to be discovered later by a chamber maid in a state of absolute ruin. But it was the hotel's poor waiters I really felt sorry for, who were embarrassed each day by the lamentable 'menu' they handed us as we plodded to our seats at breakfast. Even allowing for the inescapable fact that we were in probably the worst hotel of a small town in Cuba, the offer of a solitary slice of dry Melba toast the size of a beer mat, a stale bread roll with nothing to spread on it and a gloopy drink of an indeterminate fruit flavour, was pushing it. One morning, during the ordering charade involving the pretence of the waiters that there was some level of choice on offer, I had the temerity to ask for a glass of water, which I would have been quite happy to receive from the tap, but was refused on what I thought were the picky grounds of *'tap water not featuring on the menu'*. On another day, succumbing to hunger pangs and slowly losing the will to live, I walked into the kitchen to make a polite inquiry about the possibility of being offered something to eat other than dried-up packet toast.

I wasn't expecting the offer of a full English with a choice of white or brown toast, but I was surprised to find in the kitchen of this centrally located tourist hotel that each and every cupboard and shelf was completely bare. Complaining to the hotel management was clearly pointless, as well as possibly grossly unfair. So for this sorry state of affairs I laid the blame squarely with the collapse of the Soviet Union that led to Cuba's economic meltdown, Fidel Castro and his successor, brother Raúl, for decades of raspberry blowing across the Florida Strait, and a succession of intransigent American Presidents for blowing the raspberries back from where they came, with added interest. Yet as we have seen, this deadlock is all set to be broken.

Despite its terminal short-comings, the Santa Clara Libre had two principal redeeming features (aside from its appropriately low cost) – an excellent view from its upper floors of the lively Parque Vidal opposite and an unlimited supply of surprisingly luxuriant white towels, which benefitted each morning from our maid's artistic efforts in shaping them in the form of a swan, sailing boat or however the mood took her. For her dedication we tipped her with bars of soap brought from home especially for the purpose, following the advice of a Cuban blogger who wrote that scented western soap was a valuable local commodity. However, such excellence in the bathroom linen department demanded recognition beyond a bar of *Imperial Leather* from a Poundland multi-pack, so it was fitting that this otherwise lamentable hotel went on to become the first – and probably last – recipient of our informal 'Hotel Towel of the Year' award. So there really wasn't much to complain about at the Hotel Santa Clara Libre after all. Having said that, if any money comes the way of the establishment from the inevitable forthcoming US investment in Cuba, it may end up being not half as interesting.

When I report that my first impression of Santa Clara was of a town devoid of much to write home about, that isn't to say I was expecting the instant hit of, let's say, a Buenos Aires, Paris or Sydney. Yet on our first afternoon as we walked along the central throroughfare of Calle Marta Abreu in search of some inspiration and diversion, Amigo read aloud from the *Rough Guide* an excerpt that described Santa Clara as 'one of the liveliest cities in Cuba'. This seemed an unlikely claim as we passed by lines of boarded up shops and empty cafés, and I did wonder if the contributor of that passage had actually been to Santa Clara. At a stretch I had imagined we might find there an atmospheric old colonial town – faded perhaps and certainly knocked about around the edges, but with bohemian markets, local craft shops selling unmissable gifts and brilliant street musicians. The reality was less appealing, not helped one bit by the packs of disaffected young *jineteros* hanging out on every scruffy street corner, far more assertive in their hustling than anything we had seen elsewhere in Cuba thus far. In fact, a few hours after arriving in Santa Clara I was already wondering how we could possibly fill three days there. We found salvation in drink on the smoky outdoor terrace of Bar Europe, where we reviewed our receding options over a couple of bottles of the local, quite excellent Cristal beer, taking the opportunity while we were at it of raising a toast to our hotel for its surprise success in the towelling contest. With the general mood lightened by the infectious cheerfulness of groups of locals sitting around us, I set about making copious notes about Santa Clara, Che Guevara and our unforgettable hotel, in the hope of finding inspiration where so far it was lacking, and of somehow making a connection with this city of well-hidden charms.

Bonding with Santa Clara was proving to be a determinedly slow process, and the Bar Europe drinks only reminded us of the growing problem of food – or lack of – so we decided to brave a nearby state-run restaurant, which by definition in Cuba was not altogether promising. To be fair to the joint, there was a menu of sorts to peruse and we played it safe – or so we thought – by ordering cheese pizzas (there was no suggestion on the menu that a tomato might feature in the recipe). After what felt like several light years, when the pizzas were finally brought to our table I was surprised that our waiter wasn't rigged up in a protective suit as if entering the aftermath of some terrible nuclear accident. The two platefuls of fluorescent yellow matter masquerading as examples of Italy's national dish put me in mind of freshly-produced, Friday night town-centre vomit viewed on the pavement under the glare of a streetlight. So it is fair to say that the food in this 'state restaurant' fell someway short of being fit for human consumption, but was colourfully photogenic and provided a quirky subject for a holiday snap. We finished our beers – which had gone straight to our heads from the lack of food – paid the bill for what we hadn't had, tipped our waiter for being a nice person and left, carrying with us the novel sensation of walking out of a restaurant feeling hungrier than when we had arrived. Our only compensation was that our obliging *camareros* might be given the chance – if they were feeling particularly ravenous and weren't especially picky – to help themselves to the returned food. Twenty-four hours on and still there wasn't a hint of a decent meal to be had in Santa Clara. With Amigo's mood plummeting as a result, we did come close to consuming something passable with a couple of 'baguettes' we bought made with dry crusts and a reddish, rubbery material described by the street vendor who prepared them as 'fine Dutch cheese'. Our inquiry about the possibility of including a tomato in the filling drew a blank look, which I didn't put down to my wayward Spanish pronunciation – the tomato was evidently a rare and precious thing in these parts, or at least one out of season.

So it was with some desperation that Amigo – a man not normally known for toughing things out on an empty stomach – thumbed through the *Rough Guide* in search of an appetising option somewhere in the vicinity of the town. Leaping from the page came Los Caneyes, a mid-range tourist hotel situated a temptingly-short ten minutes away by cab from Santa Clara's centre. You will forgive our lack of adventure in choosing Los Caneyes over the indigenous – but frankly not very appealing – options in town. Hunger can do funny things to people, and the advertised self-service all-inclusive buffet seemed just too good an opportunity to turn down. As it turned out, both the venue itself (built to resemble an indigenous village) and the food were wonderful. When we entered the restaurant through a door connecting it to the poolside bar (a little sheepishly it has to be said – at this moment we did not feel like intrepid travellers), I was surprised by my over-reaction to the sight of a large tray of ripe, freshly-sliced tomatoes. However, my over indulgence of the red vegetable (or should that be fruit – my long uncertainty about this was ended with some brief research revealing the tomato to be for culinary purposes a vegetable, while botanically a fruit), brought on an untimely bout of hiccups, which probably served me just about right. Whatever the genres of the colourful foodstuffs laid out on tables straining under their weight, as an added bonus we were treated to heaps of warm and wholly unpretentious Cuban hospitality. Our exceptionally jolly waiter, Bruno, his beaming face turning a little tomato-like as he received our tip, performed a celebratory jig around the table to the delight of the entire room. For that moment alone, the cab fare and entrance fee to Los Caneyes was money well spent. More than that, Bruno's spontaneous outburst of joy squashed the touch of inadequacy we felt at choosing to eat in a tourist hotel over something authentically Cuban. The truth was, we just couldn't face another day in Santa Clara on an empty stomach.

The following morning, fortified by our gluttonous adventure at Los Caneyes, we hit the Che Guevara trail by schlepping a mile or so out of town to the big bold concrete memorial that houses his remains – as well as those of twenty-nine of Che's brothers-in-arms killed alongside him during efforts to kick-start an uprising in Bolivia in 1967. Once Che's body had been exhumed and returned to Cuba, a vast concrete plaza in Santa Clara was chosen as the most fitting place for his mausoleum, in recognition of his exploits during the Revolution at the Battle of Santa Clara in December 1958. To find out more we moved on from the memorial to the nearby *Monumento a la Toma del Tren Blindado*, marking Che's finest hour in the town. During the Battle

OUT OF OFFICE

of Santa Clara, an armoured train carrying a battalion
of General Batista's troops was derailed by Che's men
using – of all things – tractors, one of which sits on a
plinth as a striking (if somewhat inelegant) reminder
of the event. The battle is also celebrated in a novel exhibition presented in one of the original derailed trucks.
For a meagre entrance fee we were provided with our
very own tour guide, a stern, world-weary *mujer* called
Mercedes, who I managed to offend by enquiring how
old she had been at the time of the battle – an ill-judged
question that earned the snappy reply that she wasn't
in fact born until two years *after* the event. During
Mercedes' lively presentation of Santa Clara's eponymous moment, it was evident that for her the narrative
of the Cuban Revolution was fixed – one side benevolent
and entirely good (local hero Che's, of course), the
other wretched, deserving of death and absolute defeat
(the loathed Batista regime). It wasn't that I necessarily
disagreed with her, but my gentle challenging of this
moral certainty was dismissed without ceremony.

The entertaining slice of Revolution propaganda we
enjoyed at the train museum set me thinking a little
more about the man behind the legend. Before I actually
visited Cuba and saw for myself the Revolution's austere
gift to its people, I had been willing to accept the easy
and comfortable image of Che Guevara as one of life's
eternal good guys – the poster boy of the Revolution,
wholly dedicated in words and deed to a selfless struggle against decadent, oppressive opponents in support
of the common man. It is also true that only a few
weeks before I had been spurred to travel to Cuba by
Che's image gazing at me from a scruffy poster in a side
street in Granada. Then I had seen in Che only that

implacable symbol of protest, that enigmatic bearded bohemian, that ubiquitous fashion accessory – in every respect the marketing man's dream, pinned on students' walls the world over. But now, immersed in the life of the island Che laid his life on the line to liberate, I began to question some of this. I suppose what really got me thinking was looking up some of Che's best known quotes from the multitude available. These pearls of wisdom have secured his reputation as a nigh-on untouchable hero of the left almost as much as the iconic Alberto Korda photograph, which alone has established the man as a global brand – an image as recognisable throughout the world as the stylised font of Coca Cola or the golden arches of McDonald's. Here then is the man who told the world so stirringly, '...*the Revolution is not an apple that falls when it is ripe. You have to make it fall'*, and '*I would rather die standing up than live on my knees'*. Yet less impressively so you might feel, Che also owns the view that '*the black is indolent and a dreamer; spending his meagre wages on frivolity and drink'*. Not, in that instance, did our heroic Argentinian, Ernesto Raphael Guevara de la Serna, display quite so convincingly the colours of a left-wing hero. Nor indeed on another occasion did he when he attributed black racial purity – somewhat bizarrely – to '*an aversion to bathing'*. So I mostly turned a blind eye to the Che Guevara keyrings, fridge magnets, the mass-produced Andy Warhol silk screen print and the multitude of other tourist tack exploiting Che's image, preferring to think of him as a fascinating historical figure and flawed human being. I didn't mention any of this to Mercedes though.

We shook off the shadow of Che by taking a *Viazul* bus further south through Palmira and Cienfuegos to the UNESCO World Heritage Site of Trinidad, a charming old colonial town in the Sancti Spiritus region. Founded in 1514 by the Basque landowner Francisco Iznaga, modern Trinidad is a major centre of the Cuban tobacco industry and with its picturesque cobbled streets, also thrives as a centre of tourism. As we left the bus at Trinidad's dingy downtown bus terminal, inevitably we ran into an unruly posse of youthful *jineteros* offering the usual spoils of cigars, taxi rides and subsidised family restaurants. At last finding a way through the scrum, we were bundled by an older man into a car that he assured us was 'authorised'. The car inched its way through the mob, the contorted faces of the rejected *jineteros* pressed up against the glass, their fists banging madly on the tinny roof, still screaming offers of their goods and services as we pulled clear. We didn't quite have the mop cuts and the guitars, nor was there a single camera flash to capture the moment, but all I could think of as we drove away from the chasing pack was a New York side street in 1964, as the Beatles left Carnegie Hall amid the hysteria of their first US Tour. Chance would be a fine thing.

Our exceptionally chatty driver, Alfonso (his name was a dead giveaway, tattooed along the full length of his right forearm), dropped us outside Las Cuevas, a large complex of commodious concrete cabins clinging to a hillside overlooking the town with a distant, tantalising view of the Caribbean coast and the Ancón peninsula. Before he left us, Alfonso didn't pass up on his opportunity to introduce us to the option of a box or two of fat Havanas from his family cigar emporium in town and left his card should we need another cab, something to smoke, or indeed anything else he could get his hands on. Our allocated cabin belied its exterior nuclear bunker appearance by offering a comfortable well-padded interior – a perfect base in fact for forty-eight hours of poolside slothfulness and grazing on the non-stop, tomato-laden hotel buffet. Before we got stuck into any of that, we walked back into the beautifully restored sixteenth-century centre of Trinidad to explore its undulating traffic-free streets, which after the grime of Santa Clara were an absolute joy. The pretty Plaza Mayor, set around its wrought iron-fenced gardens was enchanting, although no more than a five minute walk in any direction from this tourist centre we found neglected streets shot to pieces by the nation's poverty. Beyond Trinidad's chocolate-box centre, if anything the privations of the Castro regime seemed more apparent here than in Havana, which accounted for the far more assertive tactics of the omnipresent Trinidad *jineteros* – as bold a bunch of chancers I had ever come across.

However, it was the unlikely bait of a family size bag of Walkers crisps, rather than a bundle of CUCs, that seemed to bring out the worst one evening in a pack of hungry hustlers as we walked from Las Cuevas towards the centre of town. Unbeknown to us at that point, the common crisp – that crunchy symbol of capitalist decadence – was a luxury consumable hard to come by for most Cubans. Once the group of six approaching youths spotted our teasing pack of ready salted, they descended into jeers and unflattering hand gestures – harmless stuff, but merely a warm up for the less tolerable antics that followed. As we attempted to walk round the group, the bigger and bolder members began jostling us, pretending to wrestle the crisps from us and pick our pockets. In the end, it was all simply a charade. With nobody else around, this *jinetero* mob could easily have made us the first ever victims of a ready salted crisp-mugging, or worse taken our cash, cameras and given us a good hiding to boot. In the event, none of that ever felt close to happening, and about all we did receive from that salted-snack deprived mob was a bit of mocking hostility. We emerged from the encounter physically intact but with our pride severely dented. Every convertible peso and item of value remained on our person including the offending, unopened pack of Walkers that I still clung to pathetically in my left hand. Eating them was now out of the question, of course – they really would have choked me. Neither could I throw them away – not with so many more deserving takers around than we were. We settled the dilemma by leaving them prominently on a wall for a passer-by to help themselves to, without any need for hustling. Hours later as we plodded back up the hill to our accommodation, we were amazed to find that our abandoned crisps remained untouched and in the exact same spot where we left them. Hardly earth shattering stuff, I know, but this innocuous incident seemed to me to exemplify much about the dignity of everyday Cubans – from the absence of any genuine threat from the economically destitute *jineteros* we brushed with earlier, to the refusal of any passer-by to take advantage of the free opportunity of an oversized bag of an elusive indulgence.

From the small terrace at the front of our bunker-come-chalet, we spent a couple of hours one evening gazing across at the distant Ancón Peninsular, which we knew from our guide book boasted a fabulous beach of pure white sand. There was still more than a week before our flight from Havana back to London, so we made the not terribly difficult decision to end our trip treading the sand of that beckoning Caribbean paradise. Turning up the following morning in Ancón at the hotel of the same name in the back of a smoky 1980s eastern European saloon – converted for use as a Cuban cab – was apt, for on first sight of the hotel we might as well have been rocking up at a favourite beach resort of the East German Stasi. The hotel building, which from a distance resembled an ocean liner, up close offered all the charmless, imposing concrete hallmarks of the type of brutal monstrosities erected all over the former Soviet Bloc countries in the 1950s and 60s. There was no doubting the influences behind the hotel's construction, although its former battleship-grey façade had benefitted from a recent exuberant makeover with daubs of bubble-gum-pink masonry paint. The hotel was still an eyesore – but at least now a cheerful one. Grinning at the receptionist in this pink paradise once more did the trick and we were despatched through the hotel grounds to find what she described as our 'superior' room in a newish annexe alongside the sumptuous beach. Given that the blue-green waters of the Caribbean were all but lapping at the door of our room, we happily overlooked the fact that our view was of the hotel's rear service area and a squadron of wheelie bins, rather than of the ocean itself. Nevertheless, looking beyond the skips of rubbish lay the narrow sprawl of Trinidad, providing us with the pleasing symmetry of the exact opposite view to the one that had inspired our choice of Hotel Ancón in the first place. In truth though, aside from its numerous ping-pong tables and round-the-clock option of all-inclusive heavy drinking, there was precious little for guests to actually do inside the hotel. Having no real desire to be detained in the liver unit of a Cuban hospital, we embarked on a sleepy, mood-compatible daily routine of breakfasting at nine-ish, followed by a few lengths of the hotel pool before ten, then recovery until lunch in a prostrate position on a sun lounger, in my case still enjoying the company of Deborah Devonshire. These lazy hours were punctuated by short swims out to Los Campeónes, a novel floating bar where we soon got the hang of drinking Mojitos while staying afloat by doggy-paddling – for what it's worth, a useful string to your bow to carry on any trip to the Cuban seaside. Every afternoon at around four, our peace was shattered by the arrival of a comi-cally inept dance troupe performing to an imaginary poolside audience. Each time, without exception, within five minutes of their routine starting, everyone had left to escape the din. As awful as their act was, I did feel sympathy for the poor members of the troupe – each one of them looked thoroughly jaded, indifferent and more worryingly still, painfully underfed.

After fleeing the dance troupe one idyllic afternoon, I lay on a lounger on the beach, sheltered from the dipping sun by a straw parasol. My mind wandered idly. Expecting at any moment a 'Bounty Hunter' to emerge from the calm Caribbean water, I reflected on my decision to pack up my work station, shred the paper waste of my nine-to-five and walk away. Perhaps the memory of that timeless TV advert for the coconut-filled chocolate bar had made me a little nostalgic, I couldn't really say. But the navel gazing (an activity almost impossible to avoid when lying on a Caribbean beach in the benign warmth of a late afternoon), reminded me that had I stayed within the confines of the office (an unlikely supposition I admit, but bear with me), it was about the time of year to have faced that phoney construct of management control – the annual performance appraisal. In the main, my own appraisal meetings had been fairly excruciating affairs played out in cramped meeting rooms waffling over performance indicators, training needs and objectives set and targets met. Personally, I always felt that my work performance couldn't be measured with any real accuracy by the S.M.A.R.T objectives I was being judged by. In fact, I found it nigh-on impossible to relate – with any degree of credibility – what I did on a day-to-day basis with my clients (those real, hard-up and often highly stressed students I would go to great lengths to help), to the management prescription of Specific, Measurable, Achievable, Realistic, Time-bound. In any case, I hadn't the faintest idea what any of that really meant.

I don't think it is arrogance to believe in the quality and value of the work that I did. And with organisational 'concerns' (and there were always plenty of those) coming for me a pretty poor second to the real life concerns of my clients, I became adept at playing the appraisal game, flexing my responses to the demands of the process in a bid to leave the room as quickly as possible, with my dignity intact and still on the payroll. Never once did I feel any guilt about this mild deceit – there was no need. For also complicit in this harmless little fraud were the majority of the managers who had the task of appraising me. In fact, I can be certain that most of them would have baulked at the prospect of one of their team members taking the process *too* seriously.

In such an instance, and when carried out precisely to the book by the keenest of managers and the most earnest of employees, an appraisal could easily last for half-a-day – time that could and should have been spent on actually doing the job. Mercifully, my own appraisals were generally done and dusted within an hour. For this economy of scale I am especially grateful to one past manager's loose approach to the process. On each occasion, he would simplify matters by placing a firm tick in the 'Excellent' box for every performance category bar one – regardless of how deserving a score it was – demoting me one year to a 'Very Good' for 'Training and Development' on the grounds that it would make the appraisal *look* more realistic. Fabulous! To this day I have no idea what I did wrong – or even right – that year to warrant only a second-tier rating for 'Training and Development'. I never bothered to ask, but this genial corner-cutter was certainly my kind of manager. Anyway, back in the pseudo-reality of that tropical beach, my efforts to self-appraise with some S.M.A.R.T targets of my own fell all too easily by the wayside. In the heat of that paradisiacal moment, I could manage no better than the somewhat facile S.M.A.R.T targets of basking in the glorious Sunshine sipping a Mojito in Ancón on a Recliner in the hope of returning home with a Tan. Short-term targets indeed, but at least realistic and enjoyably met.

Feeling foolishly rewarded by all of this, I took my thoughts away from the beach to share them with a lobster-red Amigo, who I suspected was building up a head of steam to draw up a few absconding plans of his own. After we had caught up on 'first world' affairs in the hotel – through the lazy means of CNN and that network's extraordinarily telegenic news anchorman, Anderson Cooper – Amigo regaled me with a tale of some ghastly-sounding new management initiative in his workplace involving sending members of staff out on 'thinking days'. The idea behind the scheme is that, let's say, a stroll along the South Bank of the Thames or a walk in the park followed by a team lunch, might inspire workers to greater ingenuity and heightened productivity. I shuddered at the thought of my former line manager rolling a piece of flipchart paper out on a lunchtime table of a local branch of *Prêt à Manger*, her team tasked with bullet-pointing the objectives of a new initiative just dreamed up on a blustery Tuesday morning walk along the river. Celebrating our agreement that life is simply way too short for the frippery of a corporate 'thinking day', Amigo and I felt about ready to fall off the crisp wagon we had ridden for all of four days since our unsettling brush with the hungry *jineteros of* Trinidad. Checking over my shoulder for potential crisp-muggers, I exchanged a fistful of convertible pesos at the bar for two potato-sack-sized bags of salt-and-vinegar and returned to my seat with the said purchase and a round of drinks. We were immediately surrounded, not this time by young hustlers, but by members of the hotel staff with eyes fixed on the salty mound piled high and wide in front of us. Suddenly the most popular punters in the bar, we offered them round to the posse of cleaning ladies, receptionists and barmen, sharing with them the mouth-tingling sensations that only a salt-and-vinegar crisp can deliver. There was a pleasing spontaneity about this small Caribbean crisp-fest, and rarely have I been among a group of people who looked so contented. Come to think of it, rarely had I felt so contented myself.

At moments like this there was really only one thing for it. I had spent rather too much time horizontal in Ancón, that lazy paradise of sand, sea and socialism. It was time to move on – time to revisit and build on my out-of-office plan. Earlier that day as I lay reading by the pool, eyes flicking between page and an uninterrupted blue sky, I reached a momentous passage in that Varadero-flood-rescued story of the mischievous Mitford sisters. It told of the afternoon when they risked all by taking tea with Hitler, a timely reminder that I had included as an immovable part of my plan a long-outstanding mystery to solve – a mystery set in a cooler location than Cuba, but one with a story to tell of its own schisms and privations of twentieth-century history. This was a mystery called Berlin.

JFK - a 'man of Berlin' or a sugary donut?

'The minute you know you're on safe ground, you're dead'.

David Bowie

– 3 –

Berlin Bitte

During the tortuous ten-hour flight back to London from Havana, I took a decision to jettison air travel for the time being in favour of the train. I was tired of the boarding passes that refuse to print, the greedy lure of duty-free and the hours of heel-kicking in the departure lounge. The other self-evident disadvantage of flying is the inability to break your journey. My next destination was Berlin, but how dull a journey it would be to fly over most of western Europe to get there. So this time I would travel leisurely, mood-compatibly and in my own time. But I needed detail and by performing a contortionist act in my economy seat between the Caribbean and London, I managed just enough elbow room to sketch out – literally on the back of a boarding pass – the plan for my leisurely route to the German capital. This would be a journey about more than the destination itself – a journey to be properly savoured on solid ground, simple in its itinerary, rewarding in its execution. When I had completed my scrawl, the rear of the boarding pass revealed a pencilled confusion of place names, approximations of timings, mazy lines of railways and possibly the worst outline map of the European Continent ever drawn. Nevertheless there was method in the mess, and my route to Berlin would take me by Eurostar from London to Brussels, then by a Belgian Thalys service through Aachen towards Cologne, and northeast in the reliable charge of Deutsche Bahn to Hannover where I planned to drop-in on the scene of an earlier highlight of my meandering CV. Nostalgia satisfied in Hannover, I would head due north to Hanseatic Hamburg and then east to Berlin where I had that mystery – if not perhaps entirely to solve – to at least have a very determined and enjoyable go at investigating.

Just shy of a fortnight after the flight from Cuba, I sat on an early morning Brussels-bound Eurostar service ready to depart London's railway cathedral at St. Pancras, considering the happy irony of continuing my new 'off-the-rails' life sitting firmly on them. An even happier – nay, miraculous – thought was that of being able to board a train in the centre of one European capital to alight a couple of hours later in another. Thanks to rail technology Paris for lunch was an affordable reality, although today I would make do with Brussels, a less self-assured substitute perhaps, but I wasn't complaining. Just about any journey I have taken by rail, however spectacular or routine, has captured my interest. Bolt upright for three days and nights in steerage class across Australia from Perth to Sydney, strap-hanging with stressed-out commuters between Barking and Gospel Oak, the thrill of Spain's high speed link from Madrid to Seville, the five-minute shuttle between Brighton and Hove – there's always a tingle of excitement there. But I can hardly think of a more propitious beginning to a rail journey than leaving from St Pancras in the direction of any major European city. In fact, given a choice between an expenses-paid excursion to outer space or a window seat on a continental rail journey, for me there would be no contest.

Before boarding my train, I felt it only right to spend a few moments in the company of the saviour of St. Pancras – the former Poet Laureate John Betjeman – at the foot of his striking bronze statue. I followed Betjeman's gaze, looking upwards in awe at William Henry Barlow's vast arch of glass, which on completion in 1868 became the world's largest single-span structure. Unfathomably, a century later the demolition of the stupendous arch and the majestic station at its front became more a probability than possibility. Following the 1960s electrification of mainline services serving the north of England – a modernisation that included the concrete re-development of the neighbouring, utterly charmless, Euston Station – St Pancras was considered obsolete. The prospect of demolition for Barlow's arch and George Gilbert Scott's monumental station frontage – the former Midland Grand Hotel – was too much to bear for Betjeman, who led an unrelenting, ultimately successful campaign to have the station's buildings saved for the nation, an achievement alone to warrant his status as an enduring national treasure – even if he failed with a similar campaign to save the 1837 Doric arch at Euston. As I sat under the St Pancras arch on the outdoor terrace of *Carluccio's* waiting to be served a budget-busting breakfast, I wondered with horror what steel and concrete monstrosity may have taken the place of this monumental structure had Betjeman failed. Much more could be said about the station itself, but suffice it to say that the refurbished St Pancras may well be the most beautiful transport terminal on earth, and for me a thrillingly grand stage to begin the latest leg of my post-work journey.

If, like me, you have spent dreamy hours (perhaps at your work computer when you ought to have been doing something else), browsing Mark Smith's guide to European and world rail travel, *Man in Seat 61,* you will understand that the position of your randomly allocated seat is crucial to the enjoyment of the trip. As I left St Pancras, I wasn't so lucky as to be sitting in the first class comfort of seat 61, in coach 7, 8, 11 or 12, as recommended by the author of that absorbing work, but my seat was at least aligned with a window rather than a panel – the potential ruination of any rail journey. I had also followed his advice by packing three of the essential accessories to fulfilling rail travel – a good book, a bottle of wine and a corkscrew. Before eight-thirty in the morning was maybe a tad early to be putting the latter two items into service, but Berlin lay a long way off and my journey was young. So after zipping along HS1 through east London (Britain's solitary stretch of high speed track until HS2 comes along to join the party), then Ebbsfleet, the Thames Gateway and across the Medway Viaduct to the Channel Tunnel, the train sped towards Brussels all too quickly in a shade under two hours.

I arrived in the Belgian capital in the mid-morning of a high summer day. Yet in truth, the city felt drab and barely awake. I wanted it to be different – vibrant and energising as a capital city should be. I had only a few hours in Brussels before catching my connecting train to Cologne, so in the hope of discovering the city's evidently bashful vibe I walked away from the traffic-choked streets around Midi station towards the quainter narrow lanes and alleyways of the Lower Town. I reached the focal point of tourist Brussels – the outstanding Grand Place – a full-scale riot of opulence dominated by the extravagant Hôtel de Ville looking down imperiously on the much smaller, frilly façades of a collection of baroque seventeenth-century guild houses. Due to the tight train connection, my appreciation of medieval Brussels had to be a rushed affair, and hungry from the journey I bolted lunch in the tourist-magnet café-bar, Le Roy d'Espagne, perched warily on a bar stool under a novel ceiling decoration of inflated animal bladders. I banked on them being empty and for decoration only.

I left the café bone dry to call in on another of the city's bladder-themed attractions, the Manneken Pis – a frankly unexceptional, sixty-one centimetre-high figure of a urinating urchin stuck high up in a niche behind an impenetrable iron fence. Since the original figure was put in place in 1619, this quirky emblem of Brussels has, for a reason I couldn't quite fathom, been stolen on no less than seven occasions, the last time in January 1963. Better protected these days, the current incumbent has been cheerfully pissing from his niche since 1965, but in all fairness offers little else to entertain its visitors. Discovering some of the legends behind the creation of the Manneken Pis proved to be more rewarding than actually seeing it. Of these, my personal favourite is the story of an early seventeenth-century boy who woke in the night to discover a fire, which the quick-thinking youngster extinguished by urinating on, thereby sparing his family from burning and in the process preventing the fire spreading to the nearby king's castle. If you can believe the tale (and frankly, a bit of faith here does add something to the modest reward of this Brussels attraction), the small figure now sitting in the niche for tourists to gawp at is there in his honour. Nowadays, the Manneken Pis is occasionally given a style makeover by the 'Friends of Manneken Pis', a worthy body of volunteers (possibly loveable eccentrics) that keeps hundreds of outfits in which to dress the urchin depending on their mood or the occasion. The pick of the outfits selected over the years include the garb of a Hungarian Hussar, the yellow jersey of a Tour de France winner, a Mozart suit and the regalia of the Mayor of Brussels. Although it wasn't drawing gasps from the crowd when I was visiting, I guessed the popularity of the Manneken Pis rises considerably on the days it is hooked up to a barrel of beer, cheerfully urinating local brews into mugs for passers-by to sample. I missed out on that particular perk but the figure did give me an idea as a solid entry for a book that could be compiled with a title along the lines of *Overrated Tourist Attractions*. This would be the sort of book to sit eye-catchingly at a bookshop till alongside *Britain's Crappiest Towns* and *The Worst Cars Ever Sold* – a small tome destined surely to become a bestseller in all good charity shops. While we're on the topic, also included in the book might be Copenhagen's Little Mermaid (an attraction so unremarkable that during a visit to the Danish capital I walked straight past it without noticing) and the Mona Lisa (after an interminable queue to enter the Louvre, Paris's po-faced must-do art attraction is virtually impossible to view from behind a sea of heads). As for an image for the front cover of this yet to be published book, I can think of nothing better than the Manneken Pis urinating in beery full flow, dressed to kill (as it was recently), as local celebrity politician Herman Van Rompuy, the man who holds the dubious honour of being the very first President of the European Council.

A lesser known Brussels attraction is the Comic Strip Route – a celebratory walking tour of Belgian comic strip art, an entertaining art-form that found real purpose during the Second World War as a reaction to the occupying Nazis' restrictions on American comics. The art's most famous exponent was Georges Remi – better known as Hergé – the creator of Tintin and his faithful dog Snowy, whose characters and images (often set against the backdrop of well-known buildings and streetscapes in Brussels) became as recognisable across post-war Europe as Mickey Mouse. During the occupation, Hergé was permitted to publish his magazine, *Tintin,* in the Nazi approved newspaper *Le Soir* leading – somewhat inevitably – to post-war accusations of collaboration. In the end, following careful scrutiny of Hergé's work that showed the author to be sufficiently 'moral' in his story telling, the taint was removed. Chief among Tintin's early outings was the 1930 publication *Tintin in the Land of the Soviets* – a story with an anti-communist plot that has our quiffed boy-detective and four-legged assistant on location in the Soviet Union sniffing around the dubious humanitarian activities of Stalin and his Bolshevik government. Nowadays, Tintin is an absolute cult hero in Brussels, and thanks to Hergé the visual highlight of my brief lunchtime stopover in the city came by way of a giant four-storey mural adorning the side of an otherwise nondescript building on the Rue de l'Étuve, showing Tintin chasing his foil,

Captain Haddock, down a fire escape. Brussels probably wouldn't make it onto too many 'bucket lists' of must-do European capitals, but without the time to follow the entire Comic Strip trail, or even to visit the Hergé Museum in the southern suburb of Louvain-la-Neuve, at least now I had a compelling reason to go back.

I had spent so little time in Brussels that by the early afternoon I was already speeding east towards the German border. A little more than an hour out of the city I passed through Aachen, Germany's most west-erly city and once the hub of Charlemagne's great late eighth-century empire. As reassuringly fast, com-fortable and reliable forms of transport go, a German train is hard to beat. Without slipping into too many clichés about Teutonic efficiency, suffice it to say that Deutsche Bahn trains are clean, beautifully appointed and, in the main, run bang on time. Changing at Cologne (an exhilarating station to arrive at – its gargantuan High Gothic cathedral is almost touching distance from the platforms), I leaped aboard my Hannover bound high-speed Inter City Express (ICE) service, its red livery and bold DB lettering the monikers of a proudly unified national rail system, those sleek carriages the last word in civilised European travel. Feeling in the mood for some on-board adventure, I shunned my pre-booked seat and headed instead for the bistro café in search of refreshment and kindred spirits. The café was well stocked with both, so I spent a lively chunk of the three-hour journey to Hannover as I sped through the provin-cial towns of Hamm, Gütersloh and Bielefeld, propping up the bistro bar with Daniel and Ana, a rugged and well-travelled couple in their mid-fifties from the northern Argentinian city of Resistencia. Putting up no resistance at all to their wandering urges, the pair had taken year-long sabbaticals from their jobs to travel across Europe. Mine was a willing ear for their foot-loose story of self-discovery – a story that began in pres-surised office environments engulfed by target-led initiatives, constant monitoring and exhausting account-ability. We spent an agreeable hour together as the train rattled through the North Rhine Westphalia country-side, sharing our indifference for office politics and our respective travel plans – with the unexpected dual bonus for me on this German train of the opportunity to flex my Spanish and an invitation to a future Argentinian homestay. After muddling through in the heavily-accented environs of Seville and Havana, it was hugely satisfying to add to my Spanish immersion experiences having a bash at being understood by a pair of up-beat South American adventurers on a speeding continental train, whose linguistic quirks included replacing con-ventional Spanish sounds with the pronunciation '*sh*'. This meant that the simplest of phrases, such as *yo me llamo* (my name is) became *sho me shamo* – a slurring of words not, by the way, connected to the potency of the bistro pick-me-ups Daniel and Ana were so enthusiastically knocking back.

I left my Argentinian *amigos* to drink the buffet dry and reclaimed my reserved seat for the final stretch of the journey up to Hannover. Having lived and worked in the Hannover area during the 1990s, I was eager to return for nostalgic reasons, even if the city's lack of a dominant architectural landmark – a major monument, towering cathedral or even a grand square – ensures that tourism there is a little thin on the ground. By way of compensation, Hannover does boast a magnificent railway station, restored to its former glory by a make-over for the city's hosting of Expo 2000. But if railway architecture isn't really your thing, try the station instead for its distinctive odour. Though I accept that this could rank as something of an acquired taste, there's nothing quite like the waft of sweet waffles and hot greasy bratwurst drifting around your nostrils to evoke the spirit of German rail travel. As I left the train at platform six – by the way at the exact location and time promised on the timetable by the good people of Deutsche Bahn – that familiar smell was my 'willkommen to Hannover' moment. Suitably intoxicated, I spent an hour or so hanging around the station with a variety of other dubious types taking in the sights, sounds and perfumes of the vibrant concourse, before indulging in that great pleasure of any railway station – the departure board. I drooled as the roll-call of enticing destinations flashed up on the giant screen above me: Berlin, Wien, Köln, Budapest, Paris, Amsterdam, München, Bremerhaven, Dresden, Minsk, Smolensk, Moskau – the latter triumvirate illustrating Hannover's historic importance as a major hub of European rail travel. I could hardly write fast enough as I scribbled each city destination on the back of my used DB ticket, musing that I would quite happily sit on a train for hours or even days for the reward of arriving at any one of them.

I eventually reached my hotel – the promisingly named Hotel Harmony – despite the forgivable fraud on the hotel's website describing it as being 'a ten-minute walk' from the station. Walking briskly, it was a conservative twenty. But harmony was quickly restored by the beaming receptionist, who handed me a complementary bottle of water and a golden delicious apple with my room key, perhaps in compensation for the location fib and the exterior of the hotel's resemblance to the pre-fabricated reception area of a budget car hire company. Yet for all its architectural limitations, the Hotel Harmony lived up to its name in about every other respect. Once I got my bearings, even the location impressed, with the walk back into town taking me through a typically Germanic urban-scape of wide busy streets, cycle lanes, pedestrian crossings and ubiquitous yellow trams rattling along a spider's web of tracks. A vibrant metropolis Hannover is not, and to be fair the reconstruction effort after its wartime near-obliteration has left it with a pretty charmless modern centre. Fortunately though, a sliver of medieval Hannover did survive the onslaught – or was at least rebuilt after it – and the small Altstadt (old town) area of half-timbered houses around the fourteenth-century Kreuzkirche, along with the magnificent early twentieth-century Neues Rathaus, were both well worth a diversion. The quirkiest feature and biggest draw of the castle-like Rathaus is the inclined lift that takes intrigued visitors to the summit of the building's giant dome. Opened by the fun-loving Kaiser Wilhelm II in 1913 (who, according to a German friend in the know, was content to allow the slaughter of the First World War to get under way for no better reason than to satisfy his insatiable boyish hunger for adventure), this fascinating piece of elevator engineering boasts a curious sloping floor and climbs its shaft at an angle of seventeen degrees, hugging the exact angle of the dome as it ascends. Before taking the ride to the Rathaus summit, I stopped off in the lobby to view the display of three matchbox models of Hannover, first as the city looked in 1939, then in its armageddon state of 1945, and finally today following the decades of its post-war reconstruction. The planners are doubtless proud of what they have achieved in Hannover by restoring life to a decimated city, but as I looked out from the Rathaus summit at a grey skyline of concrete and glass, it still felt close to tragic to witness just how much of the city's medieval soul has been lost.

If post-modernism architecture or even colossal railway stations aren't really for you, Hannover offers its visitors plenty in the way of urban green space. This is best experienced in the lavish gardens of the Schloss Herrenhausen, serving the dual purpose of a brush with nature while learning a bit about the often parodied German bloodline of the British royal family. I walked the couple of kilometres out of town to Herrenhausen and made straight for its principal attraction, the Großer Garten. I wandered its hedged avenues, meandered through the open air Gartentheater then on to take an open-mouthed gawp at the great fountain, which at eighty-two metres is the highest water jet of any garden fountain in Europe. Interestingly, the less formal Georgengarten is a nod to the English countryside complete with lake, elegant bridges and trees planted randomly for a naturally rural effect. Here, Hannover meets Herefordshire. Once this corner of a Hannoverian field that could be forever England was completed it was named after young Georg Ludwig, the son of Sophia of Hannover, the heiress presumptive to the English crown. Following the 1701 Act of Settlement that ensured the continuation of a protestant monarchy, Georg was next in line to the English throne after Princess (later Queen) Anne. Sophia's death in June

1714 – followed later that summer by Anne's – allowed the lucky Georg (or luckless, depending on how much he valued his liberty) to become the German speaking King George I of Great Britain. Although Georg never took the trouble to master English (he just couldn't face learning all those pesky phrasal verbs), we should thank him for bringing another Georg – Georg Friedrich Händel – over to London from Hannover with him as his court director of music. Gifted the best gig of his career, Händel moved into a smart town house at 25 Brook Street Mayfair, where he lived at the then exorbitant rent of £60 a year until his death in 1759. Intriguingly, the house next door at number 23 was occupied two centuries later in 1968 by another musical luminary of a quite different vintage – one Jimi Hendrix – until his own characteristically rock and roll death in a psychedelic blaze of vomit and barbiturates two years later at the address of a female admirer in Notting Hill. Before any of that, Hendrix is said to have been so awestruck at discovering the identity of his previous illustrious neighbour that he visited the One Stop record shop on nearby South Molton Street to pick up Händel's seminal *Water Music* and *Messiah*. Some Hendrix devotees have even claimed to have heard Händelian influences in some of the wild axe-man's later guitar pyrotechnics. If only the innovators Händel and Hendrix had rocked up in Mayfair in the same year – what a jam that might have been!

Back in present day Hannover, I found a table on the windy terrace of a branch of the *Nordsee* chain and chewed over my Händel-Hendrix musical fantasy with a lunch of everyone's favourite fish finger sandwich – given a Germanic twist with a liberal splatter of thick mayonnaise and a couple of eye-wateringly tart 'spree-wald' gherkins. I mention this only because breezy Hannoverian al-fresco dining had been a regular feature during a high water mark of my CV almost twenty years previously, when I landed a job with the Ministry of Defence to manage two careers centres on army bases in Lower Saxony. The work to deliver careers advice to the children of UK armed forces personnel stationed in Germany was arranged via a quirky contract with an English Local Authority – a deal that sank out of trace quite literally once the contract was sold on somewhat oddly to a company that built submarines. The two centres in my charge were part of army schools established in the post-war period when this part of northern Germany was incorporated into the British sector of occupation. The most far-flung of the two schools was part of the Hohne garrison, fifty kilometres north of Hannover adjacent to the site of the former Nazi concentration camp, Bergen-Belsen. This curious juxtaposition of workplace and former hell-on-earth internment camp provided the fascinating, if somewhat sobering image as I arrived for work each day of the extensive camp grounds. As I passed the camp's former entrance on my way into the office, it was difficult not to ponder that had I been around at the point the camp was liberated in April 1945 I would have been greeted, not by a boisterous crowd of schoolchildren, but by the sight of mounds of rotting corpses.

Rinteln-an-der-Weser, a small town roughly equidistant south west of Hannover, provided the rather less infamous location of my second office, and also the location of my army-subsidised apartment. As a Careers Adviser working on an army base, I was deemed worthy of an honorary equivalent military rank of Captain (despite my eyebrow-raising about this at the time, nobody was able to explain how on earth that system worked), which 'entitled' me to a completely gratis, bills included home in the charming half-timbered town of Rinteln. To keep me in the sort of comforts befitting a Captain, the sixties apartment was kitted out with bulky, rather beautiful pieces of G-Plan furniture and a not-so-beautiful garish-pink three piece suite. Fortunately though, I wasn't required at any point to either salute or wear a uniform. This was just as well – the rhythm and obedience that would have entailed might well have finished me off.

In truth the job itself was a bit of a dream ticket, replicating an adviser role in a regular school in Britain, but shunted a few hundred miles east into the army community of post-war Germany. Two decades later, one unexpected feature of my out-of-office life had been the odd nostalgic pang I felt as I recalled workplace highlights from the past. It had happened in Seville, in Cuba and now on a windswept pavement in Hannover. For a few moments I harked back to my mid-ranking days in sleepy Rinteln, to the long bike rides I took through forests and woodlands and to the weekend getaways in Berlin, Cologne, Frankfurt, Kiel or to wherever the mood took me, courtesy of a deal in place at the time that allowed travel at week-ends to and from any point on the German rail network for 35 deutsche marks (remember them?) Hard to believe maybe, but back then I had even quite enjoyed departmental meetings. This wasn't so much for the content of their agendas (which I have no recollection of now), but for the thrill of being flown back to

Hampshire in a military plane to attend them. With twenty years of hindsight, those days when my performance at work was about more than targets and face-fitting now seemed positively halcyon. What's more, with the job of Careers Adviser hardly being one normally laden with international travel opportunity, for two quirky years my CV was adorned with the novelty of living and working in a foreign country. Sitting on that windy Hannoverian terrace, I felt the irresistible urge to retrace the steps of my younger self, and so decided to take a daytrip to Rinteln. Well someone has to.

It took an hour by a two-car regional train through the Weserbergland to reach Rinteln, via Hameln (in English, Hamelin) of Pied Piper fame. Arriving at the town's sleepy station offered nothing of the smells and excitement of Hannover's vibrant Hauptbahnhof, but had its own reward in the suburban peace and quiet. I found my former home in a modern apartment block on Schubertweg, part of an estate of unremarkable provincial streets named after Germanic composers. Much to the curiosity of a woman cleaning the inside of her windows wondering why there was a strange man staring at her home, I stood outside my old billet reliving a few memories of the evening I arrived in Rinteln. I rocked-up in the town at eleven on a rainy Friday night after a twelve-hour drive from London, with my elderly car straining under the full weight of the welter of my life – way too many clothes, piles of books, a portable black and white TV (that in Germany could pick up only one channel – the military's own BFBS), a collection of vinyl LPs and CDs, together with a bulky music centre to play them on, an acoustic guitar and a mountain bike, the latter somehow crammed in under the car roof leaving behind it an indelible oily smear as a motif of the journey. The school bursar, Scotsman Dave, had left a note taped to the main door of the school to greet me. The note was an invitation to the regular Friday night get-together of teachers at the nearby flat of a bearded geography teacher whose name I cannot recall but who looked a lot like Jeremy Corbyn. A veritable baptism of fire, I walked into a living room full of strangers to semi-drunken applause – an anxiety eased by the tumbler of gin and tonic thrust into my hand by the wife of the said geography master. We were an eclectic bunch that evening, sat randomly around the spacious room of officer-rank furniture and garish fabric. Two of my new colleagues – teachers of music and domestic science respectively – sat in a corner knitting, while others just got on with the serious business of advancing their levels of pre-weekend inebriation. I soon gathered that along with buying expensive army-subsidised cars, gratuitous consumption of alcohol was a popular pastime among the army school teachers marooned in the northern German countryside. One of the finest exponents of both, Geordie mathematician Roger, seized the opportunity to escape the party by showing me to my flat and helping me drag the contents of my straining car up three flights of stairs to the top floor of the building. Worn out from the long journey by ferry and then the drive across Belgium, Holland and westernmost Germany, I fell into my Captain-sized bed and woke the following morning to bright autumn sunshine streaming into my madly-oversized three-bedroom pad – a good twice the size of the flat I had left behind in London.

After a long application process to actually get the job and then the solitary drive to arrive, it was quite a moment to catch my first daylight sight of that little German town. After London, its sedate pace took a bit of getting used to but the Germans do enjoy a drink, so there was a small but energetic bier-keller scene in town, easy access to beautiful countryside, and crucially the railway station from which I often set off around the country on those über-reliable red-liveried DB trains. Drinking dens and mother-nature aside, Rinteln was a little short on other forms of entertainment, but did boast an intriguing local museum. I would like to report that I was a regular visitor there and provide a detailed account of its contents to tempt you into searching for travel options to the Weserbergland yourself. But with restrictive opening hours of 2.00pm until 4.00pm on the third Monday of each month, the museum was almost completely inaccessible to the public. What a wonderful place it must have been to be employed at, unless of course the museum's under-worked staff spent the rest of the week in dull meeting rooms agonising over whether two hours per calendar month of opening hours represented good value for public money!

I came to the job in the German countryside after several years of head-banging against brick walls in the challenging inner-city London environments of Newham and North Kensington. By comparison, the pressures of guiding the offspring of squaddies in their career choices felt light. My time was split – and crucially, at my own behest – between the two schools in Rinteln and Hohne. This meant a twice-weekly two-hour drive in a spearmint green Ministry of Defence Vauxhall Opel, enabling me to carry out the routines of my job in combination with a bit of wartime sightseeing at Bergen Belsen. As I ploughed up and down the speed-limitless autobahns with Kraftwerk on a loop in my brain, struggling to keep up with the shiny super-quick Audis and BMWs, I got through it all on the daily high of feeling like I hardly had a real job at all. What's more, the arrangements for the supervision of my work were blessedly light touch. My line manager, who I rarely saw, worked on another military base two hundred miles south near the French border, and was far too busy with his competitive cross-country running to be overly interested in me. Working to my own hours and methods, I was left in peace to get on with my job, which I did properly but with plenty of scope for 'me-time' – a fortuitously brilliant working arrangement that allowed for plenty of two-wheeled adventures in the Lower Saxony countryside. One of my regular rides took me up steep wooded slopes to the Rinteln *Klippenturm* – a curious twenty-metre high, nineteenth-century observation tower that watches over the town like a toytown sentry post. During my military service in Germany, the 'Klippie's' cafeteria often provided refuge from the office and the venue for strategy meetings attended by a team that consisted of, well, usually just me, in sole charge of my own self-driven agenda.

Twenty years later, I climbed that same hill and reached the summit of the stone tower to look down on the handsome little town I used to call home. As I surveyed the grey felt roof of the school where I had worked, I felt oddly elated, remembering that there had been little of the conventional trappings of a full-time job during those days of my German self-determination. Team meetings, micro-management and random targets – they barely featured in my working day. In the event, revisiting my old working life in Germany helped me understand a little more of why, since then, I had been so resistant to settling for life in the controlled environment of a corporate nine-to-five. The reason was straightforward enough. My first experience of working abroad had incorporated work with adventure – a near-miraculous lifestyle I had been unable to replicate since. Until now, that is.

Much as I love to connect with nature, climb Victorian stone follies and explore the quaint medieval centres of small provincial towns, at heart I am a city person. And there was no better place in northern Germany to head for a fix of urban noise and social chaos than Hamburg – Germany's second metropolis of close on two million people. Travelling through the countryside of Lower Saxony and Schleswig-Holstein at a brisk 200kph, my immaculate ICE service from Hannover reached Hamburg in just an hour and twenty minutes. Once I had arrived at the city's Hauptbahnhof, it proved tricky to leave – a whole hour in fact from stepping off the train to finding the station exit. Built in 1906 as a replacement for the city's four previous main line stations, this is Germany's busiest station, beaten only by the Gare du Nord in Paris as the busiest in continental Europe. Standing on the elevated gallery gave me a perfect view of the maze of tracks, multi-coloured signals, points and island platforms showcasing the station's importance to Europe's rail system. Like a boy admiring his Hornby train set, I stood for a while with eyes fixed on the deep-red DB locomotives and carriages rolling in and out of the busy platforms, taking on and disgorging their passengers in a perpetual motion of human activity. The bold blue letters of the monumental *PHILIPS* logo illuminated the station's arch at the far end as I looked, telling me little about the giant multi-national company it was advertising, but far more that I had arrived at the railway station of a city of real significance. Why else would an enterprise of that size invest so much on a single advert? Indeed, if you were to judge a city by your arrival at its main railway station, you would be forgiven in thinking that Hamburg was Germany's capital. I could quite happily have stayed for hours trainspotting from that gantry, but I was beginning to attract the stares of a group of French students propped up against bulging rucksacks sipping coffee from polystyrene cups, who I sensed were wondering what could be holding my interest for so long.

I prised myself away from this railway fantasy and walked towards the station's elevated Wandelhalle shopping mall. Now shopping centres aren't really my thing, but drop one in the middle of a vibrant European railway hub and you might just get me interested. The bonus here was that by looking down from the parades of bling, it was also still possible to keep an eye on the incessant comings and goings of the trains. The station's 'retail experience' was enlivened further by the piped tones of Vivaldi – a musical innovation from Deutsche Bahn introduced to deter the activities of drug pushers and other low-life of the kind that tend to gather in and around large railway stations. It was difficult to tell just how much of a deterrent to illegal activity *The Four Seasons* was proving to be in Hamburg, but I was mightily glad to find that the station hadn't been sanitised of that signature scent of the German national rail carrier – my old friend the grilled Frikadelle sausage doused in a curry sauce, with fragrant overtones of sugar-coated waffles. As if facing an ocean breeze, I breathed in that sweet Deutsche Bahn air for as long and as deeply as I could.

On a previous visit to Hamburg, I spent two dreadful nights in a leaking tent pitched on a campsite under a flyover. Worse even than it sounds, the likelihood of getting any sleep on my semi-inflated airbed was further reduced by the boorish mob of drunken Borussia Dortmund football fans in the neighbouring tent, in town to watch their team take on FC St. Pauli. With memories of that discomforting trip in mind, I had pushed the boat out this time by booking into a small, relatively salubrious (in the sense it wasn't under canvas) hotel on Ellmenreichstraße. It is amazing what a location near the back entrance of a railway station can do to bring down a hotel room rate and consequently attract my patronage. Just as I had previously in Rome, Vienna, Buenos Aires, Sydney, Vancouver, Los Angeles and others, I found myself in Hamburg on the wrong side of the railway tracks – but well the right side of my budget in an area recommended by my guide book in the same euphemistic sentence, as being both 'formerly sleazy' and 'up and coming'. Although the same guide's description of Hamburg as 'The Gateway to the World' bordered on hyperbole, the city can at least stake a claim to being one of the world's great port cities, which might I suppose amount to the same thing. In case I needed reminding of Hamburg's seaside location, I could feel the draught of low-swooping gulls around my ears as I walked along Spitalerstraße and Mönckebergstraße towards the Rathaus and the city's well-preserved Altstadt. I spent an un-taxing couple of hours wandering around the Altstadt, stopping first to admire the giant façade of the baroque Rathaus and then walking over and along the Alsterfleet and Bleichenfleet canals that flow through the district's industrious streets. Tiring quickly of map checking, I relied instead on the nose-following method of exploration, which took me to the Speicherstadt archipelago, lined by the world's largest continuous complex of warehouses – an impressive collection of industrial buildings built in the late-nineteenth century of Gothic-style Wilhelmine red brick on a precarious-sounding foundation of oak logs. The sun-drenched red-brick façades took on a new fascination once I discovered that as well as housing various tourist attractions, including a model railway museum and the Hamburg Dungeon, they recall Hamburg's great trading days as a Hanseatic port by still operating as fully functioning warehouses for the handling of staple goods such as tea, coffee and carpets.

I lingered for a while opposite the warehouses on Hohe Brücke to take a look at the row of restored fourteenth-century merchant houses on Deichstraße – notable as Hamburg's oldest surviving street. Deichstraße is also notorious as the starting point of the city's Great Fire of 1842. When the fire ignited, it was carried by a stiff wind towards the northern end of the street, which was quickly engulfed in a fireball allowing in turn the survival of the houses at the southern end. The preservation of this section of Deichstraße is another reminder in fact of Hamburg's merchant heyday and the city's membership of the prosperous Hanseatic League. A powerful trading and defensive alliance, the league protected the economic health of some of the principal trading towns of northern Europe for four hundred years between the thirteenth and seventeenth-centuries. By 1400 this medieval forerunner of the European Union – also known simply as Hansa – prospered from the membership of as many as 160 cities, which besides Hamburg included Lübeck and Berlin, Bergen, Riga, Tallinn, Stockholm and Gdańsk. Interestingly, in what by today's 'Eurosceptic' standards would seem an uncharacteristic dash to be at the heart of a European economic clique, several English towns also came eagerly to the lucrative trading party, including York, Ipswich, Yarmouth and Hull. Hansa also left a legacy in the name of the German national airline Lufthansa, the Bundesliga football club Hansa Rostock and the Hansa recording studio in Berlin where the late, great David Bowie recorded his 1970s album trilogy – *Low*, *Heroes* and *Lodger* – with the help of Brian Eno and longtime producer, Tony Visconti. A little over six centuries have passed since Hamburg's Hanseatic power-house days, but Deichstraße is evidently still a place to do business. I looked on as groups of smart-suited, designer-clad businessmen and women smiled and clinked glasses on the terrace of the café Alt-Hamburger Aalspeicher, more than likely toasting their upwardly mobile bonuses, and quite possibly too the vibrant, wonderfully preserved cityscape around them.

Another circuit of the archipelago later, and a few steps beyond the Rathaus along Bergstraße, brought me to one of the most beautiful city sights I had seen in a long time – Hamburg's two great city centre lakes, the Binnenalster and Aussenalster. The inner lake – Binnenalster – formerly lay within Hamburg's old city walls, the outer lake unsurprisingly outside the walls, although today the lakes are divided by the modern road and rail crossings of the Kennedybrücke and Lombardsbrücke. I was stood on the northern shore of the inner lake, taking photographs of the brilliant cityscape of medieval spires, their forms distorted by the ripples in the water as if reflected in a hall of mirrors, when I got into conversation with a young traveller called Kota. An international student from Osaka, Kota told me that he was studying on a post-graduate marketing course at a well-known central London university – an institution incidentally that had recently gained notoriety in the sector for some creative accounting in the presentation of its graduate employment figures. That of course was of little interest to Kota, or to me for that matter – this was the sort of brow-creasing angst reserved for team meeting agendas that I had long-since concluded was best left to others. Far more interesting for both of us was lucky-lad Kota's solo three-month trip around Europe on a 'Schengen' visa that had brought him to Hamburg via Barcelona, Paris, Madrid and Rome. The Schengen Agreement was drawn up in 1985 by certain member states of the then European Economic Community to allow border-free travel on the Continent. Schengen also paved the way for international men of mystery like Kota to roam freely for limited periods within most of the EU/EEA area – but not the UK and Ireland that have, in theory at least, maintained their borders. We passed up on a conversation about how the *Daily Mail* might feel about all of this to focus on Kota's determination to stay away from his homeland for as long as possible, and to continue his nomadic lifestyle around the watering holes of Europe. Back in my office days, advising and encouraging young adventurers like Kota around such pursuits had been part of my livelihood. Yet here in the hassle free environs of a lakeside continental city, the task of helping out a foreign student felt immeasurably more rewarding. After expanding Kota's English vocab a little by explaining the meaning of the term 'Busman's Holiday', we discussed his options over a couple of icy bottles of Beck's on a terrace with a prime view of the Binnenalster. Kota's themes for discussion were his determination to remain in the UK by whatever legal means, the dramas of the English Premier League, plus his unreconstructed fascination for 'north European women'. He didn't elaborate on why the women of Italy or Spain failed to tickle his fancy, but I indulged him on his topic for as long I could bear before steering him towards his quest to avoid the marital and career man-traps being laid for him in his absence by his family in suburban Osaka. There was only one thing for it. Standing still would be fatal for Kota – he simply had to keep moving. I knew exactly how he felt.

After an hour or more of immersion in Kota's plans, I was keen to move on. I was due to leave for Berlin the following morning but hadn't yet made the requisite visit to the Reeperbahn – Hamburg's strip of ill-repute in the west of the city. In fairness, Kota was far more excited about our prospects on the Reeperbahn than I was, but if anyone was ever again going to succeed in leading me astray, it probably wasn't going to be my new Japanese friend. Kota took little persuasion in joining me on the jaunt, and was right on my heels as I dashed down the steps of the Jungfernstieg S-Bahn station to escape a sudden sharp shower and take a westbound train to the Reeperbahn. In a matter of a few short minutes and three stops, our sunny lakeside vista had been replaced by the gritty, rather drab urbanscape of the Reeperbahn's traffic-choked boulevard. This was no deterrent to Kota, and for a few energetic minutes the experience-hungry student seemed hell-bent on rolling around in the muckiest corners of the district's bloated underbelly. Within seconds of leaving the train, he spotted a strip club and its alluring drinks list advertising regular beer for a manageable €8, to the more risqué – and possibly less thirst quenching – 'strippers orange juice' *(orangensaft)* available at a more challenging €30 a pop. Something told me that an order of *orangensaft* might involve rather more than a refreshing fruity drink, so feeling a little protective of Kota's welfare and wallet, I called him back from the brink of moral ruin, suggesting instead that we spend our time looking up the area's old Beatles haunts. A keen music fan and burgeoning Anglophile, Kota temporarily put to bed any lingering salacious ideas and joined the impromptu tour.

The Beatles' experience of Hamburg was of course a lively and interesting one. Leaving economically depressed post-war Liverpool in August 1960 to discover the neon-lit vice of the Reeperbahn must have been incredibly exciting for the band. The original Beatles line up – John, Paul, George, Stuart Sutcliffe and drummer Pete Best (replaced by Ringo Starr at the end of the Hamburg tour) – arrived in town to begin what became an on-off, two-year stint of live performances on the pulsating, seedy local club circuit. In their pursuit of fun and fame, the band initially put up with the indignity of living next to a public toilet in the concrete storeroom of the small Bambi Kino cinema on

Paul-Roosenstraße. Thoroughly used and abused during their time on the Reeperbahn, the Beatles' Hamburg apprenticeship included the unexpected perks of beatings from club bouncers and the frequent bombardment of empty beer bottles from inebriated, tone-deaf club audiences. We walked north off the strip along the scruffy Große Freiheit to the rebuilt Indra Club, the venue of the very first Beatles gigs in Hamburg. Further along Große Freiheit we read a plaque marking the band's appearances at the more prestigious Kaiserkeller, before taking a brief pit-stop in the Star Club Café, built on the site of the burned-down club of the same name. Completing our circuit of Beatles haunts, we stood in front of the former site of the Top Ten Club back on the Reeperbahn – the scene of an infamous incident that landed Paul McCartney and Pete Best in a spot of bother with the local police. Unable to see anything in the gloom of their squalid living quarters as they were moving their kit following the termination of the Kaiserkeller contract, Paul and Pete improvised some illumination by taking the unconventional step of setting fire to a condom. Although minimal damage was done to the stone building by the burning rubber (apparently only a wall was scorched), the fussy club owner Bruno Koschmider informed the police. The pair were duly arrested and deported without ceremony the following day, joining George Harrison back in Liverpool who had already been kicked out of Germany for the indiscretion of being underage. We pressed on with our tour and reached the circular Beatles Platz, an eye-catching public space sponsored originally by the Hamburg radio station, *Oldie 95*. Paved in a style replicating a vinyl record, the plaza contains statues of not only the Fab Four, but a hybrid of Ringo and his predecessor as drummer, Pete Best. Pleasingly, also earning a statue in the plaza is the 'Fifth Beatle', Stuart Sutcliffe, who died in Hamburg of a brain aneurysm in April 1962, a year after leaving the band to follow his dream of a career in art. All this life stuff really is not a dress rehearsal.

Done with paying homage to the Beatles, there was little else to keep us on the Reeperbahn. Kota's enthusiasm for carnal adventure had waned and this seamy corner of Hamburg had done nothing to arouse any further his interest in European women – possibly because in the rain we hardly saw any apart from those exhibiting themselves less than irresistibly behind the plate glass of shop windows. Like me, Kota was also leaving Hamburg the following day – for Amsterdam of all places – to indulge, he assured me, in his liking for 'northern European canal-side culture', a preference lifted by the sounds of it straight from a guidebook, and the exact details of which Kota failed to specify. We left behind the sleazy nonsense of St Pauli and the Reeperbahn and travelled back to the Altstadt before parting company at the Stephansplatz U-Bahn station, not without first making those obligatory pledges about a lifetime of regular contact via social media. I enjoyed those few hours in Kota's up-beat company, and when he disappeared into the Hamburg crowds I felt – for a few moments anyway – a little the worse without his company. But I am nothing if not self-sufficient, so I headed straight for a café I had passed earlier on Deichstraße called the Alt-Hamburger Bürgerhäus and did what any inquiring visitor to this city might feel inclined to do. I ate a hamburger.

I had often wondered vaguely about the connection of Hamburg to its edible namesake. But when I took the trouble to find out more, I discovered a minefield of contradiction lying at the heart of the surprisingly lively debate around the naming of this ultimate fast-food hit. We can be fairly sure that the term 'hamburger' was first coined in 1896 by the *Chicago Daily Tribune*, which reported the growing culinary craze for placing a fried ground meat patty between two chunks of bread. At around this time America had welcomed many settlers from Hamburg, and it seems a neat and logical explanation that the words *ham* (referring to any kind of meat product) and *burg* (meaning fortified refuge) were combined by some particularly savvy, forward-thinking entrepreneur to ensure the greasy legend was born. Whatever the arguments about the origins of the burger, I was committed to believe that I was eating mine at the heart of the city where the story began. And even if I wasn't, the Alt-Hamburger Bürgerhäus didn't half serve a mean twenty-first century quarter pounder. As I was picking at its remnants, my mind had already wandered away from Hamburg and the great burger debate. I had a full stomach, itchy feet and was focused on matters further east. It was time, at last, for Berlin.

It was a shade before eight in the morning when I walked away from the Hotel Eden, over the race-track Kirchenallee and onto the breezy concrete square in front of Hamburg's Hauptbahnhof. At this most sober hour of the day, suited businessmen joined students with rucksacks and women with children on their city centre school runs, packed around tall outdoor tables in the chilly morning air, holding mugs of steaming coffee, chewing salty pretzels the size of frisbees, relishing their sizzling *bratwurst* and glugging tall measures of murky *altbier*. Only at a German railway station could such a scene be enjoyed so early in the morning. I passed on the cloudy beer, but before boarding the Berlin-bound ICE train I loaded up on supplies at the station super-market for the two hours and seven minutes of journey time promised by my timetable. As I rolled out of Hamburg, with every confidence in Deutsche Bahn that the length of the journey would be precisely that, I began to consider the modern urban mystery that is Germany's capital city.

So, Berlin. Where to start? Well, it is an odd place – of that at least I was certain. This would be my ump-teenth visit, but I have never left the city fully the wiser. Berlin is simply a hard nut to crack. I reached for an old copy of *20 Minutos*, the Seville newspaper I retrieved from the littered depths of my bag, and scribbled in the margin an attempt to define its modern mystery. My notes went something like this: following the city's meteoric rise to a level of avant-garde to rival even Paris in the fairly short period between German unifica-tion in 1871 and the tail end of the Weimar Republic in 1930, Berlin then fell into a Nazi-driven vortex of violent confusion, hate and destruction. By the end of the Second World War in 1945, more than seventy-percent of the city lay in total ruins – a wholly devas-tated place divided into American, British and French zones in the west and Soviet in the east. As if that wasn't enough to have knocked the last ounces of stuffing from the spirit and soul of any city, for Berlin there was of course much more to come. Principal culprit in the con-tinued battering of Berlin was the 1961 ignominy of division by miles of concrete wall and barbed wire policed by armed guards with a licence to kill – the desperate act of a paranoid Soviet puppet state to prevent its long-suffering citizens escaping to the decadent, free west. However, since those intoxicating scenes of the fall of the Berlin Wall flashed across the world's TV screens in November 1989, Berlin has regained its mojo to become the throbbing capital of a re-unified Germany, reinventing itself as a multi-cultural melting pot of art, music, theatre and just about anything else that might interest a human being intent on having a good time.

For me, Berlin has always been the Frank Sinatra of capital cities – *the* undisputed comeback-star city of Europe, a place entirely rebuilt both physically and spiritually. So how could one city, in such a brief passage of time, first rise so artistically only then to fall so brutally, but then recover and rise again so emphatically? During a 1926 visit to the city he loathed, that old charmer, the Nazi Reich Minister of Propaganda, Joseph Goebbels, said of Berlin, '...*this city is a melting pot of everything that is evil – prostitution, drinking houses, cinemas, Marxist Jews, strippers, negroes dancing and all the offshoots of modern art.*' Well, thanks to Dr Goebbels' review and inadvertent Berlin plug that would have made him a popular contributor on *TripAdvisor*, if I had been around in the 1920s and was thinking about taking a city break, I might well have caught the first train to Berlin. '*Poor but sexy*', is a more recent, more succinct elucidation of the city from its long serving mayor, Klaus Wowereit. But whichever way you look at it, Berlin was, is – and more than likely will remain – a bit of a mystery.

If I was to sit and make a list of the most beautiful cities in the world that I have visited, Berlin would not be on it. Or maybe it would, I just can't decide. Berlin certainly isn't especially beautiful in any conventional sense – not at all the Germany of cute, half-timbered gabled houses, for example. What's more, each time I go back there, Berlin looks different again. Whether it is new buildings appearing, familiar old relics of the Soviet occupation discarded, roads and streets moved, re-routed or simply no longer there, renamed metro stations or new tram lines materialising as if they had fallen from the sky, Berlin is a major work in progress and, once it's finished, should be lovely. Anyway, beauty, mystery or both, with custody of my time now wrestled back from my former paymasters, I had the freedom to discover at leisure Berlin's markedly diverse districts, its outstanding parkland, experience a little of its underbelly, and consider it one whole city by finally overcoming the constant urge to divide it into east and west. Whatever the outcome, I was guaranteed to relish its irresistible vibe.

To be a contented Berliner for the month I planned to stay, I needed somewhere well located and affordable to call home. So after arriving at the city's flashy triple-decker Hauptbahnhof, I took an S-Bahn train to the southern district of Schöneberg, the home of my Berlin host, Otto. As I was stood at the crossing outside the entrance to Schöneberg station alongside a woman laden with carrier bags full of *Lidl* shopping, I was taken aback by the approach of a man brandishing in the air a catering-size tin of tomatoes, at the same time offering me and other passers-by what I could only guess were unflattering greetings in German. I was well used to bizarre scenes on some of the grittier streets of south London (although the tinned tomatoes were a first), so neither the man nor his novel, admittedly potentially lethal weapon were especially alarming. In the event, if there had been the slightest lingering doubt that Schöneberg was the right choice of Berlin district for me to live, it was banished the moment the armoured tomatoes appeared.

I reached Otto's apartment on the ground floor of a 1900s artisan block on Ebersstraße without further incident, and was shown to my small cosy room at the back of the building with a view of a communal courtyard, which I clocked would make an ideal lock-up for a bicycle. Otto, an owlish, wide-faced and rather pudgy man in his mid-fifties wasn't in all fairness the warmest, most loveable creature I had met on my travels. And I soon discovered that he was nothing if not meticulous, putting me through the paces of an unexpected induction course on *Living The Otto Way*. Included in the first module was a practical demonstration of his favoured techniques of opening and closing the bathroom door – and as far as Otto was concerned, there was most definitely more than one way. Another course highlight featured the delicate maneuvering of Otto's swish-action shower curtain, which with dedication and practice he assured me could remain effective without ever putting it at the disabling risk of contact with water. Done with the bathroom, we moved on into Otto's squeaky-clean kitchen, where I was tutored in the art of moving a specially designated cloth in circular motions around the already gleaming draining board to give it an extra sheen after washing up. This Otto convention apparently *really* mattered. Next up was the hall, where struggling to remain engaged I propped open my eyes with matchsticks to endure a grave lecture

on the wear and tear risks posed to the laminate floor-
ing by the wearing of outdoor shoes. This prompted
Otto, without revealing a trace of irony or humour, to
ask if I had brought slippers to tiptoe carefully around
his home in. House slippers in hedonistic, to-hell-with-
you-in-a-handcart Berlin? Inexplicably, I had forgotten
to pack mine.

I left Otto to tend to his domestics and took a walk
around my new neighbourhood. I had chosen the quirky
suburb of Schöneberg, partly as I fancied running the
daily risk of an attack by tinned tomatoes, but also
because I wanted to live in an area of Berlin that was
central, had good transport links and abundant options
for cycling. Aside from the practicalities, Schöneberg
seemed fashionable but not pretentiously so – an area
stuffed full of cultural interest, but also ordinary enough
to be representative of everyday Berlin. Schöneberg was
also David Bowie's choice in 1976 when he rocked up in
Berlin with Iggy Pop to seek musical inspiration, anonymity and sanctuary from a cocaine-fuelled personal
crisis engulfing him in Los Angeles – an odd choice for
re-hab given that Bowie himself described Berlin as 'the
smack capital of Europe'. But something sparked for
Bowie in Schöneberg as what followed proved to be a
fabulously creative period of his career. While in town
he spent long hours in the Hansa studio, a recording
venue located a stone's throw from the Berlin Wall near
Potsdamer Platz, and known affectionately by Bowie as
the 'hall by the wall'. On one occasion, after watching
from his studio window a couple exchanging intimacies
up against the cold concrete of the wall – in full view
of the ogling East German border guards on the other
side – Bowie was moved to record his otherworldly

track, *Heroes*. In an earlier era, Schöneberg had also been the setting for Christopher Isherwood's semi-autobiographical novel, *Goodbye to Berlin* – an account of the author's life in the city during the early-1930s, when he made the very most of Schöneberg's pre-Nazi bohemian spirit – a spirit that recovered after the war and flourishes to this day. I stood for a few minutes outside Bowie's former pad at 155 Hauptstraße, staring blankly at the anonymous apartment block and ground floor tattoo parlour that was once the entrance to his home (in Bowie's day, this had been a car parts shop). In truth it was all a bit disappointing, although what I was expecting to find there I couldn't really say – a plaque to mark the block's famous former occupant, perhaps. Maybe that just isn't the German way, although now Bowie and his multitude of personas have passed away that may change. So I made do instead with a photograph of Bowie's old front door, satisfied by the thought that the sheer ordinariness of the address, and of the building itself, was in the end an attraction enough. Interestingly, when Bowie eventually left Berlin in 1978 he mused on how the very place he wanted to get lost in, ultimately had helped him find himself. It really is that sort of city.

Another fascination I had with Schöneberg was the landmark 1914 Rathaus on John F Kennedy Platz, a building that served as Berlin's City Hall until Germany's reunification in 1990. The Rathaus is best known as the venue for President Kennedy's iconic *Ich Bin Ein Berliner* speech. In the summer of 1963, when JFK came to Berlin to inspire the beleaguered communist-encircled West Berliners with his charisma and schmaltzy rhetoric, the cement on the Berlin Wall was barely dry. The despised partition had marooned West Berlin deep inside the German Democratic Republic (GDR), making it an isolated western enclave. JFK's speech, delivered from a podium in front of the Rathaus in the presence of 450,000 people, famously conveyed the message to Berliners a spirit of 'we're-all-in-this-together'. To avoid the risk of embarrassment from bad pronunciation, Kennedy wrote out his landmark 'Berliner' phrase phonetically – or at least a member of his entourage did. The irreversible result of the president's preparation was '*Ish Bin Ein Bearleenar*', inviting the ridicule of German grammar purists who claimed that the well-meaning use of the indefinite article, *ein,* had told the listening world that the president was, in fact, a sugary north German pastry, similar in constitution to a doughnut minus its central hole – an image somewhat removed from his suave persona and profile as 'Leader of the Free World'. What of course the politically savvy president meant to say was that he regarded himself as a citizen of Berlin, which in itself was a dubious claim given that this was his first – and only – visit to the city. More than half-a-century later, the grammatical debate around the integrity of JFK's speech rumbles on. So what exactly did JFK say on that June morning from his Rathaus podium? Was he a dedicated man of Berlin, or was he that doughnut without a hole? I didn't know myself, but knew a man close to home who might. Just as I expected, Otto turned out to be as fastidious about his German linguistics as he was about his kitchen surfaces. After I had first carefully removed my shoes we discussed the issue in his hallway, where Otto revealed that in Berlin German at least, the use of the indefinite article does convey the message that JFK had staked his claim as a man of Berlin, in a way that grammatically might not work in, let's say, some areas of Bavaria in the south of the country where a so-called 'Higher' German is spoken. So, albeit inadvertently, JFK got it right. Well that was one small aspect of my Berlin mystery solved, until of course someone else comes along to tell me that the president should, after all, have left the city covered in caster sugar.

When I absconded from my former job, I thought I had left my days of target driven, objective-obsessed activity behind me. But as I sat in one of the numerous Turkish *Imbiss* restaurants on Hauptstraße pouring over a map of Berlin and its unwieldy spread of disparate neighbourhoods, I attempted to set – however loose and movable – a few targets for my month in the city. Naturally I tired of this attempt at instilling order within five minutes, but not before settling on two key aims: the first that I must procure a set of wheels – two wheels to be precise (incidentally just as Bowie had when he moved to Schöneberg almost forty years earlier), the second that I would use those wheels to visit each of the districts I could see in front of me on my map. Yet after an afternoon of foot-slogging around the polluted streets of Schöneberg, I was content to leave objectives for the following day. This included sourcing a suitable bike, to which end a bit of research threw up the perfect solution: *Bike A Way*, a sort of wheeled co-operative operating in the rapidly-gentrifying former East Berlin suburb of Friedrichshain.

And now, a love story. Just like many of the best affairs of the heart, Fritz's and mine began unexpectedly. In case you're wondering, it wasn't love at first sight. In fact, when I first saw him leaning against a Friedrichshain wall, I thought he looked a little shabby, ravaged by his hedonistic Berlin habits and multiple partners. Yet there was something about his muscular frame that drew me to him – something about him that demanded a closer look. Fritz was crying out for a bit of loving care – that much was certain. Perhaps it was his wide wheels and firm chunky tyres supporting that heavy white frame that did it. Or maybe it was those thick sturdy handlebars. And when I spotted that retro dynamo light system, well Fritz had stolen my heart. I had given him his name before I even set foot in the shop, and just knew he would be mine. Maurice, the *Bike A Way* manager, was similarly infatuated with Fritz, describing him as 'the jewel in his rental crown.' So keen was I to ride away into the Berlin sunset with Fritz, I skipped haggling and paid €100 for his services, with the promise of €50 back should I return him undamaged a month later – thereby establishing Fritz, in many more ways than just financially, as my personal, unchallengeable Deal of the Century.

Quite tellingly, Maurice wore the look of someone who had been round the block a few times himself. A fifty-something American, here was another none-conformist refusenik. With a mischievous glint in his eye and an endearing smile, mid-life had evidently gifted Maurice a second adventurous wind. He was intent, he told me, on having a blow-out in Berlin as a reward to himself for bringing up his two sons alone. With parental responsibilities now well behind him, Maurice had assumed the swagger of a man at least twenty years his junior and was hell-bent on sampling the wide-ranging genres of fun and gratification in which Berlin specialises. After swapping our mutual 'you-get-less-for-murder' stories, Maurice and I parted company as friends and kindred spirits, and I left with his full blessing for my union with Fritz. Feeling a pronounced rush of freedom and movement, I cycled my new charge across the tram lines of Petersburgerstraße into the melee of Berlin traffic to begin our new life – well, thirty days – together. Fritz and I made for a perfect match – a match made, if not exactly in heaven, at least made on the cycle lanes of Berlin. Our first adventure together took us briskly across the windswept expanse of Alexanderplatz – the former epicentre of the long-defunct GDR (national motto, 'workers of the world unite!') – along past the Rotes Rathaus (given the name 'red' for the colour of its brick rather than the political colour of its pre-reunification government), and then finally along Leipzigerstraße towards Potsdamer Platz. Speaking of heaven, with Fritz and I bonded firmly even before his first well-oiled gear change, it felt to me like paradise and Berlin might just as well have been the very same place.

A new day dawned and adventure beckoned. With its vast swathes of parkland, forests and waterways, Berlin is both a twenty-first century metropolis and outstanding nature reserve – a feature of the city best experienced amid the giant green space of the Berliner Grunewald. After plotting a route on my city map rolled out on Otto's surgical kitchen table, I cycled west to Innsbrucker Platz, then through Bundersplatz and Heidelbergerplatz where I joined a section of Berlin's four hundred miles of immaculately (mostly) kept cycle lanes. Within a short time it was apparent that cycling in Berlin would be a genuine pleasure, an experience far from the urban nightmare it often presents in other large cities. In fact, as a Berlin cyclist I was treated with an extraordinary level of respect by other road users, rather than as an irritant. How gladdening it was as a long-suffering London cyclist, as I manoeuvred right from Mecklenburgischestraße onto Forckenbeckstraße, that drivers approaching the junction from my left not only gave way but stopped to allow me to complete the turn before doing so themselves. One suited man in a gleaming BMW, who came to a halt to let me pass, even gave me a cheery wave to send me on my way. As Fritz and I racked up the kilometres of Berlin's cycleways on this first excursion away from the city centre, the only thing that stood in our way – or, to be precise, ran in our way – was the progress of the Berlin Marathon, which held us up for half-an-hour at Hohenzollerndamm as the runners panted by helped on their way, like me, by a boogie-woogie band set up outside the imposing Kreuz Kirche. Once the race was down to its stragglers, I swerved around them to continue along Delbrückstraße, then across the reedy water of the Koenigsee by a small stone bridge that led into Winklerstraße, the heart of leafy Berlin suburbia. Now here was a street to admire, each elegant villa seeking to outdo its neighbour in grandeur and architectural flamboyance. A dream project for any student of residential architecture, number fifteen Winklerstraße offers Neo-Classical, number eleven English rustic, the villa at number twelve Italian Neo-Renaissance, and for a handsome example of German Renaissance, try number eight. One thing's for sure about living on this monied Berlin avenue – keeping up with the Schmidts must take some doing.

I rounded the final bend of that millionaire's row and reached the pretty Grunewald S-Bahn station, looking for all the world like a Lilliput Lane cottage dropped at the side of a railway line. Yet despite its prim exterior, the station has a sinister past. I followed a sign for 'Gleis 17' – Track 17 – to find the platform of Grunewald station used as the main point of transportation for Berlin's Jews between 1941 and 1945, initially to ghettos and transit camps in various grim outposts of the Nazi empire, but later to extermination camps in the east as the 'Final Solution' gathered pace. Established as a memorial site by Deutsche Bahn somewhat belatedly in 1998, 'Gleis 17' marks the dates and destinations of the thousands of one-way journeys made from this otherwise backwater suburban station that during those murderous times doubled-up as a commuter stop for some of the wealthiest, most well-heeled Berliners. As the movement of Jews was deliberately orchestrated in the dead of night to avoid prying civilian eyes, most wartime Berliners would not have witnessed the scenes of their petrified fellow citizens making the death march to Grunewald from collection centres like the one at the Levetzowstraße synagogue. But even so, it is hardly credible that ordinary Berliners were wholly oblivious to the movement of tens of thousands of their neighbours and former friends in this highly unorthodox way. Perhaps the rumours circulating about the fate of the Jews were just too awful, too fanciful, to believe. Selected from dozens of similar memorial inscriptions, cast onto metal treads on the edge of the Grunewald platform telling the lamentable story, I read the fate of these murdered Berliners:

13.10.1941 / 1251 JUDEN BERLIN – LODZ

8.7.1942 / 100 JUDEN BERLIN – THERESIENSTADT

8.11.1943 / 50 JUDEN BERLIN – AUSCHWITZ

Back at the front of the station, I studied a separate memorial made up of original 1940s sleepers and ballast, removed from the very track that took the Jews of Berlin on their fateful final journeys. I discovered planted among the ballast young linden trees, seeded in batches at Auschwitz and then brought from the site of the death camp to Berlin. On their arrival in the city at Grunewald, the saplings are nurtured as they take root in the ballast before being replanted randomly around the city – an organic symbol of life replacing death. Later, as I sat on the small terrace in front of the station café, I chatted a little tentatively with an elderly Berliner with clipped, precise English (a man old enough I think to have been around during the 1940s), about one aspect of the Auschwitz planting scheme that I found particularly moving. So discreet is the planting of Berlin's new linden trees, it is impossible to tell of those you walk under on Unter den Linden, in the Großer Tiergarten or anywhere else in the city, which of them originated in Auschwitz. I cycled away from the memorial into the vast space of Grunewald where I sat for a while next to a small lake in a bird sanctuary. Reclining in the warm milky sunshine, I speculated on the origin of the countless lindens laid out for hundreds of acres around me. In a scene of utter tranquillity, Berliners lay motionless side-by-side in the long grass, possibly contemplating – and no doubt bemoaning on this Sunday afternoon – the following day and beginning of their working week. I was jolted from my rest by the unwelcome bleep of my phone. The message was from a friend and former work colleague back home, relaying the news that his father had died that morning. My first full day in Berlin in the company of Fritz, bonding with the city on its pleasant cycleways and amid its verdant parkland and well-travelled lindens, had been unforgettably moving.

Back in the domestic melee of Schöneberg, Otto's tough regime included kitchen rules outlawing the preparation of any product containing meat, fish or eggs. This made the challenge of cooking way too onerous for me, but was handy as an excuse to dine out in any one of the area's eclectic range of eateries. In any event, communal dining with strangers has never been my idea of a good time – a great disappointment I suspected to my fellow guest at Otto's flat, Marie, a lanky language student from Hong Kong who, as far as I could tell from her allocated fridge space, existed on a diet of pot noodles. A keen exponent of scourer-cleaning, Marie was no doubt Otto's idea of a dream tenant. But going hungry was never a possibility in Schöneberg, particularly once I discovered the Efsane Grillhaus on the corner of Kollonenstraße – one of numerous Turkish cafés lending the area the appealing air of a scruffy suburb of Istanbul. The food at the Efsane was marvellous, served up on huge oval plates laden with a multitude of falafel, salad and meze combinations, mostly available for less than the price of a drink in a central London pub. Speaking of drink, on my first visit to the Efsane my pretension at asking for a glass for my Efes beer was met with smiling derision by the café owner, who took great pleasure in keeping me waiting several minutes for the privilege of not having to swig straight from the litre bottle (no smaller measures were available, although consuming the entire litre was of course optional). His two sons – both of them a 'mini-me' and for the time being rather slimmer images of their father – did all the graft behind the counter, while Dad would periodically haul his considerable frame from the orange moulded chair he occupied each evening surveying his empire, to help himself to a cold bottle from the bursting fridge. Whatever the motive for leaving his chair, the man never wasted a movement without also checking on the contents of the till, often grabbing fistfuls of euro notes to stuff into the pockets of his baggy trousers. On my next visit to his café – one of those enterprises where the TV is permanently switched on, flickering in a corner but with no sound – I forgot all about a glass and happily joined the rest of the jolly punters in downing beer from the oversized bottle. Needless to say, the Efsane Grillhaus was packed out every night, and by the end of the month I was on nodding terms with many of its regulars and on speaking terms with the family, particularly the younger members who were keen to try out their English. Not that I was ever once offered a glass to drink from.

With my aim in Berlin being to cover as many square kilometres of my city map as possible, I set out one sunny morning to cycle a good chunk of the most southerly areas. Setting off at a pace along Kollonenstraße, Fritz and I reached Platz Der Luftbrücke and the former Tempelhof Airport in less than fifteen minutes – an impossible mission by public transport. Once one of Europe's big three airports alongside Paris's Le Bourget and the long-defunct Croydon Airport in south London, the original terminal building at Tempelhof was built in

1927. Never a bunch to pass up on a grandiose building opportunity, during the 1930s Nazi ministers saw the potential of the airport's already considerable scale and central location to set about a massive reconstruction aimed at including it in the fantastical scheme to construct Germania – the Third Reich's impossibly hopeful world capital. The achievement at Tempelhof of Hitler's architect-in-chief Albert Speer has left us with a building of authoritarian symmetry on a quite fantastic scale. One of the original features of the Nazi makeover of the airport was a magnificent fourteen-foot imperial eagle that perched arrogantly atop a swastika on the terminal building roof until 1945. After the war, custodianship of this important Third Reich motif moved between the Soviets and Americans, before finally suffering decapitation and removal to the US where it was placed on display until 1985 in a military academy. In a gesture of friendship, the eagle's head was then returned to Germany and now sits on a plinth at the front of the main terminal building. I looked into the majestic bird's steely eyes and touched its cold iron beak, momentarily feeling the chill of making contact with the brutal regime that modelled it.

Sadly, Tempelhof is no longer in operation as an airport, and has been closed to air traffic since the failure of a 2008 campaign to keep it open. Even so, given the sensitivity of the site, I was astonished that I was able to cycle unchallenged beyond the front of the terminal building right into the hub of the 1.2 kilometre-long airport forecourt. Designed to represent an eagle in flight, the building seemed oddly reminiscent in scale, colour and form of the great Alhambra Palace in Granada. However, unlike in the crowded heat of

Andalucia, there wasn't a single other sightseer around, nor any sign of security as I helped myself to photographs, climbed up and down the terminal's stone staircases and flew back and forth with Fritz along the airport's interminable length. There were no restrictions either on entering the Tempelhofer Park that surrounds the terminal. This vast and blowy public space created from defunct runways, has been usefully transformed into a pleasure ground for cyclists and kite flyers. Another altogether twenty-first century function of the disused runway is as a 'tent city', currently providing temporary housing for Germany's swelling numbers of refugees from war-torn regions of the Middle East. We can only speculate what Albert Speer may have made of that.

Before cycling on towards Kreuzberg, I stopped for a while at the Berlin Airlift Memorial on Platz der Luftbrücke – a monument to one of the earliest and key crunch points of the Cold War. In June 1948, in an act of political spite the Soviet authorities cut off the supply of food and fuel to 2.5 million West Berliners by closing all land and sea routes into the western sector through the GDR. The allied response was an act of astonishing logistical might. Although West Berlin was marooned, fortuitously three narrow air corridors remained open as routes into the city enabling the western powers to embark on a remarkable thirteen-month rescue operation. Awarded the name 'Operation Vittles', the initiative flew hundreds of thousands of tonnes of food, coal and other essentials into Tempelhof Airport, saving West Berlin from disease, starvation and therefore capitulation. At the height of the operation in early 1949, an allied aircraft touched down in Berlin *every minute.*

The unqualified success of the mission – enabled by the excellent landing facilities at Tempelhof – may even have been some consolation to Albert Speer. The self-styled 'Good Nazi' had escaped a death sentence at the post-war Nuremburg Trials for his contribution to the decimation of his country, but was serving time in nearby Spandau Prison. Doubtless aware of the allied rescue effort taking place beyond the walls of his cell, he may have reflected that his work in the expansion of an airport with the capacity for such positive purpose had, in the end, not been altogether in vain. It is also quite possible, that as a resident of West Berlin himself at the time of the airlift – albeit incarcerated – Speer even bene-fitted from the contents of the food drops. A more gratifying thought is the gallantry of the so-called 'Candy Bombers', led by US Air Force pilot Gail Halvorsen, who on his regular food sorties had his heart tugged by the groups of hungry children he saw gathered around the airport's perimeter fence. Earning for his endeavours the enviable nicknames of 'Onkel Wackelflügel' – Uncle Wiggly Wings – and the 'Chocolate Pilot', Gail's regular rescue missions involved dropping candy bars from his plane towards the chil-dren on tiny parachutes made from handkerchiefs. Other pilots followed suit and the Candy Bombers squadron was born, to become a permanent part of Berlin folklore. The eighty British and American airmen who died during the airlift are memorialised by an odd concrete memorial I stood and admired in a small park opposite the front of the airport. In the form of a three-pronged fork representing the three air corridors, on its inauguration in 1951 the memorial was gifted by grateful Berliners the nickname that has endured ever since – the 'Hunger Rake'.

Oh my word – or more colourful language to that effect – it's a Wednesday afternoon and I really ought to be at work. That was the sobering thought that popped into my mind – before popping out again rather quickly – as I cycled away from Platz der Luftbrücke down the Mehringdamm slope towards the heart of Kreuzberg. As Fritz gleefully ate up the metres of tarmac, I weighed up the relative pros and virtually non-existent cons of spending a weekday afternoon in a trendy southern Berlin suburb, as an alternative to yet another afternoon – the latest in a series of a *lifetime* of afternoons – in a south London office block peering at a computer screen, quite possibly day-dreaming about being somewhere just like Kreuzberg. Abbreviated catchily for extra-bohemian chic to X-berg, Kreuzberg is everything commercially that the tourist centre of Berlin is not. As a feature of its rapid recent regeneration, the centre of Berlin has inevitably sold parts of its soul to commercialism – evident in the number of Starbucks, Dunkin' Donuts and Subway outlets dotted around the Unter den Linden, Friedrichstraße and Potsdamer Platz. But there wasn't a hint of corporate crudity or a global brand in sight as I looked around me from the small terrace of the Barcomi Café on Bergmannstraße watching an artsy, bookish crowd dodging in an out of the eclectic businesses lining each side of the street. I prised myself away from the café and continued across Urbanstraße, every turn of Fritz's sturdy wheels supported by a fully independent cycle lane. As I crossed the Landwehrkanal by the attractive Admiralbrücke, I was stopped in my tracks by an arresting view to my left of the beautiful Böcklerpark and its smattering of sunbathers lying out on the canal bank. This was urban cycling at its quickest, safest and most scenic.

Yet the real beauty for me of crossing this most diverse of cities on two wheels was the speed at which the culture and scenery changed. Minutes after bumping along the cobbles of Kreuzberg's affluent canal-side streets, I hit a nicely distended section of underbelly beneath the elevated railway on Skalitzerstraße. I was stopped at a red traffic light alongside rows of dilapidated apartment blocks when I witnessed a broad-daylight drugs deal in full-flow between two gaunt young men standing only feet away. They glanced a little nervously in my direction as money, a small package, but no apparent words, were exchanged. The contrast between this gritty eastern end of the borough and the canal-side gentility I had passed through only moments earlier was stark, and easily explained by the proximity of Skalitzerstraße and the elevated railway to the former site of the Berlin Wall. During its twenty-eight year existence, the scar of the wall ensured that anything in its vicinity was deemed undesirable, pushing down rents in areas like Skalitzerstraße and accelerating social decline. More than a quarter-of-a-century after most of the wall was reduced to either rubble or a tourist curiosity, remnants of this legacy of decline linger on. But Kreuzberg was good value on that workaday Wednesday afternoon, offering a dash of the bohemian, a thriving independent café culture, self-confident affluence, a smattering of inner-city decay and the grime of a live drugs deal – truly a microcosm of modern Berlin experienced in an hour-long bike ride. I looked down at my two-wheeled companion and wondered if I might perhaps be losing my grip, as I muttered something in the direction of his robust steel frame about simply not being able to do any of this without him.

It's true. In the space of a handful of days in Berlin, I had somehow managed to fall head-over-handlebars for an old and neglected bicycle. If this seems a little strange, let me tell you that now it was the turn of a bridge. The bridge and I first crossed paths as I cycled away from the seamy streets of east Kreuzberg towards the renowned East Side Gallery, a mile-long section of Berlin Wall preserved for political posterity and the daubings of youthful, extravagant graffiti. Between me, Fritz and the gallery flowed the River Spree, a key Berlin artery straddled by the unique double-decker Oberbaumbrücke, enabling a river crossing by foot, road and U-Bahn. The bridge's red brick Neo-Gothic archway and quirky twin towers are a visual treat and, according to Otto, a firm favourite with Berliners. But decorative as the bridge is in itself, the attraction for me was the constant movement of people and traffic across it, and the transfixing – nay, addictive – sight of the canary yellow U-Bahn trains criss-crossing the bridge as they entered and exited Schlesisches Tor station on the south bank of the river. As well as being multi-functional, the Oberbaumbrücke is also symbolically important to Berliners. Between 1961 and its fall in 1989, the bridge itself formed part of the Berlin Wall and so was itself the physical division of east and west. German reunification in 1990 and a makeover three years later saw the bridge restored to its former glory and reinstated as an important and popular city land-mark. Nowadays, the Oberbaumbrücke is also the only physical connection between the two areas that make up the trendy district of Kreuzberg-Friedrichshain, an unlikely union of two distinct boroughs established for administrative convenience in 2001. Whereas during the east-west partition Kreuzberg (west) and Friedrichshain (east) were – quite literally – worlds apart, since 1989 the rivalry between the two has been mocked up by an annual anarchic vegetable fight on the handsome Oberbaumbrücke, pitching teams from both sides of the Spree in a riot of rotten foodstuffs. From what I gathered, once the turnips start flying in this most unusual local derby, few prisoners are taken and little love is lost. In the equally frenetic surrounds of the council chambers during tense negotiations to establish the formalities of the new district, the highly partisan authorities of the rival boroughs couldn't even agree a location for the city hall. Eventually, after much hand-wringing, countless meetings of poker-faced officials and apparently little compromise, the dispute was settled, not this time by the deployment of decaying vegetables, but by the indisputable finality of the toss of a five-mark coin. Friedrichshain called heads. Heads it was.

I propped Fritz up against the side of the bridge and waited for the first train to pass in whichever direction, hoping to get a photograph as the front of the train reached the exact half-way point between the two neo-Gothic towers. My first attempt at the snap was thwarted by the head of an unwitting tourist, the second by the untimely arrival of an open-air tour bus that blocked the view, and the third by my hopeless mistiming and loss of patience. Twenty minutes and three trains in each direction later I got the photograph I wanted, albeit marred slightly by the inconvenience of the sudden appearance of a dark cloud. Worryingly, even in possession of my 'holy grail' photograph, I still couldn't tear myself away from this prime viewing position. I even considered waiting until two trains passing in opposite directions appeared on the bridge simultaneously, a strategy I decided against amid growing concerns around the onset of an obsessive compulsive disorder. This, I think, is what can happen to one's priorities outside the discipline of a nine-to-five routine – a curious but not altogether unwelcome thought!

Once I reached the East Side Gallery, it seemed to me at least at first sight to consist of little more than packs of tourists stood around multi-coloured murals, gurning into mobile devices for selfies or buying magnetic fragments of the wall and replica GDR military memorabilia from the lines of souvenir stalls. However, once I got near enough I could see that the art splayed on this remnant of the Berlin *Mauer* (the largest section still standing), isn't just art for art's sake – there is a real purpose. Many of the politicised daubs draw attention to the still-standing Palestinian Wall – with which the history of its Berlin counterpart has obvious parallels – and a host of other long-running global injustices, to form a colourfully right-on, uniquely Berlin attraction. But keen to flee the crowd, Fritz swept me away from the gallery along Grünbergerstraße towards Boxhagener Platz – the centrepiece of grungy south Friedrichshain – to lie out on its lush little meadow with a takeaway bought from a lively student-hangout on trendy Simon-Dach-Straße. Apart from a group of gossipy young mothers peering into pushchairs, Fritz and I were quite alone – a rare and precious thing in a city centre square.

I had spent most of the morning captivated by a triumph of pre-war Nazi architectural vision at Tempelhof. Heading north from Boxhagener Platz I was now confronted with a construction resonant of Berlin's

post-Second World War Soviet era. I took a left from
Warschauerstraße courtesy of a superbly smooth and
safe configuration of cycle lanes into Karl-Marx-Allee,
and save for the showroom-shiny Audis speeding by,
I might well have been back in the Soviet-era. Originally
named Stalinallee, this colossal Berlin boulevard was
renamed Karl-Marx-Allee following the completion of
a major communist rebuilding programme in 1961.
Whatever the aesthetic and political motives of its
designers, at eighty-nine metres wide and two kilometres long this is a truly great thoroughfare, flanked
either side by brutalist yet rather beautiful eight-storey
apartment blocks resembling a parade of towering concrete wedding cakes. Thanks to its iconic status and
central location, during the communist era the boulevard was often the Berlin focal point of anti-Soviet
protest, most notoriously in June 1953 (when it was
still named Stalinallee) when a workers' uprising was
stamped out by a small army of tanks and troops with
the loss of 130 lives. Wide and flat and therefore
topographically perfect as a parade ground, Karl-Marx-
Allee was later used as the venue for displays of military
muscle-flexing at the GDR's annual May Day celebra-
tions. The old parade ground is also a highly effective
wind tunnel – so effective in fact that Stalin's inner-
city autobahn felt rather longer than its official two
kilometres as I cycled towards what before 1989 had
been West Berlin, struggling against a stiff west-
east head-wind whistling along the boulevard from
Alexanderplatz. Yet by the time I reached Alexanderplatz,
my limbs a little shaky from the effort of pushing Fritz's
fifteen-kilos head-on against the elements, I felt ener-
gised – elated even – to be at large, right at the very
heart of my perennial Berlin mystery.

The artistically defaced section of Berlin Wall at the East Side Gallery may be the longest chunk still standing, but by far the best maintained authentic stretch of wall runs along Bernauerstraße in the Mitte district of the city. Years before, a colleague at one of the German advice centres I worked – a very well-liked Berliner called Dietmar, a man memorable for his daring work attire of tight-fitting leather trousers lighting up our team meetings – told me a fascinating story from his childhood. In August 1961, eight year old Dietmar was taken by his parents from their West Berlin home on the annual family holiday to the north Frisian island of Sylt. A fortnight later the family returned to Berlin, refreshed by the bracing North Sea air, but dismayed to discover that flung up in their absence was a 155 kilometre barbed wire and concrete monstrosity dividing their city unnaturally into east and west. The aberration of the wall was of course no passing fad and it was a full twenty-eight years before relatives and friends of Dietmar's family living in the eastern, Soviet occupied areas of Berlin could once again pass freely into the west – and vice-versa. In an effort to afford it a level of political legitimacy it hardly deserved, the GDR authorities initially christened the wall, both pedantically and a tad farcically, the *Antifaschistischer Schutzwall* – the Anti-Fascist Protection Rampart. Much more than a protective rampart, the construction of the wall was the regime's sharp response to the threat of economic meltdown posed by the daily hemorrhaging of manpower from east to west – a constant brain and muscle drain that over time amounted to 3.5 million escapees, fully twenty-percent of the GDR's entire population. This loss of manpower was addressed by shoring up the soft

East German border that passed through Berlin – a weakness that had allowed thousands of people to escape to the west through the city. So for the Soviet puppet state the wall served its purpose perfectly, and by the 1970s the total number 'lost' to the west numbered less than a thousand each year. Yet despite the anger of West Berlin's mayor Willy Brandt at the affront of the wall when it appeared apparently from nowhere to blot the Berlin landscape for close on three decades, the United States and its allies rather too quickly reached the conclusion that a wall was better than another war. Their best response was to do nothing at all.

When it was complete the Berlin Wall consisted of more than simply one single barrier, and included a no-man's-land 'death strip' running between two separate, parallel sections of wall containing anti-vehicle trenches and other defence apparatus. To find out more I cycled to the Mauerpark memorial at Bernauerstraße, which occupies a 1.5 kilometre strip along the former east-west border, utilising its section of preserved 'death strip' to house a fascinating open air exhibition. A watchtower spared from demolition after the demise of the wall reminds visitors of the ease with which East German border guards were able to take fatal pot-shots at would-be escapees to the west, on the back of an explicit government 'shoot-to-kill' order. As a result of this licence for Berliner to murder Berliner, at least ninety so-called fugitives died. The total number of escapee deaths during the life of the wall is unknown, but estimates of the umpteen incidents of drowning while attempting to swim the treacherous River Spree, or from any number of other brave, sometimes foolhardy, methods of escape attempts run into several hundred.

The wall divided a city, its families and in some sections even single streets, including Bernauerstraße where I now stood, which formed part of the border between east and west. Whereas the houses and apartment blocks of the street were situated in East Berlin, the pavement and street surfaces were in the west. Cue chaos, confusion and multiple escape attempts. Quite understandably under such circumstances, many people resorted to jumping from the upper windows of buildings in a desperate bid to land safely, unscathed and with both feet planted firmly on a western pavement. In some of the luckier cases, successful escapees enjoyed soft landings on bed sheets held open for them by firefighters on the street below. Tragically though, the very first Berlin Wall death came as a result of just such an attempt. On 22nd August 1961, the unfortunate Ida Siekmann jumped from a window of her fourth floor apartment at number 48 Bernauerstraße, not to freedom as she fervently hoped, but to oblivion. Attempting to join her sister Martha on the 'better' side of the wall, the fifty-nine year old nurse threw eiderdowns from her bedroom down to the street, a strategy that failed as she missed her target and landed heavily on the road surface causing multiple fatal injuries.

The story of the Berlin Wall does of course have a positive ending, albeit one that came about somewhat accidentally when it fell under the sheer weight of history and pick-axes on the night of 9th November 1989, to kick-start yet another reinvention of this most intriguing of cities (by an eerie coincidence on the anniversary of *Kristallnacht*, the Nazi anti-semitic pogrom). As I stood in the bleak no-man's land of the former 'Death Strip' on Bernauerstraße, I imagined that for those communist-weary East Berliners who stepped through the broken concrete and twisted barbed wire of the defunct wall on that landmark November evening, it must have felt akin to making a first intrepid step on the moon. To escape for a few moments the gloom of the memorial and a steady drizzle of the type that soaks through layers of clothing within minutes, I found a pitch in Bernauerstraße's famous Ost-West café. I squeezed up alongside other 'wall' tourists huddled at tables in front of steamy windows, warming their hands around large mugs of coffee bearing the legend, *I Love Berlin*. I looked out at the rainy street to an old East German Trabant car stood on the pavement outside, no longer spluttering its two-stroke path through the drab cobbled streets of East Berlin, but given new purpose as an icon and exhibit of the GDR. But as powerful an image the fluorescent fibre glass 'Trabby' is of Berlin's recent traumas, as a single physical motif of my Berlin mystery, the wall is surely its most potent – initially on its construction as a symbol of the city's non-negotiable division, then after 1989 of its rebirth, reconciliation and complete reinvention.

I retrieved a damp and rather disconsolate Fritz from a rammed bike rack to cycle back to Schöneberg along the race-track of Potsdamerstraße. When I walked through the front door of the apartment, I was greeted by another great incontrovertible mystery of Berlin – my über-house-proud host, Otto. Having spent the afternoon considering the oppression of millions of his Berlin ancestry, I wasn't prepared for an inquisition that would have served a police state well, on my apparent contravention of a raft of his domestic bye-laws. Since moving in I had taken great care in avoiding inappropriate – or indeed any – use of his kitchen, I had followed a clinical bathroom routine and had broken the habit of a lifetime by the daily making of my bed – a chore that included smoothing out the wrinkles from the sheets in the very likely event that at some point Otto would run a spot check of my room. So having worked so hard to please my host, I was perplexed to be facing a 'kangaroo court' accused of stepping out of line in the footwear department. When the case for the prosecution was read out, I could hardly deny a thing. Hurrying out of the flat one morning in a bid to reach a small café on Hauptstraße before it ran out of its habit-forming *apfelstrudel*, I had left my city map folded up at the side of the bathroom sink. Thinking I might just this once get away with re-entering the flat without first removing my shoes, I trod lightly down the hallway and into the bathroom to retrieve the map. However, not only did the observant Otto somehow detect my bathroom trespass, for the purpose of evidence he also took a photograph on his phone of the faint print the sole of my trainers had left on the tiled floor of his smallest room. My second bookable offence, deeming necessary a stern red-card-warning lecture, was to leave his front door slightly ajar during the thirty seconds duration of my transgression. Now, I am not one to play on national stereotypes, but Otto really could not, had he tried, been any more Teutonic in his approach to detecting my infringements and then prosecuting them. As well as showing me the damning evidence of a zoom-in of the footprint photo, I was given a short refresher course complete with practical demonstrations in the hitherto underestimated art of door closing – all delivered, by the way, without the

merest trace of irony or humour. I resisted the temp-
tation to suggest to Otto that he think about taking up
a time consuming hobby of some description, bluffed
an apology and left the flat to double up outside in
painful laughter over Fritz's crossbar, wishing it was
possible to share the story to its full effect with a steel
frame on wheels.

I quickly put the humiliation of *shoegate* to one side
and spent much of the following day on the more
important business of locating some of Berlin's innumerable sites of memorial to Germany's twelve-year
moral hiatus of 1933 to 1945. I began at the most
visited of them all: the American designed Holocaust
Denkmal (memorial), the hugely expensive and quite
overwhelming monument to the Jews killed by the
Nazi state. Mesmerised by its scale and complexity,
I walked for a while among the memorial's undulating
rows of grey concrete plinths, placed on a sloping site to
represent tombs in a cemetery. As inexplicable and disorienting as the crime it memorialises, the Holocaust
Denkmal left me cold – physically so at the touch of its
solemn concrete, and aesthetically for its dour mono-
chrome. I wandered up and down the narrow passageways of the memorial – an unrestrained, hands-held-up
statement of culpability for the German nation's greatest crime. I then followed packs of tourists down a staircase to visit the subterranean exhibition centre, where
I gazed at countless, all too familiar scenes of death and
atrocity arranged on an exhaustive collection of display
boards. Placed in the middle of the capital city in the
shadow of the national monument – the Brandenburg
Gate – the memorial is an unavoidable reminder to
Berlin visitors of the murder of six million European

Jews. But perhaps more importantly for twenty-first century sensibilities, it serves as a daily reminder to millions of ordinary Berliners, quite intentionally leaving them with no room for any ifs, buts and maybes in relation to their dark inheritance of the Nazi period. Not for a minute could Germany be accused of failing to face up to its guilt in engineering one of humanity's greatest crimes. If anything, the graphic form of Berlin's very public act of penance felt to me clichéd, somewhat forced and at times even a little wearing, as if Germany was trying just a little *too* hard. Part of this collective national atonement is the conspicuous absence in Berlin of any noticeable form of memorial to the sufferings of ordinary Germans, who of course also died in countless numbers at the hands of the Third Reich regime, from allied bombing, and then at the end of the war from Soviet invasion. It seems that the German nation, having inflicted such damage on the world during its twelve-year Nazi period, can hardly bear to claim for itself even a little of the victim territory. All efforts are focused instead on the remembrance of the persecuted minorities, and I left Berlin sure in the knowledge that every memorial effort I saw was part of the wider attempt to make the best of what had been in the 1930s and 40s – as far as modern Berlin is concerned – an exceedingly bad job. Nowadays, in a spirit opposite to 'don't mention the war', Germany cannot stop talking about it. While the conversation goes on, reparation continues apace.

I left the Holocaust *Denkmal* and moved on to the equally deflating 'Topography of Terror' exhibition on Wilhelmstraße, built on the site previously occupied by the three most dreaded institutions of the Nazi state – the Gestapo, the SS and Reich Security. The single-storey installation focuses the visitor on the wide-ranging activities of the Third Reich during its twelve violent years, presenting panel after panel of text, victim testimonies and photographs exposing the brutal purpose of the Nazi machine's three principal instruments of terror. Despite the familiarity of the desperate Holocaust images I had seen in other exhibitions in Germany and elsewhere, during my time in Berlin I found their capacity to shock and instil disbelief unabated. I moved swiftly between each memorial – there were only so many photographs I could stand of emaciated victims staring through barbed wire, or of the tortured faces of children dragged screaming from their parents, helpless in rags and bereft of care.

I pressed on and reached the eastern edge of the Großer Tiergarten, where I found the memorial to Nazi-persecuted homosexuals, a curious grey concrete cube which at the time of its construction in 2008 was the cause of quite a local stir. Two groups in particular were up in arms. One of these was made up of members of the Jewish community who objected to its location directly opposite their own memorial, suggesting that official recognition of the suffering of homosexuals undermined the much greater scale of their own persecution. Before I read this, I had never before thought of memorialising to be subject to a pecking order, and wondered what else might lie behind the resentment of the unassuming homosexual memorial cube. Few would deny the Jewish community its high profile memorial in the centre of Berlin, but to object to another placed close by in recognition of another persecuted minority, seemed to me churlish at best. More surprisingly

perhaps, the second opposing group consisted of
members of the lesbian community, affronted at their
exclusion from the memorial's original plans. But after
much hand-wringing in the Berlin gay community, it
was decided to include women in a video playing on a
loop at the memorial showing scenes of canoodling
men. During the ten minutes I queued with other visitors to watch the short movie through a tiny window
built into the side of the memorial, I witnessed a level of
disrespect that had been absent from every other memorial site in Berlin I visited. This was hardly pernicious
homophobia, but the group of smirking teenagers
queuing in front of me left me wondering about the
suitability of a short, pseudo-soft porn film to memori-
alise the dead. While on the one hand the clear message
of, 'some people are gay and they didn't deserve to
die for it', is spelled out loud and clear, surely a small
fountain or solemn inscription on stone would have
been a better choice. But then again, this was Berlin…

Buried under an otherwise nondescript car park close
to the square kilometre of memorials to victims of the
Nazi regime, lies the former site of the *Führerbunker* –
the last hiding place and the scene of the demise of the
man who did more than anyone to create the need for
the cluster of memorials that now stand in the vicinity.
In truth there wasn't much to see – no plaque or other
marker to indicate the bunker's exact position. Yet even
though I was looking at no more than an approxima-
tion, it still felt disquieting to be so close to the scene of
Adolf Hitler's final days and downfall. I eavesdropped
on a young Australian guide leading a 'Third Reich
cycling tour' (such enterprise!) who pointed at a yellow
VW camper van parked at the spot where it is thought

Hitler's body was set alight by jubilant soldiers of the victorious Red Army. When the Soviets arrived at the Berlin bunker to finish the Führer off, they would have found a complex dug fifteen metres underground and covered in several layers of concrete. This was a building clearly meant to last. I looked down at the ground in frustration trying to imagine what lay below, but it was all guesswork. So well protected was the subterranean hideout, there must surely be some of the warren of corridors and airless rooms still intact below ground – a fascinating tomb of Nazism that we will probably never be permitted to see. But given the unlikelihood of developers moving in on this prime bit of central Berlin real estate (laying foundations would be a logistical problem due to the vast hollowed out space below the surface), it seems likely that the car park will remain as the only vague marker of Hitler's feeble last stand. I cycled away from the site of the former Führerbunker feeling a tad deflated by it all, unfulfilled by the photograph of a yellow camper van being the scant reward of my hopeful visit. Just like that covered-over Nazi hideaway, the mystery of Berlin seemed deeper still.

It is probably fair to say that my memorial day hadn't been the most uplifting of my travels thus far, so in the evening I awarded myself a mini-bar crawl around upbeat Nollendorfplatz, a short stroll from Otto's apartment. When I mentioned this to my host, he most interestingly introduced me to the term *kiez*. According to the Otto 'mine of information', *kiez* is the word used in northern German cities (principally Berlin but also in the livelier areas of Hamburg and Hannover) to identify areas of concentrated bar, club or art culture that are considered trendy or avant-garde. With an eclectic bar scene offering something for just about everyone, Nollendorfplatz fits the *kiez* bill perfectly. I hung around for a while in the well-named Slumberland Bar, watching games of table football playing out noisily in the back bar, a space memorable for its floor surface of several inches of golden sand – a curious tropical beach theme I came across in several of land-locked Berlin's drinking haunts. In one of these – the Strandbar Mitte nestling on the banks of the River Spree – I sat for an hour one day sipping a beer in a seaside deckchair bearing that omnipresent city motif, *I Love Berlin*. Embracing this amorous sentiment to the full, my thoughts turned intermittently to the frustrations of my old office-bound lifestyle, then back again to the reality of the here and now and that enjoyable and rather ludicrous Hawaiian-themed city beach bar – an odd juxtaposition of thought that only reinforced my belief in the choices I had made.

On my way back to Schöneberg and Otto's quirky hospitality (wondering en route about the severe penalties about to come my way for depositing grains of imported sand in his hallway), I stopped on the super-cool Akazienstraße at a smart and affordable Italian restaurant called Don Antonio – an enticing little eatery marred only by a dough-faced waiter who glowered in disapproval at my modest order of a pizza and single bottle of beer. On one of several visits I made during the month, I had only enough coins to leave the man a tip slightly short of the regulation ten-percent, an affront that earned me an invective spat at me in German that needed no translation. I have no name for this frosty waiter so will settle for calling him Herr Flick, in recognition of his feat in engineering an unconvincing blonde quiff from the remains of his hair. Otto told me later that the waiter's attitude was perfectly normal, and all part of the famed, charmingly-named *Berlin Schnauze* – 'Berlin Gob' or 'Berlin Snout', depending on your translation – an inoffensive (supposedly) and eccentric dialect that manifests in coarse humour and gruff, standoffish behaviour. 'Berlin Gob' was evidently a communication style popular with restaurant staff, so I was happy to assume that the pizza waiter's snarl was a sort of local expression of his endearment – and well-disguised at that.

Demonstrating Berlin's unlimited capacity for intrigue and quirky entertainment, the following Sunday morning as I was cycling past the Blue Boy Bar on Eisernacherstraße on my way to another great surviving Nazi monolith – the *Olympiastadion* – a man wearing a pair of underpants on his head, and nothing at all around his waist, ran out into the road in front of me. I never got to visit the Blue Boy Bar while I was in Berlin, but it had the look of a place where pretty much anything might go, and judging by the state of its early morning clientele, a place that may have more varieties of pick-me-ups on sale inside than would generally be considered beneficial to your health. As I cycled from the scene I looked back to see the man taking a long lug from his bottle of beer, before scuttling back through the bar door to continue his early morning bender. I had no idea if the underwear pulled over his head belonged to him, or whether there might be some other similarly inebriated punter inside the bar wondering what on earth he had done with his. There was clearly entertainment value to be had in Sunday morning Schöneberg, but Fritz and I had other business. How wonderful though it felt, just at that moment, that after five decades of living it life could still conjure such surprise!

Built for the 1936 Berlin Olympic Games (awarded to Germany prior to the Nazi seizure of power), the *Olympiastadion* is a colossus. On Hitler's own insistence, construction of the stadium was carried out only by selected non-unionised Aryan builders (although the inspiration for the build was clearly Roman), with the resultant spiralling costs eventually exceeding twenty-seven million Reichsmarks. The Nazis of course did nothing by halves, and on completion the stadium boasted a total of 110,000 seats – in its day an astonishing capacity – and included, unsurprisingly, a special section of grandstand for the sole use of Hitler and his servile entourage. But as the regime's biggest propaganda opportunity yet, the Berlin Olympics were in reality a bit of a damp squib. The games may have afforded the Third Reich some level of worldwide political legitimacy, but the sporting prowess of non-Aryan athletes such as the African-American Jesse Owens – who famously won four gold medals in front of the fizzing Führer (prompting chief Nazi propagandist Joseph Goebbels into characteristic hyperbole by claiming that as a result of Owens' success, *'white humanity should be ashamed of itself'*) – was clearly not what Hitler had in mind as his Olympic legacy. Thankfully though, it was the stadium and not its creators that survived the war virtually unscathed, and after 1945 it was used initially as the headquarters of the occupying British forces, until later becoming the home ground of local *Bundesliga* football club, Hertha Berlin.

As it turned out, a game was taking place on the day of my visit. I propped Fritz up against one of the two

giant pillars that stand in front of the stadium supporting the giant Olympic rings, and stood talking for
a while to two fans of Hertha's opponents that day,
Lokomotiv Leipzig. We hit it off straight away. Günther,
a portly red-faced man of a certain age, wore the
look and carried the midriff of someone rarely having
refused a drink. His twenty-something, thus far rather
slimmer son, Paulus, a beer in one hand and battered
bratwurst in the other, looked a good bet to be heading
the same way. I told Günther that as a boy growing up
in England during the 1970s, I found the names of the
best known East German football clubs – Dynamo
Dresden, Carl Jeiss Jena and Günther's own Leipzig
club – a tad sinister, as if the players from those clubs
were involved in some kind of footballing espionage.
This was partly a figment of my young Cold War-era
imagination, but Günther – who conveniently for me
had an excellent command of English – seemed to
understand exactly what I meant. For his part, during
the same period he told me that he had associated the
names of the great English clubs with notions of
glamour, wealth, and above all of freedom, adding
pointedly that he still did. We approached the stadium's
iconic bell, originally housed during the Nazi heyday in
its very own granite tower that acted as a store for
reams of classified Third Reich documents. The tower,
like much else in Berlin at the time, was set alight in
1945 by vengeful Soviet troops, rendering it so unstable
that once the area around the stadium was occupied
by the British, it had to be demolished. Fortunately,
the British had the foresight to salvage the bell, even
though the damage to the tower had left it with a huge
crack. The bell hasn't sounded a note since, but sitting

in a proud and prominent position at the front of the stadium, it presents a fascinating pre and post-war motif. The sight of the eagle astride the Olympic rings cast into the bronze bell naturally has a far greater personal resonance for Günther than for me (I have no idea what might have happened to his parents during the Nazi period, or indeed after the war), yet I still felt a tangible chill as we stood beside it. Without hesitation, football fanatic Günther pointed a derisory finger at the swastika, albeit sanitised now of its Nazi association by the post-war filling-in of two of its spider legs. How much better though, I suggested tentatively to my new East German chum – and how much more honest – it had been to have simply doctored the symbol's potency, rather than removing it altogether.

Much as I was tempted by Günther's offer to don a blue and yellow scarf and join him and Paulus for the game, I had set a challenge for Fritz. This would take us on a grand sweep of Berlin from west to east, away from the Olympic Stadium, through leafy Charlottenburg, gritty working class Wedding, bohemian Prenzlauer Berg and finally to the former Soviet era East Berlin district of Alt-Hohenschönhausen. My final and rather ominous destination would be the former GDR Ministry for State Security *Hohenschönhausen Memorial* – the dreaded Stasi Prison. This most fascinating cycling route initially took me past Charlottenburg's seventeenth-century Hohenzollern palace, a baroque palace built for (and named after) the Prussian Queen Sophia Charlotte at the end of the seventeenth-century. The largest building of its kind in Germany, the palace is nowadays a mainstream, highly popular Berlin tourist attraction. I continued on a far less-beaten track due east along the riverside cycle path close to Levetzowstraße (from where many of Berlin's murdered Jews began their journey to Grunewald station and the death camps), then followed a taxi driver's dream elongated route up Stromstraße through the grey suburb of Moabit, before reaching Wedding.

The district of Wedding had long held a fascination for me, not so much for its English-looking (but not sounding) name, but as the setting for Hans Fallada's 1947 novel, *Alone In Berlin*. Fallada's compelling read tells the true story of Otto and Elise Hampel, an ordinary working-class Berlin couple motivated by the death of their son at the eastern front to actively resist the Nazis through the rather quaint, yet extraordinarily brave method of writing and then distributing postcards around the city containing anti-Nazi messages. The majority of the treasonable cards, written in plain and simple language riddled with spelling and grammatical errors, were left on apartment stairwells and in other public spaces for public consumption: *'Why suffer war and death for Hitler's plutocracy?' 'Hitler's war is the worker's death!'* protested two of the cards written in Otto Hampel's faltering hand. Unfortunately for the Hampels, most of their work was turned over to the Gestapo by their terrified recipients before they were widely read. In April 1943, after a year of covert resistance, Otto and Elise were betrayed, put on trial for treason and beheaded in Berlin's notorious Plötzensee Prison, to join a list of 3,000 other opponents of the Third Reich who met the same fate.

Fallada's novel portrays 1940s Wedding as a shabby inner-city suburb of mean streets and grey apartment blocks. In the intervening years, little seems to have

changed in the area at least outwardly, although
with thirty-five percent of the area's population born
outside Germany – the highest ratio of any Berlin
district – a young and artsy cultural scene now thrives.
Frayed around the edges it may be, but the gentri-
fication of Wedding is well underway, including on
Amsterdamerstraße where Otto and Elise had lived
during the war. I stood outside the Hampel's former
home, delighted to find that their risky endeavours had
earned them a memorial plaque. Not that Wedding had
at any stage been a Nazi stronghold. Known in the
1920s and 1930s as Roter Wedding – Red Wedding –
the area was awash with Communists and Social
Democrats, returning a paltry National Socialist vote
at Berlin's final free elections in November 1932, only
two months before Hitler became chancellor. I picked
up this snippet of Wedding's history from the unlikely
source of Athenian artist and fellow cyclist Stelios, who
I met as we waited patiently for a green light in the bike
lane at the junction of Pankstraße and Badstraße – one
of those mesmerising Berlin crossroads where Fritz
and I were frequently disoriented by signs that seemed
to advertise only the *existence* of other areas of the
city, rather than their direction. Before pointing me the
right way, Stelios told me that he had come to Berlin
to escape the economic turmoil currently engulfing
Greece's ancient capital – 'the anxiety of Athens' as he
described it – to join an enclave of compatriot artists
seeking better fortune. In fact, Stelios had found such
artistic impetus in the relative economic calm of this
city, that he had established a blog community of similarly Berlin-inspired artists, writers and others of a creative persuasion called *Daily Lazy*. I promised Stelios

that I would look it up later in the day in the sure knowledge that from its title alone, I would find something in it worth reading.

Stelios sent me pedalling along Schönhauser Allee, which true to his word took me in the general direction of Prenzlauer Berg. Just as I had searched out Wedding for its setting in a famous piece of Berlin literature, so Prenzlauer Berg had long intrigued me as the East Berlin home of journalist Peter Millar, from where he delivered his gripping 1989 account of life in the former GDR capital, *The Berlin Wall: My Part In Its Downfall*. Since then Prenzlauer Berg has shaken off its dour image to become one of central Berlin's most sought after postcodes and these days enjoys a natty, abbreviated nickname of Prenzlberg, given to it by a young and trendy generation of Berliners who have made the area their home since the fall of the wall. Nowadays, Prenzlberg ranks very firmly as a Berlin *kiez* and place to be seen. Its desirability was much in evidence as I walked along the elegant Rykestraße, a long residential street of apartment blocks refurbished to their former nineteenth-century grandeur, and judging by the lines of gleaming BMWs and Mercedes parked alongside them, now home to well paid, upwardly-mobile professionals. More interesting still was the beautiful 1904 synagogue that sits among the well-heeled mansion blocks. The largest synagogue in Germany – despite being looted and desecrated during November 1938's *Kristallnacht* – it escaped total Nazi destruction thanks to its proximity to the neighbouring Aryan-inhabited apartment blocks. Beginning to feel pleasingly at home in Prenzlberg, I tethered Fritz and walked the short distance to the perfectly-named local landmark of 'Thick Hermann' – a squat 1877 British-built water tower. I was glad of the English translation on the display board at the front of the tower, explaining the clever adaptation of the rooms beneath the storage tanks for use as homes for machinery operators. In fact, when the water tower function was removed in 1952, the rooms continued to be used for housing and are now regarded as highly desirable residences. As I read the dense text, it was a relief to be at last faced with an aspect of modern Berlin history that did not include a memorial to – or at least an account of – some or other atrocity of the Third Reich or its GDR successor. Sadly the relief was short-lived, and my heart sank like a stone as I reached the bottom of the panel to discover that the boiler and engine room of the Wasserturm Prenzlauer Berg had, in fact, served as Germany's very first (albeit small scale) concentration camp. All too predictable, and British built to boot.

Fritz and I continued through the leafy lanes of Prenzlberg until we reached Immanuelkirchstraße, where we took a pit-stop at one of the most welcoming cafés I think I have ever visited. I was served by an obliging waitress called Greta, who didn't betray even a smidgen of annoyance at my request for a variety of sandwich that wasn't ready made and already on display. I found a cosy corner window seat with Fritz in full view outside, eyeing each passer-by as a potential bike thief (old London and Seville habits die hard). As I watched everyday life go by, I was surprised by the volume of buggy and pushchair traffic ploughing up and down the street, something I hadn't really been aware of in other parts of central Berlin. This was evidence, Greta told me in fluent English with barely a trace of an accent as she handed me a slab of shop-baked stollen, of Prenzlberg's growing reputation as the capital's 'nappy valley', the only district of the city in fact with a growing birth rate. There was no real reason why this should put me off the area but I did wonder if, in a parallel universe of me actually living in Berlin (this was not beyond the bounds), I might be better off opting for the grittier charms of neighbouring Wedding. Anyway, that was a conundrum for later. For now, it was time to reclaim Fritz and continue our journey to the Far East.

At the time of my Berlin adventure, the twenty-fifth anniversary of the fall of the Berlin Wall had just passed. Nevertheless, the long stretch of Landsberger Allee I cycled along to reach the Stasi prison – a bleak expanse of tarmac lined by rather brutal Soviet-era apartment blocks – could have been the location of a 1970s Cold War documentary, with not only architecture left as a reminder of the GDR years. Negotiating the heavily rutted surface of the cycle lane (by far the worst maintained I had ridden on in the city and which deteriorated the further east I went), I passed a huddle of down-trodden middle-aged men sharing cigarettes outside a thrown up building bearing the legend, *Moscow Supermarket*. I felt a little self-conscious taking a picture of the scene, but the men smiled at me content perhaps for a small distraction in what I guessed might be straitened lives. Pedalling on further through the bleak post-Soviet landscape, I began to feel as if I had travelled so far east as to be about to hit Germany's border with Poland. I was someway short of that of course, although an enormous sign hanging in the sky advertising the proximity of an *IKEA* store suggested

I was now well out of town. At last I reached the landmark I had been aiming for – the modern Allee Centre shopping complex at Lichtenberg, where I crossed a tram line into Genslerstraße and cycled another two hundred metres towards the site of the former Stasi Prison. For its bleakness and seclusion alone, the location had evidently been well chosen. Somewhat ironically, before the Stasi moved in the Nazis had put the site to a somewhat more admirable purpose. Before its adaptation by the Soviets as a post-war internment camp – and then its transformation to a Stasi prison in 1961 by the addition of a stark grey pebble-dashed quadrangle – the buildings had served as a National Socialist People's Welfare soup kitchen, demonstrating the Nazi government's now mostly forgotten capacity for selective social responsibility. The ragbag collection of cell blocks and shabby offices now finds itself sandwiched between an asylum seekers' hostel and a row of genteel bungalows, the latter evidently built and occupied well before the prison's closure in 1989. I looked up and down the row of neat little homes with their trim bushes and manicured lawns, and wondered how the residents might have felt before 1989 about their former neighbours from hell. Doubtless they kept an inquisitive eye on the sinister goings-on across the street but always, I would hazard a guess, from a safe distance behind sets of nervously twitching net curtains.

At the height of its oppressive powers, the principal instrument of terror of the former GDR – the East German Ministry of State Security, the Stasi – had 91,000 full-time employees and 189,000 unofficial informants, a disproportionately high number of snoops for a fairly small country of around seventeen million people. As well as spreading beyond the divide of the Berlin Wall, the Stasi informant network (with 3,000 of its snitches even operating from inside *West* Berlin), reached as far as professional football. In 1988, Steffen Freund, then a promising young player with BSG Stahl Brandenburg – a modest outfit based close to Berlin – found himself in a darkened room sat in front of two Stasi heavies shining torches into his eyes. Demanding that the seventeen year old *wunderkind* work for the Stasi and 'tell us about your teammates', they may have been astonished by his outright refusal to play ball – a defiance that the talented midfielder claims he got away with on the grounds that the authorities were unable to pin any other significantly subversive behaviour on either him or any member of his family. Undoubtedly though, the fall of the wall allowed Freund to forge the sort of career in football that would not have been possible given the strictures of his GDR citizenship. As well as realising his playing potential through spells with top German and English clubs (he currently holds a coaching role with Tottenham Hotspur), Freund went on to win twenty-one caps for the re-unified German national team. Other East German players were not so fortunate, with some even banned from representing their country abroad for fear of their defection. One of these, Falko Götz, an attacking midfield player with East Berlin's FC Dynamo, became so paranoid about the levels of Stasi surveillance that in 1983 he did indeed defect to the west while travelling with his club to play a European Cup tie against Partizan Belgrade. And his reward from FIFA, the beautiful game's governing body of dubious repute? A one year ban from all football activities, which he served before resuming his career in 1984 with Bayer Leverkusen in the then West Germany.

Thanks partly to its obscure location and deliberate omission from official Berlin street maps, the Stasi Prison at Lichtenberg – unlike other institutions of the state – was not stormed by protestors during the revolutionary fervour of November 1989. This allowed the authorities enough time to destroy much of the evidence of culpability for what had gone on within the walls of this key component of the GDR's system of political oppression. Fortunately for interested succeeding generations, the buildings and many of the fixtures and fittings of the dreaded institution remained intact, as have the memories of some of its victims. I joined a tour led by the personable Joachim, a former inmate of the prison who throughout his commentary betrayed not a shred of bitterness towards his former captors. He didn't volunteer information about what he had allegedly done to so upset the regime – and it felt too rude to ask – but I guessed from some of his comments and views he expressed, his 'crime' had been political opposition, way more than enough in the paranoid world of the GDR dictatorship to warrant a roughing-up in Lichtenberg. Joachim showed us into a garage that housed a Stasi van previously used to transport prisoners from their homes or place of arrest to the hell of the prison. Until the GDR was forced to sign a human rights accord in 1975, inmates were often holed up in 'submarine cells' in six inches of water, causing their skin to rot and peel off. In Joachim's time, intimidation was of the more psychological variety. Once in their grasp, the Stasi guards certainly wasted no time in exerting emotional pressure on their unfortunate captives, which began during the terrifying journey endured to these far reaches of East Berlin in the small grey van I now stood beside. Regardless of where the prisoner was picked up – from any Berlin location east or west, or from another part of the GDR – the van would drive for at least an hour, turning left, right and left again many times, deliberately disorienting the wretched captive it was carrying. Even a journey from one of those anonymous little bungalows in the adjacent street would have taken a highly circuitous route of an hour or more. When the confused prisoner was finally bundled out of the van into the glaring white light of the prison garage, they were wholly unaware of where they were and, we can guess in many cases, even *why* they were there.

Joachim described how his own psychological punishment was dished out through sleep deprivation, long periods of isolation and worrying threats to the safety of friends and family. One aspect of this strategy seemed to me particularly cruel, almost bizarrely so. By way of an ingenious red-green traffic light system installed at the cross-over of the prison corridors, the guards were able to ensure that no prisoner ever saw or had any kind of contact with another human being besides their unsmiling captors. As well as exhibits that you might expect to see on a tour of a former prison of a communist dictatorship – two hundred cells and interrogation rooms, three watchtowers and a twenty-eight bed hospital with a caged exercise area known to inmates as the Tiger Cage – the prison buildings now also house what ought to be turned into a Berlin museum of 1960s and 1970s kitsch decor. Despite the harsh realities of the complex's purpose, I walked the

disinfected corridors between cells, my eyes drawn con-
tinually to the flamboyantly-patterned linoleum floor-
ing – a dedicated study in straw yellow and beige. Given
that this style is somewhat back in vogue today, the
retro floor covering and décor of coloured telephones
and original print curtains on the windows of the interrogation cells affords the prison buildings a curiously
artsy, contemporary feel. This was terror in technicolour! Later, it occurred to me how this Stasi hint at
modernity seems an absolute world away from the
depravities of the immediately preceding Nazi period.
I contrasted the yellows and beiges of the Stasi prison
with the black and white scenes of Third Reich atroci-
ties committed at Auschwitz-Birkenau, Dachau and a
hundred other places that I had confronted a few days
earlier at the 'Topography of Terror'. After a couple of
hours immersed in the kitsch psychedelic patterns of the
Stasi period, it seemed to me that when presented
without any colour, barbarity of the kind delivered by
the Nazi state can appear yet more otherworldly, yet
more incredible, than even in reality it was.

Apart from the dazzling décor, if one thing remains
firmly in my mind about the Stasi prison tour it will be
Joachim's solemn, yet ultimately uplifting tale of a
fellow prisoner and friend. He didn't divulge his pal's
name – the man is still very much alive, kicking and
happily making a nuisance of himself in and around
Berlin. But several decades ago, as a political dissident
and homosexual (a dread combination in the GDR), he
was picked up by the Stasi and held in the Lichtenberg
prison. Starved of human company and enduring in
his case both physical and psychological torture, the
unfortunate man was eventually released shortly before

the prison closure in 1989. After the fall of the Berlin Wall he continued to live in a manner consistent with his personal and political leanings, and found work in the city's famous *Kaufhaus des Western* department store – the *KaDeWe* – as an assistant in the men's fashion department. Some years later, his principal Stasi torturer walked into *KaDeWe* shopping for men's attire, only to come face-to-face with his former victim. We can only speculate how surprised Joachim's friend was to be confronted once more with his old nemesis. Yet the same fellow Berliner who had once beaten the bottom of his feet, subjected him to a form of water boarding, deprived him of light and companionship, and neglected his every human need in the course of a day's work, was now seeking his victim's advice about a shirt and tie combo. In the conciliatory environment of the re-unified Germany, and in the context of the collective and largely unspoken 'Reconciliation and Trust' initiative, no action was taken against former Stasi members for their crimes against fellow Germans. Even so, it is hard to imagine that at the moment when the eyes of the two men met once more – victim and perpetrator now living their lives on wholly equal terms – how some form of spontaneous retribution wasn't delivered. Instead, in an impressive act of forgiveness, the tortured man revealed his identity, but then reached out to his doubtless startled former tormentor and shook his hand. Among the multitude of monuments to the persecuted dotted around Berlin as the city's wounds continue to heal, there surely cannot be any one more meaningful or powerful than that.

Leg-weary from the long cycle and a little terror-worn by exposure to the Nazi and Stasi states, I was once more in need of a good night out. Luckily I had a timely date with Gisela planned for that evening. My German *amiga* was of course a lover of all things Spanish, not to mention a veteran of hours of intimidation at the hands of the Spanish 'subjunctive mood' in many an Iberian classroom. More pertinently, Gisela was also a survivor of the travails of her home city, Berlin. We met in the rarefied atmosphere of the lounge bar of the reconstructed Hotel Adlon Kempinski, part of a shiny new development at the western end of the Unter den Linden in the shadow of the Brandenburg Gate. Oh, the luxury of it! As we sat on the bar's opulent terrace in the warm evening sunlight with glasses tinkling, Gisela told me something of her Berlin childhood. Born in the sophisticated borough of Charlottenburg in 1938, Gisela recounted her wartime memory of being carried each day out of the family home in a wooden box down to local street shelters to escape the incessant British and American bombardments. So this was quite a memory. During the latter stages of the war, Gisela was taken by her family away from Berlin to the safety of Flensburg, a city close to the Danish border, and incidentally the location of Admiral Dönitz's short lived emergency government during the disintegration of the Nazi state in the spring of 1945. Over a drink Gisela recalled the extraordinary moment when she learned of Hitler's death, sat around a radio with her mother and aunt listening to the grave institutional announcement of his suicide in the Berlin bunker, only a weighty stone's throw from where we now sat. Her sharp blue eyes lit up as she recalled her seven year-old self dancing around the room with her mother in unrestrained joy at the news, while her Nazi-sympathising aunt was slumped in an armchair dissolved in tears, for that moment at least a broken woman.

After the war Gisela and her family returned to Berlin to find their home still intact and the area of Charlottenburg now part of the occupied British sector. Things could have turned out a whole lot worse for Gisela's family, of course, but post-war Berlin was a fractured, unhappy place to be and as she grew up she became increasingly unsettled. Ever resourceful and determined to stay one step ahead of events, in 1961 just as the Berlin Wall was being flung up, Gisela moved to Barcelona to begin her life-long passion for Spain. She told me of her high adventure in the Catalan capital where she worked as an assistant to a fearsome-sounding exiled former Nazi called Herr Wilhelmi, a former high grade military man of the Condor Legion, that ragbag wartime army of fascist-leaning members of the Luftwaffe and Wehrmacht. Having backed the winning horse during the Spanish Civil War of 1936 to 1939 as a member of General Franco's Nationalist forces, Herr Wilhelmi headed back to Spain in 1945 in search of a brighter future than was likely in the shattered environment of the immediate post-war Germany. Linking up once more with the diminutive *El Generalissimo* as a member of his personal guard, this opportunistic man evidently had a keen eye for a business plan and used Barcelona as his base for running a successful tissue-making company, where Gisela was employed as an assistant. As a committed fascist, the Havana cigar chain-smoking 'Don Juan' – as he was known to his cowed colleagues – may well have been a little low on close friends in Barcelona. However, one member of Wilhelmi's team who was not to be intimated by the man, his politics or his reputation was the young and feisty Gisela. Likening herself at the time to the positive-thinking Sally Hawkins in *Happy Go Lucky*, Gisela brought to Barcelona her optimistic demeanour and adventurous free-spirit. After two years under the charge of *fascista* Don Juan she returned to Berlin with that positivity of thought and spirit imbedded, with her appetite for adventure whetted for much more. In the decades that have passed since, nothing about this aspect of Gisela's character has changed. We moved on to the glitzy Kurfürstendamm – Gisela's old Berlin stomping ground – and pitched-up in a chain Spanish restaurant, where she regaled me with more stories of post-war Berlin, her dismay at the city's forced division between east and west and how she eventually left it behind to retreat to the small town comforts of Nordrhein-Westfalen. As we parted company later in the evening outside the Adenauerplatz U-Bahn station, my only regret was that I hadn't known Gisela years before. We did, however, draw up one of those hastily conceived back-of-a-fag-packet plans that were fast becoming the mini-handbooks of my life – a plan that included a pledge to meet again soon, next time in the balmier climes of southern Spain.

The following morning, as I sat reading the sports pages of an English newspaper in the public library on Schöneberg Hauptstraße, I was distracted by the engaging sight of two red squirrels scampering up and down the trunk of an oak tree in a frantic pursuit of food and frolic. Feeling a little that way myself, I took a mood-compatible decision and rode Fritz away from the grime of Schöneberg along the wide, expansive Hofjägerallee to reach the golden statue of Siegessäule. Originally constructed to mark victory in the Danish-Prussian War of 1864, the winged victory goddess – whose pet name in Berlin of Golden Lizzie sounds to me more like a brassy bar maid than an important city monument – sits atop a column that was increased in height to sixty-seven metres by the serial-tinkering Nazis. The 1930s government did, however, have the good sense to move Lizzie from the relative obscurity of her original position on the Platz der Republik, and placed her instead on the grand axis stretching towards the Brandenburg Gate and Unter den Linden – all part of the grandiose, ultimately aborted, plans for the Third Reich capital, Germania. One more Berlin sight ticked off the notional bucket list, I continued along Hofjägerallee in search of a little piece of Berlin greenery where I could lie out, eat a sandwich and think through my next moves. For this most important business I chose a lush glade on the Großer Tiergarten close to the Brandenburg Gate, propped Fritz up against a tree and lay down on the soft luxuriant grass, a welcoming surface warmed beautifully by the early afternoon sun.

For several minutes, Fritz and I were perfectly alone and I was content to simply listen to the grass grow. Presently a smartly dressed office worker arrived on his expensive-looking *Schauff* bicycle, which he too leaned against a convenient tree before beginning a ritual that I wasn't expecting in this central city park. The mid-fifties man of portly build, and certainly no adonis figure, began by removing his jacket, undoing his tie and then unbuttoning his shirt. There was nothing especially interesting about that, of course. I had seen it done – and done it myself – a thousand times in many parks and squares when the sun had shone on London.

However, my fellow lunchtime sunbather had bigger plans. First the shirt fell off his back, to be folded neatly on the ground next to his shoes, socks and tie. His belt was then loosened, his fly and waist button were undone in an open invitation for the trousers to fall around his ankles, which he then – a little inelegantly it has to be said – stepped out of. The job, I thought, must be done, so please god leave the underwear alone! But no, the Calvin Kleins were next to go, discarded onto the growing pile of his corporate uniform. Quite casually, the naked executive then opened his briefcase, took out a homemade baguette wrapped in silver foil, carefully undressed that too and began to eat as he reclined in the sunshine, looking as if he had been lifted straight from a Beryl Cook painting, his white belly extending upwards towards the brilliant blue sky.

Before the man's baguette was finished, two other lunchtime revellers had joined him in the innocent little strip show. Now it was me cutting the conspicuous figure in my sober midday attire of jeans and long-sleeved shirt. How English I suddenly felt, how buttoned up in every sense I was as I gazed straight ahead at a distant linden tree, diverting my eyes in my anxiety not to appear voyeuristic. *'Don't look Ethel!'* implored Ray Stevens as the immortal line in that saucy 1970s novelty hit record, *The Streak*, rattled through my mind. After half-an-hour or so of his naked sun worship, the man carefully replaced his clothing, attached his briefcase to the rear pannier of his bicycle, re-mounted it and rode away in the direction of the corporate glass towers of Potsdamer Platz. I could just make out the names of Deutsche Bahn, Panasonic and Sony on the side of the buildings and wondered which one of them was his paymaster. Noticing the man's self-satisfied little smirk, aimed perhaps in my direction as he left me to my fully clothed bemusement, I guessed that after his trouser-free lunchtime respite from the pressures of a career, nothing about the office *realpolitik* would be daunting him that particular afternoon. If ever a man were the embodiment of his city, then surely it was he.

Lying out in the Tiergarten, my mind was far too distracted by the brilliance and unpredictability of Berlin to be thinking too seriously about my next destination. I turned my thoughts instead to the reasons I had travelled to the city in the first place, and in particular that Berlin mystery that had fascinated me for so long. For me, part of the aura of Berlin had always been the impossibility of pinning the city's past – and indeed its present – down to a satisfactory, coherent narrative. Contrast the history of, say Britain and London, to that of Germany and its capital city. In Britain it is possible to learn, understand and interpret a comfortable passage of dates, names of leaders, changing parties of government and victories (mostly) in battles and wars. In Germany in general – and very much so in Berlin – this is impossible. So tormented is its recent history, so heavy the burden of its wartime guilt, that the physical and emotional scars of war on this once utterly broken city are still evident on every street corner. Yet thanks to its astonishing comeback from ignominy and adversity, Berlin is today an endlessly fascinating, wonderfully contradictory place to visit and, I can be fairly certain, to live in too.

Equally certain, just as love affairs begin unexpectedly, so they can end just as abruptly. So now it was time to say *auf wiedersehen*, Fritz. As I looked back

over my shoulder at my faithful friend for the last time
– now returned to his rack outside the *Bike A Way* store
in Friedrichshain – my loss felt deep. Fritz had given me
much to be grateful for in our short time together –
companionship, absolute reliability and, priceless on
Berlin's wide and lengthy sprawl, wheels! After sharing
with Fritz close to three hundred kilometres of Berlin's
cycleways (his odometer had counted each and every
one of them), it was a strange, although not entirely
unwelcome sensation to be now negotiating the city's
long hard streets on foot. Give me cycling over walking
any day, but at this reduced pace at least now I had
more time to peruse the shiny glass and steel emblems
of Berlin's rebirth as a forward-looking European
metropolis, albeit one amassed with contradiction.

Germany may have been re-unified for a quarter of a
century, but take a walk along the tourist strip of
Berlin's Unter den Linden, continue over the Spree
towards Alexanderplatz and then further east along
Karl Marx Allee to view the boulevard's brutalist architecture, and you could well be back in the Soviet Sixties.
Then stroll along any affluent avenue of former West
Berlin to discover little brass plates the size and shape of
cobblestones – known as *Stolpersteine* – set into the
pavements in front of apartment blocks, inscribed with
the names of Third Reich victims who once lived there.
These were the innocent residents of Berlin dragged
from their beds not so very long ago, to become trauma-
tised passengers on the death-camp transports. Notice
also rows of little white crosses dotted randomly across
the multifaceted patchwork quilt of Berlin, bearing the
names of some of those murdered as they sought escape
before the demise of the wall.

So in search of a solution to my single-city mystery, I had instead found in Berlin three cities for the price of one: a gargantuan open-air museum of remembrance, a post-war Soviet relic, and finally the city that has matured into the modern über-cool European capital it is today, where subculture thrives, ethnic diversity reigns and world-class museums and the avant-garde flourish cheek by jowl. To coin the phrase of its mayor, '*poor but sexy*' Berlin may well be. Yet I would leave the city, for now at least, satisfied to conclude that its extraordinary mystery remains firmly intact and, very happily for me, resolutely insoluble.

This way or that? Forever lost in Venice

'Making a big life change is pretty scary.
But, you know what's even scarier? Regret.'

Anonymous

– 4 –

Fast-Track Italia

I had been so determinedly wrapped up in the intrigue
of Berlin, that it wasn't until my final few days in the
city that I began to consider the consequence of having
arrived by way of a one-way train ticket. Far from
problematic, the lack of a return portion to my ticket
was consistent with a yearning to act with spontaneity,
contrary to the steady-as-you-go, risk-averse environment of the nine-to-five. What's more, the month in
Berlin had cemented my view that operating outside the
normal scheme of things adds a certain bohemian spice
to life. Although I was constantly on the move between
its disparate neighbourhoods, I had perhaps become a
little too settled in Berlin, and with only forty-eight
hours remaining of my tenancy with the footprint-
sleuth Otto, it was time to revisit my options. I set
about this task inside Sony's corporate marquee on
Potsdamer Platz in a branch of that unmentionable west
coast coffee chain – you know, the one that doesn't
cough up its fair share of taxes, but stakes a claim for
redemption for its ridiculously comfortable seating.
I jotted a random list of potential next stopovers, my

finger poised to click my way through to a series of one-way tickets to new destinations and fresh uncertainties. Cue decision fatigue. A couple of hours east of Berlin and I could cross the Polish border to drop in on Warsaw and Gdansk, but how about Dresden, Leipzig and Prague to the south, or the allure of a longer train journey into Switzerland to ride one of those spectacular alpine routes?

The dilemma was in reality an enviable one, but still seemed impossible. With the clock ticking on Berlin I even regressed for a few ill-advised moments to the idea of returning home to find temporary work through an agency, allowing me to pep-up my energies and bank balance for a resumption later in the year of my corporate-free lifestyle – yet in the process bringing the entire 'Project Freedom' to an abrupt and shuddering halt. With a vision of staplers and paper clips looming menacingly in my mind, I trawled through a couple of well-known job sites before hitting on a vacancy that on paper at least matched perfectly with my experience and (former) work interests. I fretted through the opening lines of the job specification – the power verbs *engage, perform, develop* and *co-ordinate* leaping out towards my wary eye – before I was gripped by the gnawing anxiety that would often kick-in when faced with other such gobbledygook in the workplace. I restored calm by clicking off the vacancy and switching off the device, reaching instead for my well-worn copy of the *Thomas Cook Rail Map of Europe* which I unfolded carefully in front of me, attracting the curious stares of the young French couple sitting opposite. My guide was mood-compatibility, and after a month in that most absorbing of northern European capitals, Berlin, I fancied a return to the temperate climes and glorious light of the south, where I could once again ruminate my lot on sun-kissed terraces. So I allowed my gaze to drop towards the southerly reaches of my map, from where the prime contender decisively leaped. This was a destination decision made easily, even perhaps a touch lazily. But who would say no to a helping of *La Dolce Vita*?

Packed and ready to leave Berlin, I stood defiantly in outdoor shoes on Otto's shiny floor, bade him a fond *auf wiedersehen* and made my way by S-Bahn to the Hauptbahnhof to catch an early morning train to Milan. After a thirteen hour schlep through Wolfsburg, Frankfurt, Basel and Bellinzona – the Italianate, Swiss alpine town notable for its riot of castles – I arrived at Milan's monumental 1931 Stazione di Centrale. Fascist built, but based on the design of Union Station in Washington D.C, Mussolini's imposing station is second only in the city in size to the landmark Duomo, Milan's venerated cathedral and principal tourist attraction. Having chosen Italy as the latest stage of my freedom-flight, I began in Milan for no other reason than it was a major European city that I had never visited. As a major rail hub, Milan was also a convenient start-ing point for my planned fourteen-day sprint up and down the boot-shaped nation through Bologna, Naples and Venice. Indecent haste is no way to fully immerse in Italian life, but then again even a month in Berlin had pushed it a bit for this restless spirit – a spirit unfurled by my recent four-line letter of resignation. Anyway, sometimes in life less can indeed be more, and making what I could of four Italian cities in such short a space of time was an opportunity to sharpen-up my waning time-management skills. *Living La Dolce Vita in a fortnight.* Now there's an idea for one of those office-based, time management training courses.

On the train I had spent a little time thinking about work, and concluded that at this point there wasn't an awful lot about 'the office' I was missing – five o'clock on a Friday perhaps, or the entertainment provided by drunk senior colleagues at Christmas parties. Speaking of training courses, I did used to quite relish those corporate away-days with the free lunches (and before the cutbacks, there were such things), and pilfering those little packets of bourbons and custard creams. Apart from the complementary food and the chance to escape the office for a day, my other training event high-lights included those toe-curling 'icebreakers' often used by the facilitator to get proceedings underway. Among these, I had two favourites. One was the mayhem of the ball-throwing between colleagues that often exposed otherwise maddeningly competent, motivated keen-beans as hapless butterfingers. I am happy to admit that I have always had a sneaking admiration for col-leagues with the capacity for taking their jobs *really* seriously. But can they catch a ball under the pressure of being watched by their team willing them to fail? Not a chance. Another favourite 'icebreaker' was the ritual humiliation of disclosing to the rest of the assembled group a cheek-reddening, off-the-wall fact about your-self that others may find in some way remarkable. In other words, a time for showing your colleagues what a cool dude or complete plank you really are. Golden moments in my catalogue of these include the fifty-something, otherwise quite steady-Eddy senior manager, who left a group of his underlings with dropped jaws following the revelation that away from the straitjacket of the office he was – as he blurted out in a high-camp affectation – *'a massive Kylie fan'*. Nothing at all wrong with that of course, except that the poor man was never taken seriously in the organisation again.

Back to my journey, and in hindsight ten o'clock at night was probably not an ideal time to arrive in Milan by train. My unease as I picked my way gingerly along Via Galvani past a collection of prostitutes, beggars and assorted dodgy geezers was heightened by the need to empty the contents of my bag containing money and my passport on to the pavement to retrieve the directions to my hotel, scrawled in haste on the back of a cappuccino receipt in a Berlin coffee shop. After a couple of hairy moments spent lurking on dark street corners I found Viale Lunigiana, a task made easier in the dim light by following the railway and defunct tram lines, the latter not benefitting as far as I could see for having been turned into a dumping ground for derelict Fiats. *Che sorpresa* to find myself once more on the wrong side of the station! My budget hotel was the Villa Melchiorre, built in the style of a Swiss chalet with verandas and wooden shutters, cutting an incongruous presence on that dingy Milanese street. The more I travelled, the more I appreciated that in life you usually do get what you pay for, and rather than looking out at an alpine scene (admittedly an unlikely prospect from a hotel room in an insalubrious suburb of Milan), my room faced the eight-lane motorway that is Viale Lunigiana. My request for a move to a room at the back of the building was met with an indifferent shrug from the lugubrious receptionist Luigi, who eyed me with even greater suspicion when I shared with him my plan to take a nocturnal walk back through the seamy streets around the railway station towards the city's focal point and recommended first port of call, the Duomo.

It was past eleven by the time I made it back to the station entrance, where a bubbly young woman keen to practise her rudimentary English pointed me down the tram-lined Via Vitruvio towards one of the city's main arteries, Corso Buenos Aires. The further I walked away from the station, the grander the Milan streetscape became. I reached the imposing Porta Venezia sitting alongside one of the city's precious green spaces, Giardini Pubblici, its gates still open but not terribly inviting thanks to a huddle of disagreeable-looking characters skulking close by. Deciding that this was one attraction better visited in daylight, I continued along Corso Vittorio Emanuele II of designer boutique fame, the first hint at Milan's status as a world fashion capital. Without the funds or inclination to part with €450 for a cashmere sweater (a whole month's rent in any one of the cities I planned to visit over the next fortnight), none of this was of much interest to me, so it was a relief to find a little further on the majestic bulk of the Duomo, dropped in the middle of the vast open space of its piazza, grandly oblivious to the heady commercialism encircling it.

Construction of the Duomo began in the fourteenth-century, but it remained unfinished until as recently as 1965 – I was astonished that it was still being built in the year I was born. Depending on your source, the Duomo – Milan's social and geographical heart – is either the third or fourth largest cathedral in the world. Wherever it sits in the cathedral league table, the Duomo is very high, and very mighty. I earned a painful crick in my neck by peering enthusiastically up the fantasy baroque mountainside of the cathedral's frontage to the summit of the main spire, marked eye-catchingly by the gilded bronze figure of Giuseppe Bini's Madonnina – just one of an astonishing 3,500 statues that adorn the Duomo. As the steady drizzle graduated to a downpour, I sheltered in a busy and appealingly warm McCafé to consider the alliterative genius of placing a McDonald's alongside a Madonna. But I soon tired of the greasy atmosphere and claustrophobia of soggy cheese-burgers and damp steaming bodies, so sprinted across the soaking piazza to shelter instead in the more rarefied space of the extravagant Galleria Vittorio Emanuele II arcade, one of the world's oldest and possibly priciest shopping malls.

In common with other nineteenth-century arcade designs – including London's Burlington Arcade – the main thoroughfare of the Galleria is covered by an arch of glass and gargantuan cast iron roof. Far larger than its London counterpart, the arcade has long enjoyed the nickname *il salotto di Milano* – Milan's drawing room – awarded for its reputation as a rare civilised meeting place in the otherwise chaotic city. Nowadays, the Galleria is home to the historic Biffi café, the Art Nouveau classic Zucca's Bar, the Savini restaurant and an all too predictable collection of designer brands, including Luis Vuitton, Gucci and Prada. Interestingly, the Galleria's second Prada store (the first ever Prada store opened here in 1913 but sold only luggage) opened in the space previously occupied by a branch of McDonald's (this was becoming an unintended theme), until the burger chain was forced out of its inappropri-ately lavish premises by a public tender. As a gesture of goodwill on its final day in the Galleria, Ronald McDonald treated his unappreciative Milanese clientele to free burgers and gassy drinks – an offer taken up by more than 5,000 people, many of whom had probably signed petitions or otherwise taken part in the campaign to replace burgers with bling. I rediscovered my inner-backpacker by sitting cross-legged on the decorative arcade floor under the huge domed roof and spread out my city map. I hadn't the time to cover a fraction of what was on offer in this urban sprawl of a million-and-a-half people, so cracking the Da Vinci code by unearthing the 'masterpieces of the genius of the Renaissance' was off limits. And given that I planned to spend one of my two Milan days at nearby Lake Como, the following day was about all I had.

In preparation for that, I headed back to the hotel to face the considerable sleep challenge posed by a night lying on a bed effectively straddling the hard shoulder of a jam-packed *autostrada*. As I walked back across the wet piazza towards the Duomo metro station, I noticed that in the space of ten minutes a thriving industry had sprung up in the sale of umbrellas and disposable macs of the quality of supermarket carrier bags. The same entrepreneurs who I had seen earlier flogging a dead horse in trying to foist dull remote controlled helicopters and soap-bubble machines onto disinterested tourists were now, buoyed by the rain, turning what looked to be a half-decent profit. Personally, I was content to take my chances in life, so ended the evening soaking wet. The unexpected bonus of that first night at the Hotel Villa Melchiorre was sleep. The champion of this was a set of earplugs that had become a trusted travel companion since managing to blot out a drunken crowd of Australian cricket fans in a cheap dive in Melbourne. Incidentally, the Australian jaunt had consumed an entire year's allocation of annual leave, leaving me with an uncomfortable Hobson's choice between the purgatory of sitting out the rest of the year in the office without further parole, of pulling a sickie or of taking unpaid leave. Going 'off sick' for the hell of it had always seemed bad karma to me, so I took the financial hit to eke out a bit more 'me-time' from the year – a painful blow to my pay-packet at the time, but in hindsight a useful dry-run for the non-salaried freedom I now enjoyed. I still hadn't quite worked out precisely how I would continue long-term in this vein, but the 'Power of Now' was currently king. Anyway, on the first morning of my Italian trip I was happily distracted from scrutinising this dilemma-in-waiting too closely as I pulled back the blinds to let abundant sunshine from a perfect blue sky flood into the room, triumphantly replacing the gloom of the previous evening.

Expecting to find the marble masterpiece yet more striking in sunlight, I made straight for the Duomo. I began my exploration by taking a long slow walk around its considerable perimeter before joining a queue to enter the massive structure under Pogliaghi's bronze statue, *The Flagellation*. The cool of the dark and rather forbidding interior was a relief from the ferocity of the sun, but also felt rather dank. To escape this air of sobriety, I climbed up to the Duomo's roof where I was treated to fabulous views stretching as far as the Alps, as well as getting a close up of many of the cathedral's innumerable statues and spires. Back down to earth, I left the Duomo to hover around the Milanese Galleria floor mosaics, waiting in vain for a gap in the swarm of bodies to take a photograph free of another tourist's head or a stray limb. This was sightseeing in a hurry, and I maintained the pace by taking the rear exit of the Galleria onto the Piazza della Scala to take a look at the façade of Milan's second most celebrated building, the eighteenth-century Teatro alla Scala. Though easy enough on the eye, I found the much-vaunted La Scala mildly disappointing, offering only the sort of middling architecture befitting a municipal courthouse or regional museum. Although it has been rebuilt more or less to its 1778 original design after its heavy wartime bombing in 1943, I was more taken by the nearby eighteenth-century Indro Montanelli Gardens at Porta Venezia, a precious green lung in the heart of Milan where I ordered a panini and a reviving Sanpellegrino Limonata on the serene outdoor terrace of Bar Bianco. I watched as office workers threw aside their suit jackets and ties to spend their lunch break playing table top football energetically in the sun. As a public exhibition, this fell some way short of the Großer Tiergarten striptease I had witnessed a few days earlier in Berlin, but as an exercise in lunchtime corporate respite, it looked to be doing the trick. The effects of my own lengthening office respite were beginning to show, too. It took me a good two hours to finish off that modest panini. Noticeably, I was slowing down.

For many Milanese, the city's other great place of worship aside from the Duomo is the famous San Siro football stadium, home to the two Milan giants, Inter and AC Milan. This ground has always held a grim fascination for me as the scene of one particularly harsh (among many) boyhood football memory, when the perennial underachievers of Everton FC were cheated out of a victory by the dodgy refereeing of one Rudi Glöckner. Somehow, Herr Glöckner's East German nationality lent him an additional suspect quality as he awarded unwarranted handballs and penalties in a two-legged tie with AC Milan. Needless to say, none of the travesties went in favour of the team in royal blue. So corrupt was Herr Glöckner's performance that night, I have often wondered since whether he had been in the pay, not just of the management of AC Milan, but also back home in the old GDR of the dreaded Stasi. For all we know, when he wasn't awarding dubious penalties around the soccer grounds of western Europe, he was blowing his whistle on politically suspect neighbours in some grey suburb of Dresden, Leipzig, or Brandenburg. Four decades later and at last I had made it to Milan and the scene of the injustice, albeit a little dismayed to find that I had barely shaken off the memory. Anyway, to reach the San Siro I took the metro to the cheerfully named Lotto station someway west of the city centre. When I left the station, I was astonished to have to ask as many as six local people for directions to the stadium before I got a definitive (or even half truthful) answer. One shifty, mischievous youth with greased-back hair who looked set for a long and fruitful career in the second-hand car market, quite purposefully sent me in completely the wrong direction. I eventually found my way by following the graffiti-daubed Viale Federico Caprilli until I reached Milan's principal racecourse, where I admired for a few moments a magnificent bronze statue placed at the entrance of Leonardo da Vinci's very own horse. Dedicated in 1999, I learned from the inscription that the statue was a well-meant gift from the American nation in grateful thanks, as spelled-out in a particularly cringing style, *'for the achievement of the Italian Renaissance'*. Ugh...

At last I reached the San Siro, a ground that was inaugurated at a match in 1926 between the two Milan giants, when Inter overcame their bitterest rivals by the resounding scoreline of 6-3. Nowadays, the stadium bears little resemblance to the 1920s original after its numerous makeovers in the intervening years, the latest in readiness for the 1990 World Cup finals. Although the financial benefits to both Milan clubs of ground sharing have been considerable, the San Siro is completely devoid of the character and unique architectural style that a truly great football arena should offer – a pity given the stature of the two clubs it hosts. The stadium is now owned by the city council, but there is absolutely nothing on its vast exterior of utilitarian concrete to suggest the identity of its tenants. There are no club crests, no stirring mottos, no murals of former players to have graced its turf, no vibrant colours, nothing at all. Truly a blank canvas, and frankly a rather grim one. What's more, the shared San Siro has evidently failed to harmonise relations between the two clubs, with visceral graffiti – some anti-Inter, some anti-Milan – daubed liberally around the perimeter, revealing the level of antipathy that exists between the rival sets of fans. I watched as a pimply youth was putting the finishing touches to some venomous artwork featuring the witless banter, *Inter Merda* – 'Inter S**t' – in the red and black lettering of his beloved AC Milan. I considered grabbing the canister off him to spray an anti-East German refereeing slogan of my own, deciding against on the grounds that I was quite possibly the only person to still remember the travesty of that game played almost four decades earlier.

Some former work colleagues have stuck in my mind, less for their exploits in the job (which rarely interested me), but for their endearing character traits. One former teammate (or should that be cellmate?) who fits this bill is one who enjoyed the office nickname 'Miss Italy', awarded to her not so much for her nationality (she was English), glamour or noticeable dedication to fashion, but for her obsession with the oddly-shaped country. Returning from a ten-day self-catering break on Lake Como (in the end it felt like we had all been on holiday with her), she banged-on interminably about the evenings she spent knocking back Grand Marnier cocktails on the terrace of her lakeside chalet, slipping into the conversation each time the three words with which she became synonymous – '*I miss Italy*'. A daily dose of this for a week or two after her short Italian adventure would have been understandable, enjoyable even. But this daily reminder of her favourite country went on for an entire calendar year until she left the department to go on to better things elsewhere. I have no idea whether she ever made it back to Italy, but I can thank her now at least for whetting my appetite for a day out at Lake Como.

To reach the watery attraction that so captivated my ex-colleague, I took an ancient bone-shaker of a train from Stazione di Porta Garibaldi to Como San Giovanni, an hour's ride to Italy's northernmost extremity. I left the train to enter an entirely different world from the centre of Milan – a world of clean, calm, well-tended streets. Minutes later I stood in front of Como's own trim Duomo, which proudly dominates its lively ice-cream parlour-lined piazza. But like anyone else travelling to Como I was there for its main draw, the Lago di Como (Lake Como), which I came across a few short steps from the Duomo in a truly lovely scene at Piazza Cavour, where the crystal clear water lapped the shore-line as if enticing its visitor to kick off their shoes and wade right in. The sky and humidity threatened a storm, so I made my way quickly along the shore, snapping madly at the postcard vistas of pretty villas dotting the hillsides on either side of the lake. Predictably, many of these are now the homes of the rich and famous and I played a diverting game guessing which of the villas might belong to part-time Como residents George Clooney, Madonna, Richard Branson and others of a similar wealth – an impossible task given that Lake Como covers an area of some 147 square kilometres, making it Italy's third largest lake after Maggiore and Garda. I walked as far as the lush Parco Di Villa Olmo, but turned back towards the town as the sky suddenly became blanketed in dense dark cloud. Wondering if I might bump into a local wide-boy with a suitcase full of rain macs to save me from the imminent deluge, I managed to get back as far as the edge of town, before the brewing storm finally visited on Como a downpour of truly epic, biblical proportions. In fact, the next hour or so delivered some of the heaviest rain I had ever seen, made more dramatic still by noisy intermissions of hailstones the size of small ball-bearings. I stood and watched the spectacle from a doorway, fascinated for a while by the force of the frozen crystals of water leaving their trail in small dents on the tinny roofs of parked cars. Once the deluge receded to merely tumultuous rain, the water falling on Como was warm enough to take a shower in. So inviting was the rainwater bouncing off the Duomo Piazza, if my soggy rucksack had contained a bar of soap, I doubt that anyone could have stopped me taking it out, removing my clothing and lathering myself from head to toe. If only this were Berlin – the whole city would have been out there showering with me! I settled instead for the drier refuge of a surprisingly deserted café that sold absolutely nothing besides paninis and cans of Coca-Cola. By the time I was done with my wedge of mozzarella and sun-dried tomato, the sun had donned its *Barbisio* hat to warm the terraces of the Duomo Piazza, full once more with ice-cream scoffing tourists. Apart from the battered roofs of a few forlorn-looking Fiats, it was as if the storm had never happened.

Back in Milan, I spent the evening around the lively Via Paganini, where I had the good luck to come across the Al Buon Umore, an atmospheric trattoria with tables draped cheerfully in red and white checked tablecloths. A pizza roughly the size of a vinyl LP duly arrived, as did a tall glass of Birra Menabrea, which I drank in an atmosphere so convivial it was a real wrench to leave. Just as it was in the end a wrench to leave Milan, a city that little by little was growing on me. As I was checking-out of the hotel the following morning, Luigi at reception printed off my Rail Italia ticket for my journey to Bologna, issuing dire warnings about the likely decrepitude and squalor I would encounter on my economy service south. For the amount I had paid for the ticket I wasn't expecting Deutsche Bahn ICE-train comfort, and the train was indeed old and slow. But what it lacked in modernity (including a WC that emptied its contents straight onto the track) was more than compensated for by its rhythmic, chugging charm. For the first peaceful half-an-hour of the journey

I spread out in a whole compartment to myself, watching the verdant Emilia-Romagna countryside drift past my window. Drift also describes well the pace of that antiquated train, and although the modern, expensive high-speed upgrade would have got me to Bologna in half the time, this relic of a bygone railway age with its worn-out springy seats and the WC through which I could see sleepers and the track, was eminently more memorable. To remind me I was on the cheaper train, I was jolted out of my slumber at Parma by a group of boisterous Italian students who, given the choice of several empty compartments either side of mine, decided to join me and end my happy solitude. I wouldn't have minded, but could have done without the lead-weight case containing a large wind instrument being dropped onto my foot without apology. I decided to befriend the gang anyway – not that I had much choice once one of them, a paunchy young man carrying the strong whiff of having overdone the garlic the previous evening, all but sat himself in my lap. On the whole, I enjoy the company of students. Not so long ago, I made a reasonable living out of spending my daytime hours surrounded by them. So I was happy to share a bit of quality time with Fabio (the owner of the offending instrument and the only one of the party to own up to any knowledge of English), talking about the benefits of an Erasmus year studying in London. Praise be, they left the train at Reggio d'Emilia, relieving my foot of the French horn or whatever instrument it was, and leaving me once more in peace for the remaining hour of the journey down to Bologna.

After my month-long sojourn in Berlin, I was well used to the curiously enduring tourist appeal of downfall and disaster. However, stood in the warmth of a perfect Bologna morning outside the city's busy central station, it seemed somehow unfitting to be faced so soon with a memorial to the brutal atrocity that had visited the city three decades or so before. The plaque I read at the station's entrance remembers the names of the eighty-five innocents killed by a shard-bomb – allegedly planted by a neo-fascist terrorist organisation – that exploded cataclysmically in the station waiting room on 2nd August 1980. That day, just like the day of my own arrival in Bologna, started out as a perfect summer's day, with the victims perishing as they sheltered from the heat in what they imagined would be their greater air-conditioned comfort. I read the names and the ages of the dead, the youngest a child of three, the oldest eighty-six, with dozens more cut off in their prime. The sheer bloody randomness of it all.

I made for the hotel on the lively Via Zamboni, checked-in and conjuring a scene from *The Shining* followed a gloomy, thickly-carpeted and seemingly endless corridor towards my room. The faded olive-green textured theme continued into the room, the carpet's geometric patterns extending up the walls and continuing in the bathroom. But I wasn't in Bologna to fret over the hotel décor so left my carpeted cocoon and wandered back towards the city's centerpiece square, Piazza Maggiore. Known locally simply as 'La Piazza', this vast and beautiful open space boasts a wealth of Renaissance and medieval gems, not least the Basilica di San Petroni and the Palazzos dei Banchi and d'Accursio. I planned to return to the square the following evening for an open-air movie screening I had seen advertised on my walk from the station, so didn't linger.

Instead, in a vain attempt to escape the intense forty-degree heat, I walked the few steps to the adjacent Piazza del Nettuno to gawp at the Fontana de Nettuno and its sun-kissed statue of Neptune, posed semi-pornographically astride random sea nymphs cooled by the falling water of the fountain.

As well as from the ferocity of the sun, I was warmed in Bologna by the signature pink-terracotta of its architecture. Walking its sultry streets, it occurred to me that Bologna – unlike similarly climate-blessed cities of southern Spain or Greece, with their characteristic whitewashed buildings – was built in *honour* of the sun, rather than as protection from it. In dire need of shade and watering, I pitched up in Café Zamboni. Mindful of some wisdom I had read recently on the benefits of time profligacy, I gladly squandered a couple of hours there sprawled on a luxuriant terrace sofa gulping mouthfuls of ice-cold water served by a stick-thin waiter. Cool, of course, comes so easily to Italians, and here was a man who epitomised his nation's style, somehow managing to maintain an air of sophistication about his serving manner even with a burning cigarette dangling from the corner of his mouth. The lazy afternoon turned into a soporific early evening, which I spent the best part of on the quite brilliant roof terrace of the hotel. I looked across in a hazy awe at the towers and domes of the terracotta-tiled skyline of Bologna, a study in glowing pink in the rich evening sunlight. By the time I dragged myself away from my rooftop eyrie and ventured out on a mission for food, the heat had brought my pace down another notch. I had gone from slow to dead-slow.

I made my way past the fourteenth-century Basilica di San Giacomo Maggiore towards the university quarter, a fair bet I gambled for finding a lively atmosphere and cheap drinks. As it turned out both were in abundance, and I was met by a cheerful orgy of *La Dolce Vita,* student-style. Scores of beautiful young people looking fantastically Italian hung-out in scruffy open-air cafés, smoking long thin cigarettes held in posed elegance between manicured fingers. Others, suave and flirtatious and accessorised to the max in loafers, pastel trousers, Ralph Lauren polo shirts and Ray-Bans, were draped over Vespa scooters mounted on the raised mosaic floors of the shady well-trodden arcades. And all of this somehow achieved on a student income. How gloriously European it all seemed along that medieval litter-strewn university strip, in a marked and fashionable contrast to the denim-clad student scene of the average UK campus, including the one I had recently hot-footed from. Curiously, the swampy urinal smell hanging in the air added an extra earthy, indefinable something to the debonair aura of this Bolognese student quarter, reminding me that I was at the beating heart of the world's oldest university. Not for nothing is Bologna known in Italy as *La Dotta* – The Educated.

The following day I made the thigh-burning ascent of the 97 metres-high, alarmingly leaning twelfth-century Torre Degli Asinelli, by way of a decidedly rickety, five hundred-step wooden staircase. If I had arrived in Bologna eight hundred or so years earlier, I would have found another 180 similar structures, the majority of them built by the wealthy merchant families of the city, probably – although no-one can be certain – as little more than status symbols or shows of wealth. These were no less the loft conversions and conservatories of their day. The emblematic tower I bust a gut to climb is one of only two of its kind still standing in Bologna. The other, much shorter, Torre Garisenda stands alongside its imposing big sister teetering to one side threatening an imminent and untidy collapse. To say that the views from the top of the Torre Degli Asinelli are outstanding – thrilling even – might sound like a tourist platitude, but I'll say it anyway. You really couldn't wish for a better city vista, with the bonus of a bit of innocent Tom-peepery as I watched late stragglers taking breakfast on the roof terrace of my hotel where I had sat only a few minutes before. As I looked out over the sprawl of Bologna's Roman street plan and its thousand red roofs glowing like the embers of a bonfire, it was possible to imagine that the whole city was ablaze.

Back down to earth, in a bid to see as much of the centre of Bologna as time and the heat allowed, I followed the Via Rizzoli back to Piazza Maggiore intending to visit the Palazzo d'Accursio and its central courtyard, from which my guide book promised 'unmissable' views of the original city beneath glass floors. But miss them I would, as frustratingly the complex was closed for the weekend. I continued instead through numerous shady courtyards to reach Via Galleria where I found the unexpected quirk of a wooden window in a wall, which I opened to a view of the Reno Canal – a sneak preview of Venice, the final destination of this breakneck Italian Grand Tour. Fully open for visitors close by was the serene Basilica di Santa Stefano, the masterpiece of Saint Petronius, the fifth-century Bishop of Bologna. Not content to offer its visitors one substantial attraction, the basilica incorporates several lavish churches: the eighth-century Church of St. John the Baptist, the fifth-century Holy Sepulchre and the San Vitale e Agricola. So rich was the diversity of the complex's interior and interlinking courts, the free admission seemed absurd. What's more, I couldn't even find a donation box. Much of what I saw at the basilica was in a state of semi-ruin and in dire need of repair, and if I had anything to do with it, the custodians of this architectural gem would start charging and get the restorers in pronto on the proceeds.

Thanks to the searing heat, I was sinking gracefully into a state of partial disrepair myself, so returned to the hotel to take a long cold shower and a Bolognese siesta – *riposo*. Refreshed, I spent my final evening in the city wandering around its arid back streets in a temperature that had barely dropped from its afternoon high. I pitched up in an attractive pavement trattoria, ate a bowl of multi-coloured, locally-produced salad and then made my way to the hub of Piazza Maggiore to join hundreds of other pleasure seekers for an offering of Ingmar Bergman at the al fresco Film Festival. I had travelled from 'al desko' to al fresco – what a transformation! In truth the movie, *Wild Strawberries*, passed me by – the Italian dubbing was of no use at all to me. But even if they had shown the original version, following it would still have been a challenge, given I was surrounded by hundreds of excitable Italians swirling their arms in wild gesticulation in front of the giant screen as if celebrating an *Azzurri* goal in a World Cup final. And all they were probably doing was simply passing the time of day in that stirring way that only the Italians really know how.

The other day while I was doing a bit of idle surfing (of the mobile data variety), I came across the astonishing stat that on average a smart-phone user checks their device 150 times each day – that's every six minutes or so in a sixteen-hour cycle of wakefulness. I learned this of course on my smartphone, so perhaps I shouldn't have been so surprised. A vibration from the device as I waited on the platform of Bologna's central station signalled an anguished plea from Amigo – he of the recent trip to Cuba – for some help plotting an escape from his current plight working in an organisation driven by un-reachable targets, oppressive micro-management and that latest shiny vehicle of corporate clap-trap, the 'Thinking Day'. Amigo wasn't ready to throw in his well-paid, pensionable towel any time soon. But following a recent performance appraisal that among other things concluded that he was an employee, *'in touch with himself and his world'*, Amigo was a man in certain need of a dollop of light relief and summer sun. More revealingly to Amigo himself on that annual judgment day, had been the assertion of the same manager that he was '...*an employee who prefers quiet, and who may devise ingenious ways of making himself invisible'*. So to prove the pertinence of his manager's words, he set about putting some distance between himself and 'the office' to join me in Naples the following day, courtesy of a last-minute knee-busting couple of hours in the care of a budget airline. As for me, the comfortable three-hour Eurostar Italia ride to the Amalfi coast via Florence and Rome avoided any of the inconvenience of musical instruments being dropped onto my feet by chortling students, even if it did seem as if I was committing a crime of tourism by passing through Florence and Rome en route without stopping. As I skirted round these two jewels of the extravagantly encrusted Italian crown (I had visited both previously), I made do with a bit of alternative escapism by watching a back episode of *A Place in the Sun* on *YouTube*. A type of travel porn, the programme showcased a British woman with a healthy budget hell-bent on picking up a bolt-hole in Florence where she planned to spend extended periods of her time, hopping back and to from Blighty as she pleased. This veritable 'Life of Riley' seemed to me like a pretty sensible approach to enjoying the crowded delights of the Tuscan capital, or indeed of any capital come to that. As for Rome, calling in on the Eternal City for the briefest of stopovers on the way to the less rarefied surroundings of Naples might have felt a tad rude – and I couldn't have that.

An hour south of Rome I reached Naples, and from the train I spilled out of the glass-fronted Stazione de Napoli Centrale onto the vast and blowy Piazza Garibaldi. '*See Naples and Die*', as Goethe first coined the phrase while on tour in the city with his Italian mistress – a sentiment far closer to reality for me than felt comfortable as I steered my luggage carelessly across the pot-holed square towards a moving bus, forcing the vehicle to perform an emergency stop a few feet in front of me. Realising that my attempt to negotiate the Neapolitan streets while listening to music was an act of the utmost folly, I removed my headphones and sat for a minute or two on my case to acclimatise to the melee of Naples, a city that was blatantly the polar opposite of Bologna – socially, economically and in most other conceivable ways. I was still in Italy of course, but by the skin of my teeth. Only a few hours before I had sat buttering toast on a peaceful roof terrace, lapping up a view of terracotta-pink roofs and leaning medieval towers. Now my vista was one of overflowing dustbins, an extraordinary volume of graffiti that covered every inch of every available surface, small herds of abandoned shopping trolleys grazing in the vast expanse of car park, and a huge Neapolitan traffic jam enlivened by the soundtrack of a thousand competing car horns. All said and done, on first impressions of Naples, I absolutely loved it.

Occupying a precarious spot roughly at the epicentre of one of the world's earthquake hot-spots, it is little wonder that Naples is so volatile. As recently as November 1980, a quake of magnitude 6.89 ripped under Irpina, forty-kilometres east of the city killing 3,000 people, injuring 10,000 and making 300,000 others homeless. And according to my mobile earthquake-tracker (activated especially for the trip), Naples had experienced several quakes measuring 1.5 or greater in the last three months alone. Smallish quakes such as these frequently ripple under the crowded streets of the city and little is made of them. In fact, as I picked my way over the deep cracks and ruptures on the pavement of Via Firenze on my way to my digs on Piazza Principe Umberto I, it seemed like a quake measuring rather more than 1.5 might have rumbled a couple of kilometres below the ground only minutes earlier.

I dispensed quickly with the hotel check-in and made my way across the square – an unruly and rather wonderful clutter of small mountains of discarded bottles and cartons, groups of bored-looking feral youths and a plethora of open suitcases offering every conceivable form of fake designer wear from jewellery and brightly coloured trainers to perfumes and retro Blues Brothers shades. Happily immersed already in the utter chaos and confusion of the Neapolitan streets (you take your eye off the ball in this city at your peril), I walked along Vias Carbonara and dei Tribunali to discover what anyone who has been to Naples would know – this is Italy at its absolute grittiest. The quite over-whelming sense of congestion in Naples is heightened by the almost complete absence of a central park or square, ensuring the city's status as Europe's most densely populated metropolis. As a result, Naples isn't a particularly good walking city, unless you enjoy foot-balls being kicked in your general direction at head height, the ubiquitous white-van-man coming at you at speed from every angle, or the constant threat of the Neapolitan teenager clad in shiny puffa-jacket astride his fizzing Vespa, joyfully revving-up to unnerve you at blind junctions. Negotiate all of that and you still have the bollards placed illogically in the middle of pavements to hinder rather than help your progress, not to mention a multitude of other animal, vegetable and mineral obstacles to relaxing sightseeing. In Naples, the pedestrian just doesn't get a look in, and even though my efforts to negotiate this mayhem of a city on foot seemed to be thwarted at every other step, I can still highly recommend it!

Despite its considerable sprawl and noisy appeal, Naples is a little low on major monuments, an initial disappointment that in the end barely mattered as the city benefits from another, altogether more welcome absentee – large groups of selfie-collecting tourists. As I picked my way through the city's streets, I stumbled across the Duomo – in truth a fairly unremarkable affair hemmed-in on a scruffy terrace of souvenir shops and cafés. Cathedral-wise, I had been spoilt by recent visits to Seville, Granada, Cologne and, a few days earlier, the Gothic masterpiece of Milan, so the pale nineteenth-century frontage of their Naples counterpart was set up to disappoint. I moved on, content to leave that particular cathedral behind with the thought that if this wasn't to be a destination of great and memorable buildings, then I would find plenty to compensate in the natural pulse of the city itself. I made my way along the obstacle course that is Via dei Tribunali (a sort of *It's a Knockout* challenge for the fashion conscious), distracted by the garish tourist-tack on display in shop windows. Kitsch catholic souvenirs, including a thousand forms and variations of Taiwan-produced Our Ladies, jostled for centre stage with inflatable Diego Maradonas – the mercurial, narcotic-loving football genius who was the face of the Napoli team between 1984 and 1991, and is now a man revered in the city as a virtual demigod. However, it was a model of two other slightly lesser-lights of the beautiful game that really caught my eye. A choicer souvenir of one's travels would be hard to find than Zinedine Zidane's duracell-propelled forehead lunging towards the midriff of a hapless Marco Materrazi. The plastic commemorative pays homage to the Frenchman's violent final fling on a football field during the closing stages of the 2006 World Cup Final at the *Olympiastadion* in Berlin – a no-prisoner-taken response to indelicate questions put to him on the pitch by the rough Italian defender about the integrity of female members of the Zidane clan. I moved on towards the Spanish Quarter through Piazza Dante, a space dominated by the nineteenth-century statue of the medieval poet of the same name, and then down Via Toledo, a traffic-choked nod to over two hundred years of former Spanish colonial rule in Naples up to the early part of the eighteenth-century – a brush with the Hispanic that felt oddly like coming home.

Just along from the muscular, fascist-built Banco di Napoli, I walked up a steep side street into the teeming Spanish quarter. This earthy world of cheek-by-jowl living was the Naples of a movie-set: belching Vespas, litter bins spilling out onto pavements, street hawkers offering illicit goods from open suitcases, and that most evocative sight of all in this, and many other Mediterranean cities – washing draped across the narrow streets, pegged on lines secured to facing wrought iron balconies. Garish pink, blue, red and white-striped bedding, bleached shirts, underwear and bloomers of every unflattering size and style fluttered so close above my head that I could smell the detergent. I could have been in the backstreets of Havana, the alleyways of La Barceloneta or the cramped courtyards of Palermo. I was fast acclimatising to Naples, coming to appreciate the human scale of the city, its rhythm and its beat. It was simply wonderful. As I walked along Via Trinità degli Spagnoli and through the quintessentially chaotic Neapolitan barrio of Spaccanapoli, I was followed by a fight-weary feral cat with chewed up ears I had just befriended by offering a slice of cheese from a sandwich I discovered at an advanced stage of decomposition at the bottom of my rucksack. Feline Diego – I just couldn't think what else to call him – stayed with me to investigate his namesake's gaudy little shrine on the corner of Via Nilo, until in the way that only cats know how, turned tails without so much as a thank-you and wandered off in search of a better offer. '*Forza Napoli*', proclaimed the banner next to the blue and white-adorned niche dedicated to Diego Maradona, a man who aside from his considerable exploits on the pitch, endeared himself to his partisan Neapolitan public (who tend to resent the more affluent areas of northern Italy, and are proud of their warmer climate and supposed greater friendliness), as a figure of serious veneration by describing his adopted city as being simply, 'not Italy'. A smart man, that Diego. I walked on, unable to resist peering through the windows of the tiny houses I passed. In one, a woman sat shelling peas at a wooden table as she gazed at a flickering TV screen. In another, I saw what looked like a father and son engaged in a furious heated argument, both with their arms and voices raised in angry confrontation, although more than likely in this cauldron city of noise and wild gesticulation, they were simply discussing the weekend's football results.

I swapped the cacophony of chaos of the Spanish Quarter for a rare Neapolitan oasis of calm and open space at Piazza del Plebiscito, where if the plan came off, I would meet up with poor Amigo. And there he was, leaning against one of the stone lions that flank the gargantuan domed Church of San Francesco. From a distance he looked weary with the world, his expression betraying a little too much time spent under the fluorescent strip-lights of a meeting room discussing, as he might put it with tongue planted firmly in cheek, *'the review, improvement, recognition and evaluation of his performance and development'*. Not to mention an 'Annual Leave masterclass' his employer had put him through recently, about which words simply fail me. Surely *taking* annual leave was all you needed to think about in this instance, but what would I know? Anyway, happily now out of sight and mind of his office travails, and with the freedom of Naples unfurling in front of him, Amigo's complexion and general outlook on life perked up quickly. No sooner had we met, we were approached by an elegantly turned out policeman with an oversize peak-cap who asked us for our passports, which on account of not being continental Europeans we weren't carrying with us. Luckily, the *carabiniere* accepted our profound apologies for being British and thus our reason for being so much in the dark about such things, as well as our explanation of the innocent business we had in his piazza. And on he went – sensibly, I noticed – to stand guard in the shadiest spot he could find, right in front of the square's other great edifice, the Bourbon-red Royal Palace.

As we walked away from Piazza del Plebiscito along the extravagantly named Via Ammiraglio Ferdinando Acton (international footballer meets west London suburb), we caught our first glimpse of the perfectly-formed Bay of Naples – a quite stunning sight that I wager would take anyone's breath away. We gathered our composure by taking a seat at a waterfront café close to the Fontana del Gigante – and never, by the way, has a name been better chosen for a fountain – and got stuck into some office gossip, a perk of the workplace I no longer enjoyed since possibly creating a bit of office tittle-tattle myself by walking away. The bay was pristine and beyond the little boats bobbing in the clear water, we looked across as far as the brooding presence of the volcanic Mount Vesuvius. Yet the only eruption worthy of a mention on this occasion flowed from Amigo himself. In a series of seismic expulsions, he described the recent takeover of his department by the group of ambitious lunatics who now controlled his particular corporate asylum. But for the greater good of his bank balance and continued rude health of the pension plan, Amigo was content for now to stay in position, holding down his tin-hat, head safely below the parapet until, as he put it, the cessation of office shell-fire. Just at that moment, amid Amigo's delirium at being away from the front-line for a few precious days, I hadn't the heart to share with him my gut instinct that in all probability, the firing wouldn't stop until there wasn't a man left standing.

We walked out to the Megaride Peninsular to take a look at the curiously named twelfth-century Castel Dell'Ovo – Egg Castle – the oldest remaining fortification in Naples. The unlikely moniker given to the Norman fort was the result of a legend around the Roman poet Virgil, who in medieval times grew in reputation as a predictor of the future, quite apart from evidently having a highly vivid imagination. The contemporary legend had the mischievous Virgil placing a magical egg beneath the castle supporting its foundations. As the fantasy went, if at some point the egg were to break under the strain of the stone castle sitting atop it (as if *that* was ever likely to happen), the castle itself would also be destroyed and, worse still, a series of disastrous events would be visited on the city. The destruction of nearby Pompeii in A.D. 79 pre-dates Virgil's legend by some eleven centuries. So unless you count the continued presence of the Mafia-like crime syndicate – the *Camorra* – as a disastrous event for the city, the odd intervening earthquake, or anything at all connected with Diego Maradona, then Virgil's egg must have had one-hell-of-a tough shell. Given the superb vantage point we found at the far end of the pen-insular, it was no surprise to meet two wedding parties lining up on the castle ramparts for photo opportunities of the spectacular bay beyond. It was impossible to distinguish which guests belonged to which wedding. Every female in both groups, young or old – apart obvi-ously from the brides – looked virtually identical: beau-tiful and petite with doll-like figures, sets of too-perfect teeth, extraordinarily long eye-lashes, all topped off with quivering fascinators. Likewise the men: all of them stick thin with pale angular faces clad in designer sunglasses, their dark hair plastered down by oily lotions slowly oozing down their foreheads in the heat. One nattily-dressed wedding guest asked me to take a snap of him and a group of his oikish friends, a couple of whom made Maradona hand-of-god gestures when they discovered I was English (reminding me of *that* goal in the 1986 World Cup finals). I thought about running playfully towards them with pumping fists, imitating Diego's ephedrine-fuelled goal celebration in a 1994 World Cup match, but decided against it. It was a long drop into the sea from the castle ramparts, and much as I was smitten by the views of the Bay of Naples, I didn't really fancy at that particular moment taking a swim in it.

The city of Naples is famously hilly – the perfect place, in fact, for building a network of funicular rail-ways. The best located and most used of the city's four funicular lines is the Funicolare Centrale. Opened in 1928 to transform the lives of Neapolitans living and working in the vertiginous commercial district around Piazza Vanvitelli, the line carries an astonishing ten million passengers each year making it, not surprisingly, the world's busiest funicular. Eager for the thrill of the ascent, Amigo and I rode at the front of the creeping train, pretending like schoolboys to steer it up the steep climb. Although the Funicular Centrale is only 1,270 metres long, it ascends 170 metres in altitude at an average gradient of thirteen percent – so quite some climb. And if the rail anoraks of Naples ever get tired of riding the Funicular Centrale, there are three other funiculars in the city to have fun on: the Chiaia, the Mergellina and the Montesanto. From the funicular's summit at Piazza Fuga, we walked to the medieval star-shaped fortress of Castel Sant'Elmo, a relic of colonial Spanish rule and a superb vantage point to take in unrestricted views of the city's dense sprawl. As spectacular views go, it would be hard to beat the extraordinarily beautiful Bay of Naples, with its brooding backdrop of Mount Vesuvius and the Amalfi coastline running into the distance towards Sorrento. But the lucky Neapolitans also have the island of Capri to gaze at, reclining elegantly in the water before us as we looked across the bay as if it were a Henry Moore figure, carved beautifully of the finest marble and lowered carefully into position.

Continuing down the slope, we passed numerous garish, flowery little shrines to Our Lady protected behind misted perspex until we reached the funicular station at Corso Vittorio Emanuele. We took the train back to Agusteo where we squeezed up in a crowded café alongside locals putting away huge platefuls of *rigatoni sofia*. Fortified by a hundredweight of pasta we entered the nearby Galleria Umberto I, a public shopping gallery reputed to have the grandest interior of any building in southern Italy. Like its Milanese counterpart, the Naples Galleria boasts a cavernous cruciform interior, topped majestically by a glass dome perched fifty-six metres high above a lavish floor decorated with mosaics of the signs of the zodiac. Yet the striking décor cannot hide the sad decline of the Galleria, clearly now more a tourist curiosity than a working, commercially viable retail environment. Of the grand old shop fronts that weren't boarded up, most now seemed to be dedicated to the promotion of the Naples souvenir industry. Save perhaps for Holy Week in Seville, I have never seen so many virgins in one place, magnetic or otherwise. So where once the Grand Tourist in Naples may have lingered in the Galleria over his choice of silk scarf or expensive perfumes, the best he could hope for today is a t-shirt emblazoned with an image of a gurning Diego Maradona, or a plastic Our Lady.

While I had been moving around the Continent in the lazy comfort of high-speed and not-so-high-speed trains, buses and the odd guilt-laden bucket flight, my nephew Michael – evidently struck with the wandering family gene – was part-way through a 5,000-mile cycle odyssey across Europe that had thus far taken him and his Norwegian girlfriend through the heart of Spain, the South of France, the Mediterranean islands of Sardinia and Sicily and now a good part of the Italian mainland. By the time they finished their mammoth five-month pedal back to their Scandinavian home, apart from quite possibly having very sore backsides, they would have seen more of Europe than most people do in a lifetime. Early one morning I received an upbeat text message from Michael who, co-incidentally, had just arrived in Naples himself – on two wheels, naturally. He had heard on the family grapevine that I might be in town around the same time, and being of an optimistic and outgoing inclination wondered if, by some outside chance, we might cross paths. I have no idea what the odds of us both happening to be in Naples on the same day were, but it was clearly meant to be. So it was that Amigo and I met Michael and his cycle buddy on the corner of a rainy Via del Sole, at a spot we had passed earlier in the full throttle of the Neapolitan day. In stark contrast, by night the area was a disappointment. Anticipating crowds of evening revellers jostling for space on pavements outside heaving smoky bars, we found instead a drab scene of closed businesses and virtually empty streets. We tried a couple of restaurants on Piazzetta Gigante, but both refused to serve us with drinks only.

Tired of peering through the darkened windows of closed bars, we made do with passing the evening in a licensed ice-cream parlour. Keeping up with the drinking pace of two thirsty long-distance cyclists was a tough ask, but between the four of us we managed to get through a fair chunk of the cafe's stock of Peroni, marking the evening for the parlour's owner as possibly his most profitable rain-blighted Monday on record. As a reward for keeping the place open for the evening (we were the only punters), we were presented with a complementary plateful of a local cream-soaked dessert speciality, which landed on our table from a height like a cholesterol-loaded bomb. A couple of spoonfuls each of the sugary gloop was about all any of us dared try. When somebody eventually bothered to check the time, it was a surprise to discover that it was a shade after one in the morning, a jolt that turned to mild panic once

Michael revealed that the last bus to the outlying area of town where they were staying left Piazza Mancini in precisely eight minutes time. In the absence of push-bikes, the only way to get them to their bus stop on time was to run – and boy, did we run. I don't know whether it was the urge to work off the drinks and that artery-clogging freebie that fuelled our city sprint. But if I had ever recorded somewhere a previous personal best for the distance – increased unnecessarily by a couple of wrong turns – then that hairy, traffic-dodging late-night tear through Naples would likely have consigned it to history. The next day, my nephew and his pedalling partner were back in the saddle and heading north towards Rome. As for me, I was just happy to be getting out of bed on a Tuesday morning to look out of a hotel window across a sunny Neapolitan square, with the only choice to make of any consequence being whether to start the day with a newspaper or by catching a train to Pompeii.

Like any journey by rail, getting to the Roman city of Pompeii was in itself a high adventure. Once Amigo emerged bleary-eyed from his room, we left the hotel with a stern warning from the receptionist about the high likelihood during the trip of an attack by pick-pockets. Aversion to small risks was something I had left in my wake in the fretful arena of the workplace meeting room. Thus I calculated that the odds of ending the day a victim of a light-fingered Neapolitan on the quaint, wonderfully-named Circumvesuviana train that rumbled down to Pompeii, seemed about equal to the odds of an untimely eruption of Vesuvius. Fortunately for me, Amigo, and all of the other hundreds of perspiring souls crammed into the hot confines of that

Circumvesuviana carriage, there was virtually no chance of our day trip being marred by a volcanic episode. The modern visitor to Pompeii is protected by the development of an apparently infallible eruption early-warning system – a miracle of technology quite obviously unavailable to the unfortunate 3,000 who were engulfed by ash and soot in the cataclysmic August eruption of A.D. 79. Secure in this knowledge, the only remaining threat to our well-being came from negotiating Pompeii's vast excavated site under a fierce sun in a temperature approaching forty degrees, with the richly deserved impediment of a thumping hangover.

As we joined the long queue of French, American, Spanish and Japanese tourists – in fact of every other nationality apart, it seemed, from Italian – it occurred to me that Pompeii, a bit like, say the Alhambra in Granada, the Tower of London or the Paris Louvre, was one of those attractions that has ceased to be *of* the country in which they are geographically located. Had it not been for the certain knowledge that we were actually in Pompeii, we could have been anywhere, if you see what I mean. At any rate, Pompeii in the midday heat was certainly one of those touristic moments for a less-is-more approach. We began our exploration on an extraordinarily well-preserved Roman road lined with the ruins of little terraced houses crushed nigh-on two thousand years ago by the overwhelming force of molten ash and soot. The ancient road was remarkable for having a streetscape reminiscent of twenty-first century town planning – every ergonomic consideration appeared to have been applied. These city remains reveal that the streets of Pompeii contained grooves for the smoother running of Roman cart wheels, cambers

OUT OF OFFICE

to facilitate the flow of water and waste, a full drainage
system and high pavements to prevent pedestrians
being sprayed by foul concoctions lying in the gutters as
they went about their daily business. However, the
feature that really brings the Roman streetscape design
up to date is the enormous stone blocks placed in the
road to give pedestrians priority over speeding carts,
thereby doubling up as both elevated zebra crossings
and the speed bumps of antiquity. The terror that visited
those crowded Pompeii streets as the eruption hit is
barely imaginable – a terror exhibited by the plaster
casts of victims who perished under the deluge of
ash we saw laid out in rows at the excavated site of the
Forum. Also well preserved for modern tourism under
the ruinous blanket of ash are the hilarious, often
raunchy scrawls of Roman graffiti artists who adorned
the walls and backs of Pompeii toilet doors with their
vulgar sound-bites. On-the-spot translations from the
Latin were impossible for either of us, but later in the
day it was fascinating to discover that among many
bawdy sentiments, we had read – '*Restituta, take off
your tunic please and show us your hairy privates*', and
another lewd, less witty boast of the type that you might
also find today scrawled in the restroom of a twenty-
first century pub – '*I screwed the Barmaid*'. And just to
show that the first-century Roman was not averse to
showing his touchy-feely side when the mood took
him, written boldly on the wall of a Pompeii hostel can
be found the line, '*Lovers are like bees in that they live
a honeyed life*'. Sweet.

We passed the well-preserved *thermae* – the Forum
baths – before reaching on the eastern edge of town one
of the highlights of any visit to a Roman archeological

2 4 1

site – the amphitheatre. The oldest surviving in the world (which in itself made it awe-inspiring), the oval amphitheatre at Pompeii in its day boasted a capacity of some 20,000. Looking at the majority of the sun-drenched seating of the Pompeii arena, on events days the Roman touts must have had a field day getting their price for the seats in the shade. We lay out on the lush amphitheatre grass with a small pack of feral dogs for company, who stuck around in the hope of liberating a bar of chocolate they had sniffed out turning molten in the heat at the bottom of my bag. We left them to the fun of devouring its runny remnants to join a horde of tourists heading for the outlying Villa dei Misteri – Villa of Mysteries. Despite being overwhelmed by ash and soot, somehow the majority of the villa's walls, ceilings and frescoes survived the Vesuvian eruption. In a room stuffed full of the most curious of frescos, we looked at scenes depicting women being initiated in the ancient Greek cult of Dionysus, the god of two of humanity's most enduring pre-occupations – fertility and wine. With so much crudity on show in the form of bar-room graffiti and the ubiquity of erotic art, it was somehow rewarding to discover in Pompeii a city that, just like its noisy Neapolitan neighbour, in its heyday was not a city given over to sobriety and restraint. As a lasting reward of our visit, we left Pompeii gratified to know that one way or another, the city's populace did at least have plenty of fun before it all went so horribly wrong.

If a visit to Naples might be considered incomplete without visiting Pompeii or the neighbouring Roman site of Herculaneum, so we weren't about to leave the city without sampling its greatest culinary invention – the pizza. As understatements go, to say that Naples is well served by pizzerias is a bit like saying that there is quite a lot of water in the average-sized ocean. So on our last night in Naples we walked along Via Tribunali in search of a genuine Neapolitan Margherita and were so overwhelmed by choice of pizzerias that we made our decision based on nothing more than a sign pasted on one restaurant door promising its clientele '*La Vera Pizza Napoletana*' – The Real Neapolitan Pizza. The name of the restaurant I cannot say, for apart from the bold letters outside advertising 'Pizzeria', it didn't seem to have one. Once we were inside in the company of bottles of cold Moretti beer (this pizzeria-with-no-name was yet another eatery I passed through on my travels that didn't offer the option of drinking from a glass), there didn't seem to be much else worth talking about other than the origins of the Neapolitan signature dish. Not unlike the low key dispute over the origins of that other global fast-food phenomenon, the hamburger, we cannot really be sure how the world's insatiable appetite for pizza began. Researching the matter briefly while waiting to be served in that little back-street joint in Naples, I was content to accept the findings of pizza historian, Carol Helstosky. In her tasty-sounding thesis, *Pizza: A Global History*, Carol recalls the development of the pizza in the eighteenth-century as a cheap means of satisfying the hunger of masses of poor Neapolitans living in the crowded areas of the Bay of Naples. According to our pizza specialist, those earliest flat-breads were used as vehicles for many of the basic ingre-dients found in the modern pizza: cheese, tomatoes, oil and garlic. However, the pizza enjoyed a serious commercial lift-off following a visit to Naples in 1889 by King Umberto 1 and Queen Margherita. In an attempt to get-down with the proletariat – and possibly because they were sick of the rich and pretentious French food of the court – the King and Queen fell into the slothful habit of ordering takeaway pizzas from a popular local supplier. A slippery slope, indeed. Although their pizzas possibly didn't arrive at the Royal Palace in a flat box on the back of a Vespa, the royals soon got hooked on the circular delicacy, as well as appreciating the bonus of having little washing up to do after they had eaten. Okay, I made that bit up, but during her Neapolitan tour the Queen did take a particular liking to the simple local recipe of baked dough topped with soft white cheese, red tomatoes and green basil – a dish presented to her ingratiatingly in the colours of the Italian flag, and which was named Pizza Margherita in her honour. Thus the pizza legend was born. Yet despite its subsequent spread in popularity in Italy, it wasn't until after the Second World War that the pizza found a foothold abroad, almost inevitably at first in America. In the late 1940s, the cities of New York, Boston, Chicago and St. Louis saw an abundance of specialist pizza restaurants opened by immigrants from Naples. Unsurprisingly, just like Coca-Cola, Rock 'n' Roll and Wrigley's, an Americanised version of the pizza re-crossed the Atlantic and spread across Europe and the wider world like the wildfire of a pizza oven. And the rest, you might say, is a very oily history.

With Amigo returned somewhat ruefully to his commitments in the workplace, and feeling as if I had only just arrived in Naples (barely three days in this pulsating place was patently not enough), I was back on a Eurostar Italia train heading north to Venice on a five-hour journey through Rome, Florence and once more

Bologna. Passing through Rome and Florence for the second time in a week without getting off, once again felt somehow wrong. Failing to get off a train arriving at Venice's Santa Lucia station would also be an almighty oversight, but for many more aesthetic reasons than the station simply being a terminus. After crossing the dramatic two-mile long Ponte della Libertà causeway that has connected Venice by rail to the industrial mainland at Mestre since 1846, I left the station to experience what must be one of *the* great joys of travel known to mankind. Emerging from the station's rather low front entrance, my eyes blinking as they adjusted to the sunlight, I beheld a city-scape so enticing as to be impossible to prepare for – the wide and majestic, 3.5 kilometre water-filled boulevard of Venice's Grand Canal. I took a Vaporetto water taxi from the front of the station travelling in the general direction of my hotel just off Piazza San Marco, feeling as I boarded like an extra on a movie set. Right at that moment, if a suave dinner-jacketed secret agent had sped past in a private launch in splashy pursuit of his arch-villain intent on world domination, I wouldn't have been the least bit surprised. As it was, I was ecstatic just to be in Venice and sailing through it on what is quite possibly the most exhilarating form of city public transport available anywhere on the planet. As the Vaporetto chugged along the congested waterway of the Grand Canal, I was quickly overwhelmed by the perfect composition of beautiful images lining each side of this watery avenue of palaces. Sitting alongside other suitably awed tourists, I passed under the graffiti-marred Ponte de Rialto accompanied by an armada of little craft – small private boats, water taxis and countless tourist-filled gondolas meandering a course along the choppy canal. Bathed in sunlight under the most brilliant blue sky, this extraordinary city presented a vision of near perfection – a scene so uplifting that it could not be marred even by the sudden intrusion of loud music piped from a passing gondola. I had been warned about the *'Just One Cornetto'* tune being the inescapable soundtrack of Venice, but on this occasion at least the crude rendition I heard floating by of the classic O *sole Mio,* came without the words adapted to the banal pleasures of cheap ice-cream.

Whoever the giant of town-planning history was that signed off the wholly improbable scheme for the construction of a small metropolis on a collection of marshy islands, really should be recognised by humanity as an unchallengeable hero. But rather than handing all the credit to the vision and genius of one individual, we should not ignore the seminal contribution to the building of Venice of the ragbag bunch of marauding fifth-century Germanic Barbarians, who rocked-up in northern Italy for a share of the spoils of the fallen Roman Empire. Understandably disinclined to the indignities of rape and pillage promised by this invasion, the Venetian population living on the mainland escaped to the nearby marsh lands. On arrival they adapted quickly to the unpromising building conditions on the sandy islands by developing the smart construction technique of driving huge wooden stakes into the ground to support wooden platforms on which to build their homes. Over the years, the building of Venice has of course required an awful lot of wood, much of it scouted in the forests of Slovenia and the nearby Balkans. That's all well and good, but given that wood wouldn't necessarily seem to be the most propitious of materials for the purpose of underwater construction, its choice for the building of Venice appeared to me a little odd. But the decay of wood, I soon discovered, is down to microorganisms such as fungi and bacteria. As these normally invasive properties are dependent on exposure to oxygen – to which they are naturally deprived under deep water – the microorganisms are benign when submerged in the muddy Venetian canals. Add to that the petrifying effect on the wood of centuries of salt water hardening, then Venice is built, pretty much, on pillars as hard as stone. Interestingly, this petrifying process is also responsible for the preservation of wooden implements discovered among the remains of Henry VIII's warship, the Mary Rose. Sunk in battle in 1545 but salvaged in 1982, the silt of the Solent kept the ship's wooden artefacts in a fair and recognisable shape for well over four-hundred years. Good news, we can hope, for the future health of Venice.

However, of very real and much graver threat to Venice is the looming danger of climate change, regardless of the number of planet-saving deals signed off by politicians. As the lagoon that has protected Venice for 1500 years rises, flooding has become the city's number one challenge. Episodes of Venetian flooding – known as *acqua altas* – occur around twelve times each year, putting at risk not merely the fabric of the buildings, but the very survival of Venetian society. Several ambitious proposals to ensure the continued existence of Venice are currently on the table. One of these, if adopted, will involve the placing of almost eighty floodgates to separate the lagoon from the perils of the rising Adriatic – a phenomenal construction challenge, but one that anyone who has ever set foot in Venice would surely think worthwhile to protect this city gem from the unthinkable fate of becoming a modern-day Atlantis. Aside from the omnipresent threat of flooding, Venice is also blighted by pollution and general neglect. In response, many UNESCO-backed organisations have been set up to support the protection and regeneration work. Although most of the money to fund this exhaustive effort comes from the Italian Government, interest in the preservation of this exceptional place is international, including support from the UK through the London-based *Venice in Peril* – a cause bolstered thus far to the tune of £2 million, helped in part by the long-standing commitment of *PizzaExpress* to donate 25p from the proceeds of every Veneziana pizza served-up in its restaurants.

Back to my own Venetian visit, I found my hotel – not for once located on the wrong side of a railway track or even of a canal – a few steps away from the Vaporetto stop at Piazza San Marco. When I entered my room, I was close to ecstatic to discover that by leaning precariously from the window I could just about take a side peek of the Doge's Palace – the fourteenth-century Gothic quarters of the Venetian Doge, the supreme Venetian authority. Leaning out further still (preferably with a chamber maid on hand to hold me by the ankles) offered a teasing glimpse of the peak of the campanile, Venice's landmark bell tower of San Marco. This was truly location, location, location. Doing justice to Venice in a little over forty-eight hours would be a tall order, but I set about the task by joining a sea of tourists moving along Merceria Orologio towards the Ponte di Rialto. Think of those aerial shots of football fans edging along Wembley Way an hour before kick-off in the FA Cup Final, add a few canals and bridges and then you'll have a fair picture of this crowded Venetian scene. As an inspiring introduction to the infinite charms of this congested city-in-the-sea, choosing to take a place in a disorderly queue of bad tempered visitors to step onto the colourfully-graffitied Ponte di Rialto was perhaps not ideal. Yet more irksome was the pushing and shoving at the top of the Renaissance stone arch as hundreds of people vied for optimum positions to take their regulation photograph of the small vessels ploughing through the sunlit water below. Despite the extraordinary human selfishness on show, the scene remained fantastically beautiful. Unsurprisingly, the original wooden bridge built on the site collapsed twice under the similar duress of medieval tourism, but once the sixteenth-century development of the Rialto market on the eastern side of the canal gathered pace, a replacement was considered essential. By 1591, when the present structure was built, the authorities had worked out that only a stone construction would do. Pleasing as it was to be stood on the famous arch – and I wouldn't go anywhere near as far as describing the Ponte di Rialto as a let-down – it was still a relief to step off it. Whereas sailing under the bridge earlier in the thrall of a Vaporetto ride had been exhilarating – inspiring even – negotiating it on foot felt a little like wading through a rush-hour commuter scrum on the Bakerloo line.

I walked away from the bridge back towards Piazza San Marco, impeded less by the crowds but by a pecu-liarity of Venice's street signage. In what looked to me like a mischievous attempt by locals to confuse visi-tors, I passed comical scrawls on walls masquerading as signs to San Marco and Rialto (the two principal orientation points in the city), pointing tourists first one way and then, completely bafflingly another way. Yet the ruse offered the pleasing pay-back of getting hopelessly lost amid the warren of Venice's ancient streets, taking me over un-named bridges and canals I may not otherwise have crossed, and through the narrowest of unmarked alleyways I may never have found – in other words, a free-spirited, follow-your-nose approach to tourism devoid of guidebooks and maps which suited perfectly my new, largely rulebook-free existence. All of this was proving thirsty work, so I repaired to a tiny bar on Calle Larga San Marco full of noisy punters at various stages of afternoon inebriation. As I tussled for standing room I bumped, quite literally, into Colin and Maureen, a rather scratchy middle-aged couple from Kingston-upon-Hull. Hot and bothered from the effort of exploring Venice on a day trip from their holiday base in the Dolomite Mountains, they sought solace in drink and a pale-skinned compatriot. I kicked-off the small talk by asking Maureen about her trip, her liking for the heat after an east Yorkshire winter and her general impressions of Venice. Bearing in mind that we had the good fortune to be holding our conversation in what is quite possibly the best preserved, most romantic old city in the world, her assessment of this watery paradise as being 'sort of alright' stopped some way short of hyperbole. Not to be outdone, Colin interjected with complaints of his own, his personal gripe being about the 'rip-off prices' in the Venetian bars. Judging by the empties lined up beside him, he must already have racked up a fair bill. Frustrated by their downbeat mood, I wondered how a travelling couple in such a beautiful place could be in such bad humour, and so unappreciative of their blessed surroundings. Maybe they were fresh from a blazing holiday row. Or perhaps they were just missing the good life back in Hull. I just couldn't tell.

To be fair to Colin, he was absolutely right about the inflated prices of drinks, especially when enjoyed anywhere within a short stagger of Piazza San Marco. So later in the day, with this in mind and in an attempt to avoid the early evening beer stampede, I headed for the district of Castello, the largest of the six *sestieri* (districts) in the historic city. Spoilt for choice and views, I pitched up in the wonderfully-named 'Crazy Bar' and sat on its crowded terrace watching a flotilla of gondolas bobbing past full of loved-up, over-excited tourists making hasty and expensive wedding plans. Equally excitable was a small group of septuagenarians gathered at the table next to mine, each one sporting a Boston Red Sox baseball cap. With the help of their Venetian tour guide, the Bostonians poured over their Rick Steves Italy guides, evidently on a mission to live up to the writer's promise I could just make out on the book's rear cover, of making their Grand Italian Tour *'more savvy, more surprising and more fun'*. With a similarly whistle-stop itinerary to my own to follow, I eavesdropped that the party had precisely forty-eight hours to 'do' the delights of Venice before heading south to get Florence and Rome similarly 'done', as if the whole tour was some onerous exercise rather than the exorbitant pleasure it really ought to have been. Anyway, to prove that this Boston-Italian adventure was indeed savvy, to the great surprise of all of those around him a lean, angular man in a Red Sox cap gazed up at the sun, before addressing his tour guide with the straight-faced query as to whether the sun above Venice was the *same sun* as the one he looked up at from his suburban backyard in Massachusetts. Not wishing to discourage this frighteningly ill-informed gentlemen from tipping her handsomely at the end of the day, the startled guide answered that yes, she thought it probably was the same sun, but that she fully understood any doubt that may exist around the relationship between the sun and different regions of Planet Earth.

With unfortunate timing, just as the man uttered his folly I had taken an expensive mouthful of beer, which as the rising hysteria took hold, I then allowed to leave my mouth in a frothy spray. In a bid to avoid soaking those sitting close by, I aimed as best I could over the wall of the bar terrace, showering instead the heads of a surprised couple I caught in mid-embrace gliding past in a gondola. They both looked up at me, at first in astonishment, before then bursting into creased-up laughter of their own. As for the unwitting Boston comedian, he had by then switched topic to hold forth to his group on the likelihood of Venice sinking into the sea during the remaining twenty-four hours of their stay. He opined that on balance it probably wouldn't, but none of his compatriots looked in the least bit convinced by his arguments. In the hope of more of the same from the Crazy Bar's resident comic and sage astronomer, I stayed on to watch the spectacle of the setting sun, contemplating the miracle of that very same hot star having also quite recently risen in the skies above Boston – unless of course on that side of the Atlantic they already had one of their own, maybe even specially decorated with stars and stripes. After a couple of hours in the Crazy Bar, nothing in life seemed that certain anymore.

The following day I took a Vaporetto to the island of Murano, one of three sizeable islands – along with Borano and Torcello – that sit picturesquely in the Venice Lagoon. As you might expect the thirty-minute journey was nothing short of thrilling, although as the small vessel bounced energetically through the wash of the bigger craft that passed either side in both directions, I was glad I hadn't recently eaten. Famous for its exclusive crystal and glassware and general laid back quality of life, Murano felt a world away from the chaos of Venice. Making the most of the respite, I wandered along the virtually tourist-free Fondamenta Vetrai, where I took in a demonstration of glass-blowing in one of the numerous little factories and workshops lining the canal-side. I was so lulled by the island's charms that I fell for a high-pressured sales pitch tempting me to take away with me from the demo a small finely-crafted bicycle blown in orange and black glass. So delicate were its wheels, pedals and levers, that once I had paid the craftsman, I gave his work only a fifty-fifty chance of making it back to Britain in one piece. Every time it catches my eye on the shelf where it now stands, I feel eternally grateful that it did.

I spent the best part of the final morning of my sprint around Venice queuing for the crowded lift to take me to the summit of the St Mark's campanile. The present campanile structure dates from 1912, built as a replacement for the original 1514 tower which to everyone's surprise collapsed in 1902, albeit with the loss of life limited somewhat incredibly to the tower caretaker's unfortunate cat buried under the falling rubble.

The new tower's stocky, twelve metres-wide brick shaft looks unlikely to ever suffer the same fate. Yet rising from such an elegant piazza, the replacement tower seemed to me an edifice wholly out of scale and style with its surroundings, offering the incongruous, almost industrial look of a factory chimney. Place it in a Lowry painting belching black smoke into a rainy northern sky, and no-one would bat an eyelid. This thought did nothing though to detract from this sun-drenched Venetian scene, and once through the hot queue and the crush of digital-device wielding tourists enjoying their experience of Venice through a pixelated screen, the reward at the summit of the campanile was a view, as they say (but I wish they wouldn't), to die for. In the crystal clear morning light, a 360 degree panorama of the 118 islands of the Venetian Lagoon spread out before me, extending as far as a dark blur on the horizon that I was assured by another English tourist as he brushed his enormous lens past my ear lobe, was the outline of the Alps – satisfyingly much the same view I had lapped up the week before from the roof of the Milan Duomo, enjoyed this time from the opposite side.

The rest of the day was taken up with the effortless pursuit of getting lost in Venice's riot of alleyways, its countless mazy streets, 400 bridges and along its 170 canals. Even with the best of maps, which I didn't have – and in the case of Venice probably doesn't exist – the city is virtually impossible to navigate with any confidence. There are no major streets to speak of in the old centre, and with its chaotic address system creating mayhem for residents, tourists and probably for postmen too, getting lost in Venice is as inevitable an experience of the city as a Cornetto or a kissing couple in a gondola. The areas of Castello and San Polo, which I passed through repeatedly and quite unintentionally, provided plenty of scope for confusion. As did an improvised, self-guided walking tour that took me over the wooden Ponte dell'Accademia (surprisingly one of only four bridges that span the Grand Canal), to the area of Dorsoduro and its serene network of silent back streets. By luck rather than design (always more rewarding this way) I stumbled on the Peggy Guggenheim collection – or at least the monumental building that houses it – an eighteenth-century palace bought for the purpose by the American collector in 1949. Finally running out of terra firma, I reached the Customs House, set on the superb vantage point of a land-spit offering transfixing views back across the widest stretch of the Venetian Lagoon to Piazza San Marco.

Yet the enjoyment of this melee of beautiful palaces, squares and near-perfect vistas has come at a considerable environmental cost to Venice. Indicative of the damaging assault on the delicate fabric of the city by the ceaseless inundation of tourists, is the recent proposal by the Venetian authorities to ban the use of wheeled luggage in the historic centre. The negative impact on the city of this ubiquitous accessory of modern travel is self-evident – the noise pollution, coupled with the slow erosion of stone caused by a constant procession of hard plastic wheels over the fragile surfaces of ancient streets and bridges. Although the pull-along ban may yet prove unworkable in the long-term, pressure from local resident groups is mounting in the face of a perceived threat to the preservation of the city by the thirty million annual visitors. Another idea doing the rounds of Venice law makers is the imposition of a charge for entering the city, a toll that could be put to obvious good use in the ongoing preservation campaign as it crumbles towards extinction. As for me, I was hopelessly smitten by Venice, and aware that my short stay in the city was adding infinitesimally to the problem, I couldn't imagine why anyone would baulk at the prospect of forking out a modest fee to get in, so long as the income was used in the city to good effect. Quite apart from the tyranny of the wheeled suitcase and the punishing visitor footfall on the city's ancient stone, I also noticed a sloppy attitude to tourism in Venice that I have rarely met elsewhere. For one thing, from morning until night the steps of ancient churches are packed with sprawling tourists stuffing themselves with fistfuls of fast food, before casting aside the plastic and polystyrene aftermath into already overflowing bins. I noticed in Venice, too, some of the worst excesses of outdoor drunkenness I had seen as I travelled. One alleyway that I shuffled along gingerly one evening had been transformed into a long open air urinal. Even the soberest of visitors seemed to be playing their part in disregarding Venetian conventions by refusing to walk on the 'right' side of the narrow streets, although for me if anything this added to the city's enjoyable air of chaos.

At the end of this short Venetian visit, I came to the reluctant conclusion that as a viable and thriving city, Venice is simply unsustainable. Unlike other tourist hotspots I had recently visited, let's say Seville, Berlin or Bologna, Venice isn't these days even regarded as being a particularly desirable place to live. In 1951 the population of the city stood at a healthy 174,000.

At the last count it had dipped below 60,000. Therefore, at a figure of around 55,000 per day almost as many tourists as there are residents now besiege its canals, streets and bridges. This collapse in the numbers of indigenous Venetians now populating the city comes into stark relief at night. As a visitor, walking around the teeming streets of Venice after dark felt like an enlivening, even romantic, experience. But looking up at the hundreds of forlornly unlit windows of crumbling mansion blocks was a reminder that owning property here in the city's tourist centre is beyond the reach of most of those dwindling numbers of resident Venetians. The darkened neglected homes I saw on the tiny streets around San Marco are these days the selfish preserve of outsiders, investors and holiday-letters. Thus the community of the city is under threat of extinction as much as its buildings are threatened by sinking.

To add a dash of Italianate drama to the crisis, in November 2009 premature rumours of Venice's demise were played out in a mock funeral organised by local businessman, Matteo Secchi. This veritable merchant of Venetian doom had already been charting the city's slide in population numbers on an electronic display board placed in the window of his shop close to the Ponte di Rialto. Doing things in style – and to make quite sure their efforts didn't go unnoticed – Matteo and his co-mourners sent a coffin representing the remains of the city on a floating cortege along the Grand Canal. In a grand gesture of despair at the end of its journey, the coffin was placed ceremonially outside the city's thirteenth-century town-hall-come-palace, the Ca' Farsetti, in an effort to rouse local politicians from their hitherto shoulder-shrugging resignation to the city's fate. The world awaits a uniquely Venetian solution.

As I slid around my damp seat on the Vaporetto water taxi back to Stazione Santa Lucia, I experienced a heavy sinking feeling, appropriate perhaps to the city I was leaving behind. I identified two reasons for this: firstly that my journey back to Britain was to be by budget airline – cue a cramped two hours breathing in second-hand air – and secondly because the next stage of my post-work project was as yet unknown. 'Know thyself' went the trusted mantra I had coached myself with time and again, thus ruling out an imminent return to the workplace. As I began to hatch my onward plan during the short flight home, the only distraction – apart from the cabin crew's noisy promotion of scratch cards, microwaved chilli-con-carne and inflatable toy aircraft – was the memory of that conversation with Amigo back in Naples. Sitting in full view of the mighty Vesuvius across the bay, he offloaded about his unenviably-pressurised office-based routine of relentless strategising, target setting, and his often over-whelming desire – so far repressed but I doubted for much longer – to do what a man called Forrest Gump once did and to run, run and to keep on running until that corporate grind was far behind him. As for me, my course was already set. I was out-of-office, and assuredly out for good.

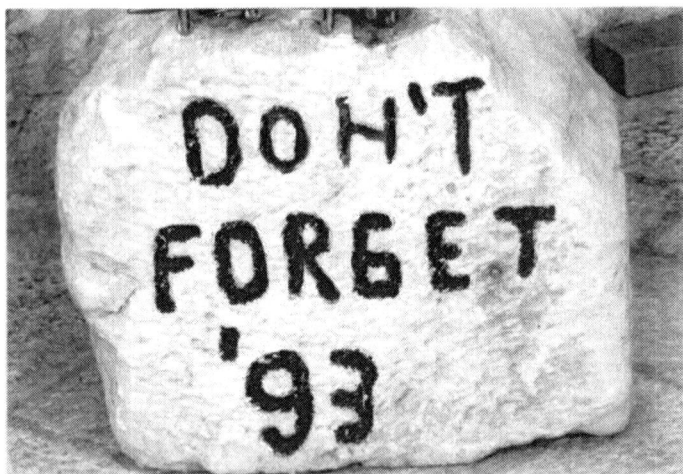

The past as present in the tortured Mostar stone

'One day your life will flash before your eyes.
Make sure it's worth watching.'

Anonymous

– 5 –

Balkan Trails

If there was one visually stunning corner of Europe that I had not properly explored yet wished I had, it was the Balkans. I first heard the mysterious-sounding name of this far-flung enclave of the Continent during history classes as a grammar school kid in the 1970s. Although scorned by many of my geeky, maths and science-loving schoolmates who just couldn't see the point of learning about the past, for me the twice-weekly periods with historian extraordinaire Mr Walker were right on the money. So well did he enliven his subject, that when I think of the considerable amount that I garnered in his class, decades later I can still see his face and hear the northern dulcet tone of his voice. It was Mr Walker in fact who delivered as neat an explanation as surely could possibly be drawn for that most complex of historical complexities – the causes of the First World War. Conveniently setting aside much of the entanglement of European ententes, treaties and alliances that by the summer of 1914 made the conflict as good as inevitable, he focussed our wandering adolescent minds on the Balkans, and in particular on an obscure Serbian nationalist named Gavrilo Princip – and what a mark on history he made. In angry resistance to his country's subservience within the giant Austro-Hungarian Empire, the fanatical Gavrilo assassinated Archduke Franz Ferdinand, the heir presumptive of the Austro-Hungarian throne, during an ill-conceived troop-inspection trip to Sarajevo. The murder triggered a military response from Europe's great powers, each of them committed by the spider's web of treaties and alliances to offer military support should an ally be threatened or attacked. So in an extreme example of cause and effect, the Sarajevo assassin not only ended the life of the unfortunate Archduke, but lit the touch paper for the bloodiest confrontation yet to visit humanity. A real bite-size chunk of history if ever there was one, and just as I liked them.

Almost a century on from the assassination, a group of energetic young musicians from Glasgow thought the royal victim's name sounded cool and catchy enough to use for their fledgling band, which in the event proved a more than canny choice. Asked in an interview about naming the group *Franz Ferdinand*, founding member Alex Kapranos recalled, '*he* (Archduke Franz) *was an incredible figure. His life, or at least the ending of it was the catalyst for the complete transformation of the world*'. Not holding back either in an assessment of the band's potential to transform the world of rock music, drummer Paul Thomson said of its association with the Archduke, '*I like the idea that if we become popular, maybe the words Franz Ferdinand will make people think of the band instead of the historical figure*'.

That might well of course depend on your age group, musical tastes or general inclinations. Nevertheless, whenever I catch sight of the band's eponymous self-titled 2004 debut album sitting among my CDs – with the name of the deceased Archduke emblazoned diagonally on its cover – I do think first of the excellence of the record. But the album's defining tracks – *Take Me Out* and *Michael,* for instance – also conjure in my mind an image of the extravagantly mustachioed Archduke. So the prospect of retracing his final steps on that sunny Sarajevo morning a full century before had a lure about it that I had no reason to resist – especially now without the obligations of the workplace standing in my way. As for the impact of the moniker 'Franz Ferdinand' on both the destiny of the world and the progress of Scottish rock music the rest, as they so often say, is history.

Whatever the mystique surrounding Archduke Franz Ferdinand's trip to Sarajevo to inspect the imperial Bosnia and Herzegovina troops, one thing is certain – he didn't arrive there by budget airline. For my own visit to the scene of his murder – and, I hoped, to see much else besides – neither did I. However, I did opt for that charmless knee-breaking mode of transport to start my Balkan trail some 300 kilometres from the scene of the crime, landing with an economy bump in the Croatian city of Split. A few days later, I planned to follow by road Franz Ferdinand's ill-fated journey to Sarajevo – the city that in the Archduke's day had been the frontline between the empires of the Muslim Ottomans and Christian Austro-Hungarians. I would then head south by train to the bridge-famous town of Mostar, before crossing back into Croatia to one of the genuine 'lookers' of the Adriatic, the celebrity seaport city of Dubrovnik.

I arrived in Split in the early evening light-fantastic of a dazzling day in June. Budget-wise I had reached the stage of my travels where room-rates were everything and mistakes unrectifiable. So for the amount I was allowing for my digs, if I ended up being allocated a room with a mattress on the floor (as did happen to me once in Singapore. Nor, incidentally, did the room have a window – this was a proper cell), then that is precisely where I would stay. As luck would have it the Hostal Spalatus turned out to be the perfect choice, which I located on reaching the centre of Split thanks to a helpful suggestion on *TripAdvisor* to follow my nose towards the smell of raw fish emanating powerfully from the nearby market. A double-booking bungle by the receptionist was my blessed, lucky moment, forcing the smooth-talking hotel manager, Ivan, to offer me the choice of either a room shared with a stranger and a partial refund, or a move to another, as yet unidentified alternative address. Given that sharing a room with a stranger would amount to just about my ultimate travel hell, I opted for the adventure of the switch. A brisk five-minute schlep alongside the long-legged Ivan up a steep hill to the north of the centre brought us to the Marin Apartments, about which I could gush for several pages. My commodious apartment – yes, that's a *whole* apartment – had two bedrooms, a fully equipped kitchen (introduced by Ivan proudly as being of an 'American style'), a spacious gadget-crammed living room and an elevated sunny terrace. All things considered, the apartment topped just about any holiday accommodation I had ever stayed in before, and was comfortably twice the size of the flat that I lived in at home. Enough said.

Feeling in particularly good spirits about all of this – and frankly at this particular moment about life in general – I walked back down the hill towards the sea and the unpronounceable Obala Hrvatskog Narodnog Preporada, Split's restaurant and bar-lined promenade that fortunately tends to be known by its easier, everyday name of the Riva. I had done very little preparation for this trip, and the name and identity of the city I had just arrived in resonated with me thus far only through its famous football club, Hajduk Split. I set about putting this right in a lively sea-facing café-bar, where I spent time genning up on the city's recent history, helped along by the pleasing background murmur of the incoming Adriatic Sea and the distant horns of tiny craft bobbing to the gentle rhythm of the water. I read that having changed hands between Roman, Venetian, Napoleonic and Habsburg rule, Split had been part of the Austro-Hungarian Kingdom of Dalmatia until that one-sided Sarajevo shoot-out in 1914 put paid to the Austro-Hungarian Empire for good. Following the First World War peace settlements – which did about as much to promote the virtues of peace and harmony as your average exploding bomb – Split was knocked about once more during the Second World War and suffered periods of first Italian, then German occupation. After 1945 Split became part of the newly created Socialist Republic of Croatia (a constituent part of the Socialist Federal Republic of Yugoslavia), and remained so until the country's breakaway during the Balkan Wars of the 1990s. Inevitably, Croatia's victory in its struggle for independence during the civil war came at a high price. As well as the loss of 20,000 of its citizens, the country's economy shrank by a quarter, and as Croatia's second city after Zagreb, Split bore its fair share of the brunt. However, since the end of the war the city's salvation has been the rapid development of its tourism industry – a belated prosperity helped no end by its fortuitously glorious position on the eastern Adriatic. The city that had once sported Nazi and Communist flags and saw its own people lying dead in the streets during a bloody civil war, is now a major tourist destination. All in all, with the gaiety of a cosmo-politan crowd around me and an international cacoph-ony of competing English, Spanish, French and German accents – not to mention the prospect of my very own two-bed crash-pad to return to – all things in Split on that first evening in the Balkans seemed to me about as good as they possibly could get.

I began the following day on the trail of Split's most famous son – Emperor Diocletian. Born in Salona, a mere five-kilometre hop from the centre of Split, Diocletian was Roman Emperor from A.D. 284 to 305. His story caught my eye as being the story of a man not temperamentally cut out for the demands and responsi-bilities of his role in the hurly-burly of the workplace. In fact, from what I could tell, Diocletian didn't carry the burden of his power at all lightly, and examples of his insecurities abound – including his hasty-sounding order in 302 to remove the tongue of the dissenting Deacon, Romanus of Caesarea, not to mention his con-stant edicts and persecutions against the beleaguered Christians. A little more than a quarter of a century later, those edicts had been reversed by the Christian Emperor Constantine, and Diocletian's legacy tarnished by the memory of him as an adversary of God. But what really grabbed me about Diocletian was his notoriety for being the first Roman Emperor to abdicate his title voluntarily by handing in his notice. Considering the furore over the resignation of Pope Benedict XVI in the more enlightened times of 2014, it is no great surprise to learn that Diocletian's admission of his own unsuitability for high office in May 305 caused quite a ruction, even without email and social media to spread the gossip far and wide like wildfire. But Diocletian didn't go quietly, and at his last ever 'team meeting', the outgoing emperor made a memorable speech. Welling up in tears like a daft Oscar winner, the absconding Diocletian revealed to his assembled generals his plan to resign, put his feet up and lead a life of seaside self-determination and mood-compatible decision making – or words to that effect. None of this, of course, went with the usual territory of being Emperor of Rome. Yet this was no knee-jerk, throwing in the towel moment. Diocletian clearly had an out-of-office plan. In fact, having already lined up his own little fourth-century 'place in the sun' here in Split, it could even be said that Diocletian invented the concept of early retirement. This man is owed a great deal indeed.

The ex-emperor's seaside 'grand design' was the Diocletian Palace, where he lived far from the demands of his former subjects, tending his roses and vegetable patch until his death in 311 at the decent fourth-century age of sixty-six. More impressive still was his outright rejection of repeated calls for him to come out of retirement to sort out the unholy mess he left behind. Evidently very much his own man, under considerable pressure to return to Rome, Diocletian proclaimed movingly from Split that, '...*if you could show the cabbage that I planted with my own hands to your emperor, he wouldn't dare suggest that I replace the peace and happiness of this place with the storms of a never-satisfied greed*'. Now there's a man who had his priorities right. In the event, Diocletian's Palace turned out to be not so much a single identifiable structure, but more a sprawl of buildings erected haphazardly over an extended period of time. Once completed the palace formed a walled citadel where living, trading, worship – and most importantly for Diocletian, cabbage-growing – co-existed cheek by jowl. Covering nine acres, the complex's disorienting tangle of narrow streets and tiny squares is the world's largest remaining Roman palace. No ruin or museum though, Diocletian's old stomping ground is now the beating heart of Split's modern city, containing over two hundred buildings and providing homes for more than 3,000 people. To find a good vantage point of Diocletian's old crash pad and of the rest of the city, I made the heart-thumping climb up to the campanile bell tower of the tiny Cathedral of St Domnius (Diocletian's mausoleum, converted by Christians after his death), via a set of precariously steep iron steps that were so casually secured to the ancient stone wall, there was a discernible swing from side to side. The effort was rewarded by a flawless view of the colourful roof-scape of Split, the pristine Adriatic harbour and a flat, blue-green sea glistening beyond.

Back on terra firma, I followed in Diocletian's footsteps around the rectangular floor plan of his palace complex streets, first along Dioklecijanova (named after the man himself) and then under the beautifully preserved Bronze Gate to the giant statue of Grgur

Ninski (Gregory of Nin). As I went, I thought about the near criminality of a recent threat to the integrity of the palace complex from city planners. Despite being awarded World Heritage status in 1979, in 2006 Split's local authority approved a lamentable scheme for the construction of twenty new structures within Diocletian's Palace to include – incredibly – a shopping mall and car park. Thankfully, common sense prevailed and in a heartening display of people power, once locals got wind of the madcap plan the protests were deafening and prolonged, forcing a hasty and sensible backtrack. To this day, Diocletian's retirement pad remains fully intact.

I reached the huge Gulliver-esque bronze statue of Grgur Ninski to make the mandatory touch of his wellworn (and exceedingly hot) big toe. Much is owed to local-lad Grgur, a medieval bishop who strongly opposed the influence of the Pope on his congregation. In 926, in a firm two-fingered salute to Rome, Grgur ensured that local people would understand religious services by replacing the Latin sermons and prayers with Croatian, while in the process easing the spread of Christianity across the country. Given Grgur's resistance to papal authority, it was no surprise to discover that during the Second World War the occupying Italians removed his statue to an obscure site outside the city. Happily, once the Italians were driven out of town in 1943, it was returned to this original position on the edge of the Diocletian Palace. As for the rubbing of the bishop's toe, the ritual is said by those in the know to bring good luck, and even though I had possibly used all mine up in Split with the replacement apartment, hoping for the best I added infinitesimally to the toe's shine by giving it a quick wipe. Feeling about as lucky as any man could after my brush with the holy big toe, I followed the crowds underground into the former palace basement, now a thriving market of locally produced clothing, leather belts and a whole host of souvenir trinkets. I left the palace at the Adriatic-facing Bronze Gate and sat for a while at a shady table of a waterfront café. As I looked at the happy faces around me, most of them whooping with partially-inebriated laughter, it was difficult to imagine the wildly chequered past of this stunning Dalmatian port city – an often violent and bloody history that has left it with an alluring sense of otherworldliness.

Feeling the onset of cabin fever and an urge to work my legs, I left the café and crossed the road to hire a bike from a quayside kiosk. Invigorated by the swift movement and rapidly changing scenery that cycling uniquely offers, I pedalled away from the crowds towards the hilly peninsular district of Marjan. The scenic road was a leisure cyclist's dream. It was never too straight as to be dull, it undulated gently but sufficiently to pose a modest physical challenge, while offering unbroken spectacular vistas over the craggy mountains of the distant Adriatic islands of Šolta and Brač. Looking for a break from the heat, I stopped off a few kilometres out of Split at Kasuni beach on the southern part of the Marjan Hill. Given that the beach was devoid of any natural form of shade, respite from the sun was impossible, so in a Reggie Perrin moment I stripped almost bare (almost being the operative word – this was patently *not* Berlin), left my clothing in a small pile on the shore and held my breath as I ran into the chilly turquoise sea, thinking about what I might otherwise be doing with my time on this summery Friday lunchtime. A soggy south London cheese sandwich, maybe. Not a great prospect, but one still someway short of bringing on the idea of faking suicide in the fashion of Reggie Perrin's fictional TV character, who once saw it as the only way out of the frustration and claustrophobia of his humdrum existence as a middle manager at *Sunshine Desserts*. For some unknown reason, as I splashed about in the bracing Adriatic water, some of Reggie's plotlines sprang to mind. In one, after faking his death to escape the rat-race, Reggie assumes a new identity as a labourer on a sewage farm, where he at last finds vocational and spiritual contentment in his role mucking out the pigs. Apart from their constant need of decent filling swill, the pigs prove to be the most undemanding of clients, suiting Reggie down to the ground in fact with not one unreachable target or performance indicator standing in his way of doing a good day's work. As far as I know, neither the pigs nor Reggie's management had the slightest call for complaint. Unfortunately for me in any future quest for job satisfaction, a career in pig farming had to be ruled out on the grounds that it would most probably involve very early mornings – another career thwarted.

I continued my cycle to the hamlet of Bene at the very tip of the peninsular, where I found a rocky outcrop from which to plunge into a warmer pool of sea water furnished with a rusty old slide, in full service at the time providing fun and games for a selection of kids aged five to eighty-five. After a couple of invigorating forward-facing lunges into the pool from the decidedly-listing slide, I sat for a while in the beachside café drying off under parasols plastered busily with advertisements for competing brands of local beer. Blissfully aware that I was at that moment the only tourist in the village, I watched groups of friends and local families chatting happily in the sun, enjoying their great good fortune of living on the edge of a thriving little metropolis that doubles up on a fine day like this as an outstanding beach resort.

At some ungodly hour the following morning, I left my slice of luxury behind at the Split apartment to meet the first coach out of town heading for Sarajevo. I was met at the harbour-side bus station by the spectacle of a glorious Balkan sunrise, the bright outlook not marred in the least by the prospect of a painstaking seven-hour coach journey ahead. After all, I was travelling. Nevertheless, looking at my map of the region unfolded on my knees as the coach pulled away from Split, unless we were about to be asked to get out and push the vehicle over the border, it was difficult to see how the road journey to the Bosnian capital could take so long. Although the terrain is mostly mountainous, it seemed quite some oversight of planning that no major road exists between the Croatian border and Sarajevo. But the lush alpine-like scenery of the western Balkan mountains eased me through the journey, even if my nearest neighbour hadn't the faintest idea about elbow-etiquette on a long coach trip. With the right-hand side of my body smarting from the constant jabbing of his bony elbow, the coach pulled into Sarajevo bus station in the middle of the sort of afternoon a 'red top' headline might describe as a 'scorcher'. As I left the bus to enter a maelstrom of revving engines and bawling hawkers, my first thought was for the ill-fated Archduke Franz Ferdinand, who at least had the good sense to make the final part of his circuitous journey to Sarajevo from Vienna by train. I spotted the railway station next door to the bus terminus, and was mightily glad to know that when I left Sarajevo a few days later on my journey south to Mostar, I too would be sitting on a train.

I set out to walk to my hotel, realising within minutes that I had been sold a pup of a direction by a young man I asked outside the railway station, who saw my question as no more than an opportunity to try out his rookie English. After some fairly aimless wandering through hot anonymous streets, I reached the banks of the Miljacka river. Using the minarets of the old town as a guide – and feeling as if I was walking towards a mini-Istanbul – I eventually spotted the garish yellow facade of the hotel on the south side of the river, right next to the Latinski Bridge. I had chosen the hotel of the same name for its handy location opposite the spot where the Austrian Archduke drew his last breath. Inside the hotel as I looked from the window of my room across the bridge to the murder scene, I felt as Lee Harvey Oswald may have done in November 1963 as he surveyed the JFK motorcade, seconds before taking excited aim at the president as his car rounded the corner beside the Texas School Book Depository. I prised myself away from the mawkish view, left the hotel and walked over to the north side of the Latinski Bridge where I found an inscription on a wall marking the spot where Gavrilo Princip fired his fatal shots. I looked around as people hurried past by me, going about their daily business as if nothing of any consequence had ever happened there. But in the certain knowledge that something significant most definitely *had* happened there, I felt a frisson of excitement that only being in such close contact with the past can create.

Although the murderer got his man, in truth the assassination was a botched, amateurish affair. Young Gavrilo was just one of a group of Serb desperadoes who travelled from Belgrade in June 1914 to murder the Archduke as he made his pre-announced, security-lax tour. As the Archduke's motorcade wound its way through the streets of Sarajevo and the royal couple waved happily to the crowds, before Gavrilo pulled his trigger three other members of the deadly welcoming party had already fluffed opportunities to release bombs and fire their pistols. One of them, Nedelijko Čabrinović, managed to despatch his bomb towards Franz Ferdinand's open-top sports car, but instead of the device exploding among the passengers as intended, it bounced off the back of the vehicle and detonated under a separate car wounding twenty bystanders. As well as with the bomb, the failed assassin Čabrinović had also been issued with a cyanide pill and instructed by his ringleaders to swallow it once he had carried out the murder, before completing an heroic suicide by jumping into the Miljacka River. Inconveniently for the hapless Čabrinović, the cyanide pill was of an economy, low dosage variety and merely induced some unattractive pavement puking. Neither did his attempt at jumping into the river do the trick, thanks to the hot dry weather of the Sarajevo June reducing the depth of the water to a paltry thirteen centimetres. As he lay face down in the shallow water heaving from the effects of the cyanide, the wretched man was dragged ashore by a policeman, who a tad unprofessionally it must be said allowed the crowd to give him a good pasting before he was then taken into custody. Reports that the Keystone Cops were also called to the scene remain unconfirmed.

Meanwhile the Archduke's car (which bore the portentous number plate, A11-11-18, the date of the First World War Armistice) was on its way to the local hospital where Franz had planned to visit those injured in the earlier failed explosion. Seizing his opportunity as the Archduke's car came to a halt, amid the confusion of the driver about the safest route he should take, Gavrilo Princip drew his pistol and fired into the vehicle, killing Franz Ferdinand with a bullet to the jugular vein and also his poor wife Archduchess Sophie, who he shot in the abdomen. Such heady times this city of Sarajevo has seen!

Historical curiosity satisfied, I set off to explore the maze of little alleyways and squares of Stari Grad, Sarajevo's atmospheric old town. Astonishingly, following the city's liberation in 1945, a woeful scheme was mooted to destroy Stari Grad's principal and most precious landmark – the sixteenth-century Ottoman bazaar. Had the plan come to fruition, in the dubious name of modernity the cultural heart of Sarajevo would have been lost forever. Mercifully, the plan stayed on the drawing board where it firmly belonged, allowing Sarajevo to remain a sort of European Jerusalem – a colourful and vibrant fusion of east and west. I walked past mosques built next to churches, in turn stood alongside synagogues – diverse people and architecture co-existing amid the wonderful chaos and confusion of the huge open-air food and craft market that is Stari Grad. I took long gulps of ice-cold water from a fountain outside the courtyard of the old town's main mosque – the Gazi Husrev-beg –and took a step back from the heat and crowded hubbub in the shady garden of a neighbouring café to read-up on some of the history of this oft-embattled city – a microcosm, no less, of the entire Balkans region.

To say that Sarajevo in recent times has been a city a little low on peace, love and understanding would be an understatement of seismic proportions. In my first few hours in the city I passed dozens of buildings scarred by shelling during the city's great modern tragedy – the Siege of Sarajevo – which terrorised the population and devastated the city's infrastructure for an agonising 1,425 days between April 1992 and February 1996, setting an unenviable record as the longest siege endured by any capital city in the history of modern warfare. Synonymous with the siege was the Holiday Inn, originally constructed in 1984 for the happier event of Sarajevo's hosting of the Winter Olympics, and which during the siege ended up being the city's only fully-functioning hotel. Positioned unpromisingly on a 'sniper's alley', once the siege was underway the hotel was regularly shelled, earning it the damning review of one of its long-term wartime guests, the BBC reporter Martin Bell, that *'from the hotel you didn't go out to the war. The war came in to you'*. A change from petty complaints about dripping hotel showers, at least. But long after the last shell was fired in the direction of the Holiday Inn and at the hundreds of other decimated buildings around the city, the physical scars of war have become colourful symbols of remembrance. When a mortar explodes against masonry, the impact leaves behind a distinct star-shape, and during the siege Sarajevo was marked by countless of these imprints of war on its roads, walls and buildings. In an act of artistic redemption, after the war many of these motifs of violence were filled in with red resin to create a floral effect known charmingly as Sarajevo Roses. Although these makeshift tributes to the city's dead are fast-disappearing as the façades of damaged buildings are gradually repaired or replaced, I spotted odd ones still intact in front of shops, office buildings and alongside open-air market stalls and churches, each one a decorative reminder of the three hundred-plus shells that exploded on Sarajevo's streets each and every day of the siege. That's an extraordinary shell count approaching half-a-million, withstood by a city roughly the size of Bristol.

The background to the Siege of Sarajevo is worth recalling. On 15th October 1991, Bosnia and Herzegovina took its chances by declaring independence from Yugoslavia. However, as the most ethnically diverse region of the former Yugoslav Republic, not every compatriot was wholeheartedly on-board with the process. At the time, Bosnia comprised a population roughly 44% Muslim, 31% Serb and 17% Croat – a tangle of ethnic antagonism that in 1992 erupted in a bitter war. In an effort to carve out their own enclave in the country, the Serb minority laid siege to Sarajevo by setting about a ruthless bombardment of the Bosnian capital, carrying out gratuitous massacres and mass expulsions of the predominantly Muslim population. To discover how one particularly cruel aspect of the war was executed I headed, quite literally, for the hills. Labouring a little against the intense afternoon heat, I made the steep climb up Kovaci Street to one of the many verdant mounds that surround the city. At the summit of a high wooded slope, I found the remains of a fort typical of the kind of vantage point used to prosecute Sarajevo's siege by the 13,000-strong Serbian force. And what a fortuitous view these forces had – a glorious cultural and architectural mishmash of mosques, minarets, synagogues and churches. Partly enabled by this birds-eye city view, the four-year bombardment of the city claimed 14,000 lives, 5,500 of them civilian. As I walked back down the hill towards the old town, I saw for myself the human cost of the conflict laid bare by numerous cemeteries, each of them packed with lines of pillar-like headstones arranged like perfect regiments of brilliant white teeth. I read the inscriptions of the names and dates of the dead on numerous headstones. Not one of those I paused to read marked the loss of a citizen of Sarajevo aged more than thirty.

Back in the heart of the old city, I visited the happily air-conditioned Official Siege Exhibition, known colloquially as the 'Sniper Alley' museum. Presented in the form of a narration-free DVD embellished with incidental music, the pitiful images told their own story. Every bit as harrowing as a Holocaust exhibition (the principal difference being that it was presented entirely in colour), amid the mind-boggling scenes of violence, one set of images were particularly horrifying. These were photographs of the work of gutless Serbian snipers camped out in the exact spot where I had sat only an hour earlier on that peaceful wooded slope. From their superb vantage point during the long siege, the snipers took great delight in aiming pot-shots at innocent men, women and children as they went about their insufferable existence in the embattled hell of the city's streets below. In graphic detail, the exhibition showed how the snipers aimed at the most vulnerable and painful areas of the body, such as the knee-cap or shin. Not content with merely disabling their victim, they then played a sick game of laying bets with fellow snipers on how far the body would crawl before finally collapsing. A further bullet to the head then finished the poor soul off for good, to become yet another fatal statistic of the siege. And they did all of this, just because they could.

Quite miraculously, since the end of its bloody nadir Sarajevo has enjoyed a complete renaissance. With a population that has recovered from its war losses to now total around 400,000, the city has become once more the social and cultural centre of Bosnia and Herzegovina. As well as Sarajevo being nominated for European Capital of Culture in 2014 (only to be beaten to the prize by the Latvian capital, Riga), the country is currently undergoing consideration for European Union membership through the painstaking 'Stabilisation and Association Process' – the means dreamed up by the Brussels bureaucrats of measuring a nation's economic, political and human rights record. But for now at least, the Bosnian capital remains a refreshing travel alternative to more illustrious European destinations. What's more, given its abundance of unspoiled charm, magnificent scenery and deep cultural diversity, I was even happy to forgive Sarajevo the inconvenience of a long footslog in the forty-degree heat in search of a place to buy a proper drink. When I eventually found one, the price tag suggested a city that was quick on the uptake when it came to the tourist buck. It may for now be a little short of decent bars – and so is spared the indignity of drunken stag parties – but Sarajevo can boast being named in a recent poll by *Lonely Planet* as 'the forty-third best city in the world to visit'. On learning this, my first thought was that if Sarajevo, with all the brilliance of its east-west diversity, architecture and summer temperatures, comes in at number forty-three, I wouldn't half mind a weekend in the city rated forty-two. But in the meantime, I had another early morning to face, a train into the unknown to catch, and at the end of the journey another notorious bridge to cross.

Slaven, the cab driver who drove me to Sarajevo station the following morning was infectiously cheerful, and just the sort of man to spend time with at six-thirty in the morning. Regaling me with stories of Sarajevo that were made funnier than they probably were by his novel take on the English language, this cabbie's joie de vivre reached a near frenzy as he came mightily close to running over an American tourist foolish enough to think he might get away with his life by crossing the road at a pedestrian crossing. I knew the man was American partly because of the beige pop socks he wore inside his leather sandals, but also because Slaven told me so. Lovely man as he was, Slaven was also one of those infuriating types confident that he knew just about *everything* – most definitely then a man to be taken in small doses. Anyway, when I arrived at the station it was already filled to the brim with tourists, many of them headed my way to Mostar. Among them strolled a rather shaken-looking man in beige pop socks and sandals who looked like he had recently had a near miss with a taxi. And just to confirm his national-ity and indeed prove Slaven absolutely right, the man sported a large stars and stripes badge sewn proudly into the side of his bulging rucksack.

Feeling the buzz of intrepidness that is never missing when I enter a foreign railway station, I took some photographs of the bulky old train I was about to board, branded boldly on the side with the insignia of the Bosnia and Herzegovina national railway – ZFBH. I had bought my ticket in advance, without any of the obsessive nonsense about compulsory reserved seating characteristic of most modern rail systems. The benefits of reserving a seat on a busy train are self-evident, but half the time with a numbered seat I seem to end up with a view of a grey plastic panel between two windows, rather than of a panorama out of one. In the event the carriage I opted for was of a decidedly vintage stock. It was also quite wonderful. As I boarded I could just make out the outline of a large number '1' scratched off the glass of the window, indicating that at some point in the distant past this carriage would have offered the luxury of first class. As I sank, quite literally, into the partially-collapsed velvety covering of my seat (effectively a battered old armchair screwed to the floor), it felt like I was about to set out on a journey in a mobile Edwardian drawing room. I was joined in my well-upholstered comfort by a group of upbeat German backpackers, whose main pre-occupation throughout the two-and-a-half-hour journey south to Mostar was to work their way through a small mountain of bread, salami sausage and an unidentified substance that may have been a local variation of sauerkraut, all of it washed down with a red wine the colour of cheap nail varnish sloshed into plastic cups. The view from my window was rather more verdant, and as I considered suitable adjectives to do proper justice to the scenery my train was rolling through, I ummed-and-aahed about options beyond the oh-so pre-dictable 'stunning'. I might equally have plumped for 'incredible', 'breathtaking' or 'amazing', but they just seemed like clichés too. So if like me your definition of 'stunning' is something uncomplicated along the lines of 'extremely attractive or impressive', then you'll settle for that as a description of the Karstic mountain scenery and the waterfalls, rivers and viaducts through and over which the train creaked and clanked its way down to Mostar. I wasn't complaining, but my view might have been even better, had ZFBH taken the trouble to show my window the soapy side of a squeegee at least once since Marshal Tito last made the same trip.

As the train rolled into Mostar station, rarely have I felt as disappointed at a journey's end. Not, I hasten to add, because of the destination I had reached, but because I could quite happily have sat on that wonder-fully saggy old train all day. The welcoming party of bawling women of all ages, offering me rooms in their homes reminded me of arriving on the island of Crete by ferry a few years before. Feeling a touch queasy after a bumpy overnight crossing from the Athens Port, Piraeus, on that occasion I took up the first offer of bargain-sounding accommodation that came my way. Abductions of forty-something British men were not commonplace on Greek islands at the time, but looking back it may have been a tad risky to get into the back of a car with a strange woman and a much younger man who I assumed was her son. As it turned out, I couldn't have been in better hands. I was driven to a large house on a hill, bundled with my rucksack into a room with an uninterrupted Mediterranean view, and spent a bliss-ful week wallowing in the hospitality of a warm and generous family. Back in Mostar, I had booked ahead and was deprived of such spontaneity. So after disappointing the welcome party at the station, I set off alone along Marshal Tito Avenue (pleased to note that the name remains unchanged – why deny history?) in search of my digs at an intriguing-sounding establishment called Muslibegović House.

As I walked along Tito's wide, rather bleak avenue, I passed numerous derelict buildings pock-marked by gun and shell-fire from the Bosnian War – long since abandoned to the elements and nowadays the draughty homes of wild-sown silver birches and maniacally barking dogs. After a couple of false dawns and wrong turns I found Muslibegović House, a grand old stone villa doubling up as both hotel and Bosnian national monument (effectively a living museum). I was greeted at the front door by the beaming housekeeper, dressed colourfully in the traditional Bosnian garb of an embroidered bodice, ushered into an elegant hallway of traditional Ottoman décor, then sent up to the attic room I had been allocated, which disappointingly had not been treated to the same authentic treatment. Evidently the hotel's turkey room, I felt certain that I had been given the cramped dark space in the eaves on the grounds that it would 'do' for a single bloke. I was in Mostar for one night only and was so keen to see *that* bridge, I didn't bother mentioning to the housekeeper that the shower was unsuitable for any adult over five-feet tall wishing to wash themselves stood fully upright. Cracking my head against the tank as I got up from a crouching position under the lukewarm water set me up nicely for my day of exploring this small – and as I was about to discover – quite exquisite city. As I left the hotel and set off towards the centre of town, my business-savvy hostess bade me a cheery farewell, reminding me that in the end perhaps all that really matters in life is a friendly smile.

With no more than twenty-four hours to spend in Mostar, I wasted no time in locating the city's most famous landmark – the re-built, sixteenth-century Ottoman Stari Most (old bridge), after which Mostar is named. Before I left the hotel I had prepared by sitting on the edge of my futon-style bed, partly to recover from the accidental head-butt of the boiler, but also to watch on *YouTube* the rather upsetting footage of the destruction of the original bridge – a spiteful act of cultural vandalism by Croat forces in November 1993 that knocked the heart and soul out of Mostar. I was so agitated as I watched the trauma of the bridge's collapse that the quite irrational thought entered my mind – and thankfully exited just as quickly – that never again could I support a Croatian football team in a World Cup match or one of the nation's ever-so-tall tennis players in a Grand Slam final. Originally constructed in the 1550s on the instruction of the Ottoman King Suleiman the Magnificent, the emblematic bridge had spanned the steep banks of the River Neretva for well over four hundred years, its stone arch rising high above the water like two sets of fingers cupped in a cat's-cradle of thought. The elegant structure had linked Mostar's Christian and Muslim communities living either side until the Croats severed the peace by firing sixty shells towards it, sending the graceful arch crashing heartbreakingly into the water of the Neretva twenty-four metres below. As a symbol of the raw pity of the Bosnian War, the obliteration of Mostar's bridge provided the watching world with the conflict's most resonant TV horror image. But as a metaphor of reconciliation and renewed hope, its near-miraculous reconstruction could hardly be more potent. A lazy thought maybe, but for reasons that are easy to define the bridge has loud echoes of the Berlin Wall.

The new crossing was opened in 2004 as a beautiful replica of the original, once more bridging Mostar's cultural and ethnic divide. For both sides of the Mostar community, the loss of their iconic bridge during the fighting was apocalyptic enough. Yet its destruction was but one violent act during a long and bloody siege that just like in Sarajevo, Mostar was subjected to after Bosnia and Herzegovina's bold declaration of independence from Yugoslavia. In addition to the loss of its bridge, the war cost this small city a Franciscan monastery, its Catholic cathedral, a library of fifty-thousand books and an astonishing fourteen mosques. Tourists to Mostar – and on the day I was there the city was absolutely teeming with them – are encouraged to consider their visit to be about more than just photo-graphy, ice-cream and tacky merchandise. This was evident as I joined a multi-national trail of visitors making the mandatory short pilgrimage to the bridge. As I walked along an ancient well-beaten cobbled path towards it, I passed a sign impossible to ignore, hand painted in black on a large round stone. The sign said, quite simply, 'DON'T FORGET 1993'. As if anyone could.

Although the bridge's reconstruction achieved near-perfection, as I approached it I couldn't help wondering that it looked a bit *too* new, even a touch pastiche. The remedy for that I suppose is to keep the bridge away from shellfire for another five hundred years or so, let it weather a bit and then no-one will mind that it is a copy. Original or not, the bridge's reconstructed pale stone form is a wonderful sight. Irresistibly photogenic with its perfectly-poised thirty-metre span, the structure is supported either side by two fortified towers known locally as 'the bridge keepers'. As I reached the top of the graceful arch, I was asked for money by one of a small gang of local unofficial bridge keepers also on patrol that day. These friendly young hustlers were probably all too young to remember much about the original bridge, but now tout a living from tourists by performing risky dives from the bridge summit into the River Neretva rushing noisily below. I watched as they entered the water in athletic twists and turns, each in a bid to outdo the last for technical and artistic merit. To get a better view of the daredevil antics of these Tom Daley wannabees, and also of a less-photographed angle of the bridge, I scrambled down the river bank to take a bit of a plunge myself. Not, I hasten to add, by leaping from the bridge into the abyss – although that option might have been under consideration had I been due back at the office the following Monday. Instead, this was a very British sort of plunge involving discarded shoes and socks, rolled-up trouser legs and pale toes dangling feebly into the icy water. I was a knotted-handkerchief-on-my-head short of looking completely ridiculous. Those Mostar divers are a bunch of tough nuts and deserve every Bosnian convertible mark (KM) they earn. It was a hot afternoon in high summer when I risked all by baring my feet in the Neretva River. But take it from me – that water was seriously cold.

The Dayton Agreement that brought the Bosnian War to an end in November 1995 has left Bosnia and Herzegovina with an uneasy peace. The three ethnic groups that were awarded 'constituent status' within the country by the peace settlement – Bosnian Muslims, Croats and Serbs – inevitably hold hugely conflicting views on a wide range of issues affecting their country. Having said that, one aspect of modern Bosnia they do all share dismay over is the post-war dire straits of the country's economy – exemplified by one of the world's worst youth unemployment rates running at a ruinous sixty-percent. Given that 100,000 people were killed and two million more displaced during the three-and-a-half years of fighting in Bosnia, this terrible legacy of economic instability is hardly surprising. And more than twenty years on from the conflict, Mostar's cultural and economic growth remains stunted by the great divide that still exists between the city's Bosniak and Croat groups. The reconstructed bridge supposedly crosses rather more than just a river. Yet despite legislation preventing employers discriminating against any ethnic group, the reality for young people in Bosnia is that unless they have 'suitable' family or ethnic connections, finding meaningful employment can be an impossible task.

The continuing ethnic tensions already holding back Bosnia's recovery from war are compounded by a worrying absence of economic growth. During the war Bosnia received a substantial amount of humanitarian aid from the international community. Since hostilities ended in December 1995 aid has continued to pour in leading, some economic critics have ventured, to a culture in the country of dependency, lack of innovation and the stifling of growth. As a result, many young highly-educated Bosnians now find themselves marginalised and unable to secure meaningful employment. As I walked away from the bridge into a less touristy zone of narrow cobbled lanes lined with abandoned war-torn buildings, I met a young man facing just that predicament. His name was Amir and he was plying an artistic trade in the sale of his cleverly painted flat stones depicting miniature scenes of the emblematic bridge. Quietly spoken and articulate, Amir told me in considered English of his dream to leave Bosnia (despite still loving his country) and travel to London (a city he regards as a hive of endless opportunity) to work for a decent living and generally enjoy a more prosperous life. I bought a couple of Amir's fine stones and told him of a hope of my own that one day I would meet him again, the next time cleaning up through the sale of his artwork for many times the price in a busy corner of Camden Market, London NW1.

When I had checked-in earlier at Muslibegović House, I was issued with a voucher for a 'free drink' at a nominated town centre restaurant – a 'freebie' I was assured that would be at the hotel's expense. Having accepted probably the worst room in the hotel, I decided that the least I deserved in return was a drink on the house. As I was down to my last dregs of convertible marks following the spree on Amir's painted stones, the voucher was a bit of a godsend. So for my only meal out in Mostar, I sat in the said restaurant clutching my voucher and calculated what I could afford to order, relying on the voucher to stand me a drink. Cutting to the chase, the bill arrived with no reduction for one of the two beers I drank, despite my determined waving of the voucher in front of the waiter as I ordered. As it turned out, the voucher wasn't really redeemable for what you would call a drink at all, unless you're in the habit of quenching your thirst by knocking back small measures of a gloopy, paraffin-coloured concoction from a shot glass. Not only was I reduced by the mix-up to being unable to leave a tip, I was still short by one whole KM of being able to pay the bill in full – an embarrassing end to my short stay in this most hospitable country. I did offer other means of payment such as washing up and clearing tables, but in the end my waiter just aimed a few tut-tuts in my direction and allowed me to leave, carrying my tail firmly between my legs as I left. When I return someday to Mostar my first stop will be the same restaurant, where I fully intend to spend and tip lavishly, having first avoided any kind of liquid refreshment the colour of candyfloss. In the event my short visit to Mostar ended on a very pronounced high. If the Stari Most is picturesque by day, by night it is positively enchanting. I joined a queue of other amateur photographers, each one as keen as I was to take home something of the floodlit splendour of the bridge, its golden arch set against a blue-black sky, suspended dreamily over the roaring current of the Neretva River – a sight, no less, of natural and man-made perfection in the most exquisite harmony.

After a superb breakfast of a multi-coloured assortment of meze served on the sunny outdoor terrace of Muslibegović House (in full redemption for the room I was palmed-off with), I left for the coach station to continue my journey due south to Dubrovnik. I got off on the wrong foot with the driver of the coach, who punished me for not having a bean of Bosnian currency to tip him with for placing my rucksack in the hold, by forcing me to spend the entire journey encumbered by it in my lap. But there were two aspects of the journey to Dubrovnik that distracted me from this modest discomfort. The first was the two border crossings between Bosnia and Croatia, the second the traffic jam of Catholic pilgrims we ran into at the first of those border points. The slow and bureaucratic formalities of the first crossing were made more intriguing by the presence of uniformed guards – a forgotten and often quite stirring feature of cross-border travel now absent in most of border-free Europe. Our attempt to cross the first border was also hampered by no less than four coach loads of pilgrims travelling to nearby Medjugorje, a small mountain town populated largely by Christian Croats. The coaches had Irish number plates, so I assumed the passengers had taken the trouble to make two sea crossings and drive halfway across the Continent to be there. Since 1981 when six local children reported apparitions of the Blessed Virgin Mary at Medjugorje, countless others have followed the same route, placing the town firmly on the map as one of the world's great centres of Catholic pilgrimage. Whether the apparitions were real or not depends of course on what you are inclined to believe, but since that Catholic red-letter day an astonishing thirty-million pilgrims have made the same trip – hoping no doubt to be dropping by just at the point Our Lady of Medjugorje decides to show here elusive face once more.

Once waved though into Croatia and travelling in the opposite direction to the hopeful pilgrims, I was treated to an indisputable apparition of my own in the form of dozens of little Adriatic Islands lying serenely in the blue-green sea. A very long and winding road eventually brought us to the second border crossing and so back into Bosnia. This oddity of geographical and political division is the result of a Dayton Agreement clause that ceded a corridor of land to the Bosnian people allowing them access to the sea, in the process cutting Croatia in two. After a further hour or so more of pleasant meandering, the coach pulled into Dubrovnik. The relief at leaving the coach was tempered somewhat by the discovery that it had terminated three miles shy of Dubrovnik's old town, requiring a taxi to complete the journey. For the ten-minute ride I formed part of an eclectic bunch squashed up in the back seat of a smoky old Fiat. Joining me for the short ride were a well-fed couple from Holland, who told me in perfect English that they had fled south to escape the incessant northern European rain, and a local woman whose only luggage was a plaintively meowing cat fastened inside a wicker basket.

If you have been there yourself, you will know that words cannot do justice to the beauty of Dubrovnik. It really is *that* lovely. I entered the traffic-free old town through the monumental Pile Gate – one of the two main entrances to this UNESCO World Heritage Site – and was instantly transfixed by its honey-stoned beauty. After his 1929 city break on the Adriatic, George Bernard Shaw announced to the world that, *'if you want to see heaven on earth, come to Dubrovnik'*. GBS was about spot on, for here lies about as heavenly-formed a walled city as you could hope to find. Nevertheless, we must hope that the Nobel-prize winning playwright had no call to use the local Tourist

Information shop while he was in town, which in my short experience deserves a far lower rating than the city it serves. Without a clue to where I was going, and not really caring enough to start foraging in my bag for a map, I popped in to ask for directions to my hotel. After having to virtually stand on my head and whistle to attract the merest flicker of attention from the deeply disengaged assistant, I was issued with a set of precise but ultimately hopeless instructions pointing me towards the 'tenth turning on the left' off the old town's crowded main drag, Placa-Stradun. The bit about turning left was sound enough advice, it was just the small detail of the turning I needed being not the tenth, but the third. Never mind, seven misguided streets in a place as intoxicating as Dubrovnik was nothing to angst about, and as there are so few affordable places to stay in the old city (I didn't take myself off the payroll to stay in expensive hotels), once I found it the location of Hotel Antic Ragusa was about as good as it could get. So well located was this hotel I happily overlooked the patchy wifi signal in my room, the 1970s polystyrene ceilings tiles, the loose dado rails, un-hung mirrors propped up against walls and the surprising lack of anywhere in the bathroom to hang a towel. There was, however, one overwhelming redeeming feature of this otherwise imperfect hotel – it was situated in Dubrovnik.

Preening itself in a sublime and lucky location on the southern Adriatic, during its sixteenth-century Golden Age as the trading capital of the affluent Republic of Ragusa, Dubrovnik had one of the world's largest merchant navy fleets. Nowadays, this pearl of the Adriatic retains its affluence, but largely because of its easy magnetism for tourists – and there are certainly plenty of those. The downside to Dubrovnik's popularity is that the price of having a good time in the town is way in excess of that in other parts of Croatia. Worse still, and of great detriment to the integrity of the city, is the fact that hardly anyone who lives in the old town these days is Croatian – not surprising, considering the cost of a sea-facing villa to be in excess of £2 million. At the last tally the indigenous head-count living within the city walls was a paltry 500, making the proportion of local residents to outsiders unhealthily imbalanced. I sat for a while on the edge of the sixteen-sided, fifteenth-century Onofrio Fountain on Placa-Stradun, once the end point of an aqueduct system that brought fresh water into town from the nearby Sumet spring. After taking a few mouthfuls of the fountain's reviving ice-cold water I walked towards Dubrovnik's sheer medieval stone walls, encircling the old town at an average height of twenty-four metres and six metres thickness. Some sections of the wall date back to the tenth-century when it was constructed to protect the old Ragusa Republic from would-be invaders. Most of the construction I looked at now was completed more recently – between the fourteenth and fifteenth-centuries – although there have been various additions and reinforcements since, including seventeen circular and quadrangle towers and the immense St John's Fortress. Highly effective in keeping the city free of undesirables, a moat originally ran around the entire outside section of the wall containing over a hundred cannons, helping to maintain the wall's record of having never been breached – an achievement that to this day remainsa source of much local pride.

Walking the full circuit of the city walls is an absolute must-do in Dubrovnik. As I began the adventure by climbing the hundred steps leading up from the Pile Gate, I was met at the top by a view so striking as to be almost unreal. Across the battlements over one side of the wall lay the lush green clump of Lokrum Island, serene in the perfectly still blue-green Adriatic. Then my eyes were diverted to another sea on the other side of the ramparts, this time of rose-red and yellow ochre roof tiles. The tiling mis-match is the colourful legacy of Dubrovnik's fate during the 1990s Balkan Wars. In 1991, during the city's seven-month siege rockets rained down on the old red-tiled roofs, a war crime so abhorrent to the 'international community' that it earned the Serbian General responsible an eight-year jail term. After the war when it came to restoring the city to its considerable former glory, the original ancient factory that supplied the red tiles locally was long gone. The compromise solution was to use tiles from further afield, that although not matching exactly the original reds, have in themselves created a new and unintentionally-alluring feature.

In fairness, compared to the Sarajevo and Mostar horror-shows, Dubrovnik's own siege at the hands of the Yugoslav People's Army was less destructive. Nevertheless, the siege cost the lives of almost three hundred Croatian civilians and military personnel, while causing severe or terminal damage to nearly seventy-percent of the old town's ancient buildings. Just as the world was outraged by the destruction of the old bridge at Mostar, so the bombardment of Dubrovnik's UNESCO World Heritage Site was a public relations calamity for the Serbs – not to mention counter-productive by encouraging global opinion to back the independence cause of Croatia. Furthermore, in another more symbolic sense the Serb action against Dubrovnik also failed. The shellfire may have damaged or destroyed many building within the city's old defensive walls. Yet the walls themselves showed remarkable resilience to the destructive power of twentieth-century weaponry, a testament to the skill – and who knows even the foresight – of their medieval builders.

Continuing my circuit of the ramparts, I peered from the walls into the back gardens of crumbling old houses where the few remaining lucky locals sunbathed, tended their gardens or played with children in the afternoon heat. Against my better nature I walked painstakingly slowly, eking out as much pleasure as I could from each of the wall's two thousand-metres of stone circumference. Now and again I paused to look out to sea for a while from various spectacular vantage points such as the Lovrijenac Fort, Dubrovnik's very own mini Rock of Gibraltar. Struggling to prise myself from this near-perfect scene, I moved on to the northern tip of the old city where I lingered again, this time at the Miceta Fort to take in the self-confident view of the entire perfectly-symmetrical city peninsula spread out before me. I soon discovered that in Dubrovnik, one idyllic view simply begets another, and then another. Somehow I got caught up in a scrum of tourists edging anti-clockwise towards a set of steps back down to the old city's streets. As I made my reluctant descent, I doubt that I had ever felt so disappointed at leaving behind a busy tourist site. In an earlier age than George Bernard Shaw's, Lord Byron – that errant, rather louche Grand Tourist we met earlier gushing his fondness for the women and oranges of Seville – was also a frequent visitor and devotee of Dubrovnik. But during that epic stroll around the city's formidable walls, my only worry was that with so much travel in me left to come, I hadn't peaked just a little too soon.

Now, Dubrovnik is not a city short on beauty at street level either. To discover more I walked along the shiny stone surface of the three hundred metres of Placa-Stradun, past its low buildings of warm pale limestone heading in the general direction of the sea – which in this peninsula city could be in just about any direction. I found a shady spot in Luza Square to take a closer look at the slender bell tower that dominates the old city's skyline. Constructed in 1444, the tower has the important job of housing two local celebrities called Maro and Baro. Cast in bronze, these two hard-working lads were installed at the tower's summit with the straightforward job description of each day striking the bell at midday. However, centuries of exposure to the salty Adriatic air has taken its toll, transforming Maro and Baro from men of bronze to men of a somewhat less-muscular weathered green. An additional oddity of the tower is its clock hands stylised in the form of octopus legs. When the tentacles reach midday, this spurs Maro and Baro into action, striking the bell to continue a tradition that has lasted nearly six-centuries. I walked on, past the Gothic-Renaissance Sponza Palace to the black-domed seventeenth-century Cathedral of Assumption. As I stood peering up at its Baroque façade, I was told by another lone, similarly impressed British visitor (who I suspected was on the lookout for someone else to be British with), that an earlier cathedral on the same site had been built partly with money pledged by Richard the Lionheart, who made the smart move of stopping off in the Ragusa Republic for a bit of R&R on his way home from the Third Crusade.

I wandered and wandered, wasting time perhaps, but while doing so feeling that I was also using the time well – a life skill I was developing nicely into something of an art. At the sea wall I followed an enticing-looking sign advertising not only 'cold drinks' but 'the best view in town'. A little sceptical that anything could surpass the views I had been dewy-eyed at from the ramparts of the city walls, I continued anyway down a steep stone staircase to find possibly the best located bar anywhere on Planet Earth. Perched on an outcrop of rocks high above the sea, Bar Buza (I know, what a great name for a bar!) provided a spectacularly splashy setting for a couple of those cold drinks the owner so wanted me to try. Oh dear. That is about where my story for that particular afternoon ends. Spend a couple of daylight hours in Bar Buza yourself, and I wager you would feel the same. When I did eventually drag myself away from my ocean-facing bar stool, I wound my way back slowly through the hot narrow streets of the old town towards my hotel. As I clambered the stairs to my third-floor room, for some reason those aforementioned towels-without-a-hook-to-hang-from sprang to mind. Perhaps these days I had just a little too much time on my hands. But sure enough, as I entered the bathroom the first thing I encountered was a pile of fluffy white linen in a forlorn little heap on the floor. Sometimes it's the minutiae of travel that's best remembered.

The most memorable feature of breakfast the following morning – apart from the ersatz orange juice made from a powdery substance that left a small dune of fluo-rescent silt at the bottom of my glass – was the short-lived encounter I enjoyed with an Australian adventurer called Cooper. Sporting that tanned outdoor-living look carried so well by many of his compatriots, Cooper could be cast in any Antipodean daytime soap opera as your stereotypical barbie-loving Aussie. Spotting me as the only other solo guest, Cooper helped himself to the chair next to mine, and as a man evidently fond of his own voice announced to all in his earshot his assessment of the hotel as being 'like Fawlty Towers'. It is true there was a distinct whiff of Basil and Sybil chaos about the place, the service was on the lax side of average, and there was a list of maintenance issues to keep any hotelier busy – so he wasn't far wrong. Cooper then helped himself to my unoccupied ear with a précis of his life story and the 'spiritual journey' that brought him to Dubrovnik.

To summarise his summary (and do be grateful this story is not in full), a year earlier Cooper had made the unsettling discovery that his wife had been getting a little too close to a family friend than was healthy for their marriage. Devastated by the infidelity and clearly not a man to do things by halves, Cooper not only fled the marital home in a fit of jealous passion, but auc-tioned his entire portfolio of possessions as a job lot through an online marketplace. Had it been possible, I am certain that included in the list of items for sale would have been his errant ex-wife. The proceeds of this fire-sale of Cooper's life were currently being spent on a disorderly round the world jaunt – thus he had traded in his old life of marital mistrust for one of adventure, mood-compatibility and powdered orange juice. Apparently, Cooper borrowed this ingenious life-changing idea from another man 'Down Under' facing a similar predicament, who had made a career and more than decent living for himself out of bothering strangers and the world's media with his story. For Cooper though, the upshot was that for the first time in his life, for the time being at least, he was both cash *and* time rich – a dream ticket for someone of his restless bent, even if his marriage now lay in ruins. For twenty minutes or so over the cereal and toast Cooper made great company, and I was grateful for the gift of his story. Having said that, I ducked out of an invitation to be his accomplice in a mischievous jape he had up his sleeve to clear the building by setting off the hotel fire alarm. I hadn't a clue what Cooper thought he might gain from his lamentable plan – a plan I thought to be especially misconceived given that at some point in our conversation Cooper told me that he was forty-seven years old.

Before Cooper had a chance to inconvenience us all by executing his plan (by then I was keen to get as far away from him as possible), I made my way through Pile Gate to find a small beach I had spotted the day before from the city walls. After undergoing a crash course in surviving a capsizing incident, delivered in broken English by a local dude in a wetsuit, I took a sea kayak out into the ocean still with barely a clue what I was doing. Once I was underway and realised that I had to get into some sort of even paddle-left, paddle-right rhythm to put an end to the perpetual circles I was travelling in, the experience was nothing less than exhilarating. After a few minutes of reasonably straight-line paddling, I glanced over my shoulder back towards the shore, partly to see how far I had travelled, but also to check that my novice paddle action wasn't the source of some huge joke among sunbathers watching from the beach. In the event, it was a bit of a shock to discover that I was way too far out at sea to tell what might be happening back on dry land. To suppress the rising panic, I took a few deep breaths, checked that my life-jacket was still velcroed to my body and rested my paddle on the side of the kayak to spend a blissful half-an-hour drifting at sea. The magnificence of Dubrovnik's city walls rose sheer out of the Adriatic before me, proud and imposing in their un-breached record of five centuries and more. In fact, so sturdy did the ramparts look, if I had been cooking up some madcap scheme to launch a surprise, single-handed attack on the city from my lime-green kayak, I may well have thought again. I was jolted back to the reality of a more immediate danger by a sudden and unexpectedly lively wave, which for a brief and thrilling moment I rode the crest of. Fears that I was about to be engulfed by a small tsunami were dispelled by the appearance of a truly vast cruise liner, the source of the turbulent water I could see making its cumbersome and rather ominous way into Dubrovnik's harbour. In this David and Goliath seafar-ing contest, there could have been only one winner. It was high time for me to turn back, and head for shore.

I have always avoided cruises, which is just as well as their prices have ensured that they too have avoided me. But cost aside, I really don't like the idea of a holiday involving being told when and where I might be allowed to leave a floating hotel, to then plod in a flus-tered group through a city's streets behind a tour guide ludicrously holding up an umbrella in the middle of

August. That sort of fake-chummy, communal tourism could never be for me. More important than that, vessels like the floating tower block I watched inching into the harbour can have a terribly negative effect on places like Dubrovnik. If you think of a cruise ship berthing in, say, Sydney Harbour and disgorging its human content on a city of four million people, then the impact isn't so noticeable. Attempt the same thing in cramped spaces like Dubrovnik's old town and there can be real problems. Apart from the obvious peril of overcrowding, tourist saturation runs the risk of turning desirable places like this into historical theme parks, allowing the demands of the influx of tourists to drive up prices, lower overall quality and alienate any locals that may still be left there. Even though the selfish thought crossed my mind that the imminent invasion of the city by a thousand thirsty cruisers might well put the kibosh on my chances of finding a decent seat in a bar later that evening, for now I was content to arrive back at Dubrovnik's shore in my own, environmentally friendly little vessel under the steam of nothing more than a wooden paddle. Those lucky voyagers about to be freed from their floating opulence to begin an orgy of consumption in the old city may have arrived pampered by a non-stop buffet, cinema screens and on-board gymnasiums. But I would still be surprised if any one of them had enjoyed their cruise around Dubrovnik harbour that afternoon anything like as much as I had mine.

As it turned out, the bars and restaurants were busy in Dubrovnik that evening, but no more so than on others. Perhaps the cruisers had been made a better offer on board. So I ate in one of the old town's ubiquitous pizza restaurants, paying a king's ransom for a humble (and not very exceptional) Margherita. Oh, to be beamed up for an hour to the back streets of Naples! I fared better in my choice of bar – an atmospheric, dimly-lit joint in a narrow alley running off Placa-Stradun. I was minding my own business on a stool at the counter when I was approached by Brit-spotters Nigel and Lynne, a talkative and energetic couple from Cambridge in their early sixties. Nigel was in high spirits on discovering that there were no smoking restrictions in the bar and took great delight in lighting one cigarette from its predecessor. His liquid appetite was equally sharp, and several litres of a particularly gassy brand of Euro Fizz and a packet of Marlboro later, Nigel made what I thought to be the surprising announcement that he was a GP – but crucially, he added with a smile and a wink, a GP *on holiday*. Lynne, a school teacher of relatively abstemious habits, wasn't really in a position to either drink or smoke very much as both activities would have required her to stop talking for several seconds at a time. For a short while anyway, Nigel and Lynne made great company. Among other topics of conversation we covered (including the grave risks to health and well-being of overwork, but conspicuously not of smoking or heavy drinking), the couple were keen to pin me down on whether I thought Nigel should retire now or wait until his sixty-fifth birthday – an odd piece of advice I thought to seek from a total stranger. Nevertheless I was happy to help out, and taking into account the good doctor's appetite for booze, fags and general thirst for adventure my advice, as you might guess, was unequivocal. As Nigel himself rather enjoyed pointing out to his small captive audience more than once during our couple of hours together, all of this life stuff really is not a dress rehearsal.

The following morning I took a hike in the heat up a steep hill leading out of the old city to the lofty cable car station at Ploce. While I was stood in the queue to buy a ticket to take the easier route back to town, I was approached by Ivo, a local charmer and committed entrepreneur. Wearing a perma-smile to show off a striking row of too-perfect white teeth, Ivo told me that he owned several apartments nearby and would gladly rent one to me for an unmissable €50 per night – a decent rate for Dubrovnik, for sure. Having already made the decision to return to Ivo's idyllic little city sometime very soon, I agreed to an on-the-spot viewing of his apartments and so followed him down the hill to a house containing three of them. Although the house was fully occupied, Ivo used his own key to open the door before – extraordinarily I thought – taking me through into a bedroom where one of his fifty-a-night guests was lying in bed, fast asleep. The young woman in the bed was entitled to look as startled as she did when she woke to find her landlord and a male stranger stood at the foot of it. I beat a hasty retreat from the room, followed closely by Ivo who closed the bedroom door with a bang, but no apology to his terrified tenant. Without embarrassment, Ivo asked me for feedback on the flat, plus an on-the-spot cash deposit of €100 to secure my booking. I don't know about you, but I have never really fancied the idea of waking up to find strangers stood at the end of my bed – not even when I am in an adventurous mood on holiday – so to avoid running that risk on my next visit to Dubrovnik,

I pulled out of the deal that never was, leaving a puzzled looking Ivo to scratch his head and wonder where it had all gone so badly wrong.

My time in Dubrovnik was drawing to a close. I returned to the old city and sat alongside the harbour wall to watch the world go by from a shady bench and to enjoy some last quality moments. Just in the nick of time, a bit of impromptu quayside entertainment unfurled in front of my eyes. A small group of floppy-hatted Japanese tourists had set up their travel-sized easels to begin painting watercolours of whichever of the many outstanding scenes around them took their fancy. From among the small gathering of interested bystanders ran an inquisitive black and tan mutt, who during his inspection of a handbag belonging to one of the lady painters, lifted his leg and did what dogs are inclined do in such circumstances, sprinkling the contents of the bag with his own distinct brand of Adriatic scent. With the exception of the distraught owner of the bag, the rest of the quayside crowd burst into spontaneous and possibly embarrassed laughter. A tad ashamed by my own chortling at the dog's mischievous deed and the poor artist's misfortune, I created a distraction of my own worthy of a guffaw or two by ripping off most of my clothing, and then climbing down some rusty steps hanging loosely from the harbour wall to take a celebratory dip in the crystal clear water. I couldn't tell you exactly what I was celebrating. Perhaps it was the overwhelming sense of relief I felt that when I left Dubrovnik, it would not be to return to a swivel chair behind a desk in a 1960s office block.

Invigorated by the swim, I climbed out of the water and lay down in the sun on the picturesque harbour wall, feeling the droplets of water dry before they could run from my body. All was apparently well with the world, apart from the niggling thought that for the moment at least I was clean out of a plan. Back-of-an-envelope itineraries were fast becoming the route maps of my life, and as I began plotting the latest in a lengthening series of these, I once more ruled out the purgatory of airport queues, boarding passes and full-body x-ray machines. My eyes half closed to the sun, I pictured in my mind instead an ensemble of one-way journeys – journeys that offered not only destination, but also scope for many rewards en route. So decisively and mood-compatibly, the next leg of my odyssey would be taken by train.

The agony of France recalled in Marseille

> '*When I wake up on a Monday morning and realise*
> *I don't have to go and work at the Civil Service,*
> *I really think I've won.*'

Paul Merton.

– 6 –

Riviera Rails

Back in Blighty, for interminable weeks the country was shrouded under the sort of moribund cloud that has people curled up on sofas building up weather-envy watching old episodes of *A Place in the Sun*. Close your eyes, turn the thermostat up a notch, pour yourself a cool drink and you too could be sitting pretty in a picturesque Tuscan square, lounging on a Costa Blanca beach or swimming off the Algarve. Well, almost. One chilly evening I sat down to spend an hour of TV escapism with a hopeful couple as they were shown by a presenter a collection of damp cottages in a windy outpost of northern England, keeping alive for the show the possibility that they might yet opt for rainy skies in preference to that 'place in the sun' they really longed for. Meanwhile another radiant, perma-tanned presen-ter was stood waiting for them under a blue sky in a lavender field in Provence, extolling the virtues to health and well-being of living in a climate boasting 300 days-a-year of sunshine. By the end of the show the smiling retirees were jubilant after plumping for a life in the ebullient climes of the South of France over the draughtier charms of an English moorland location. For the time being, shelling-out for my very own place in the Spanish or French sun was a pipedream. But a few brief clicks later, I had done what I considered the next best thing by booking a series of one-way train journeys to take me through Paris, Lyon and then towards the blue skies of Provence, along the Côte d'Azur from Nice to Marseille, before ending my sojourn in the Languedoc-Roussillon capital of Montpellier. Momentum was everything, and after a few online minutes in the company of *Société nationale des chemins de fer français* – the French National Railway, SNCF – I was all set to flee the grey skies of home and follow the adventurous TV couple on their impressive Gallic odyssey.

Sunlight, however, would keep me waiting. In fact, the sky hanging over Paris as I left my Eurostar train at Gare de Nord was more leaden than the one I had left behind at London St Pancras. 'La Ville Lumiére' – The City of Light – was evidently having a day off, prompting a little doubt on the matter of its claims to luminosity. Just as the inclement city of Sunderland has its 'Stadium of Light', so I wondered how a city as far north and as distant from the sea as Paris could be deemed a 'city of light'. Surely Valencia, Cádiz or Palermo would be more deserving candidates for such a moniker. Paris's light association has of course little to do with meteorology, but far more with the Age of Enlightenment in which the city played a leading role. More prosaically, the shining reputation of the French capital is also down to its pioneering role in the installation of gas lighting, when in 1820 the city's previously gloomy streets were illuminated in an attempt to reduce worryingly high levels of crime. The labyrinthine SNCF timetable didn't allow time for a Parisian stopover – I had barely enough time to cross the city by métro from Gare de Nord, let alone be let loose on the sights. But the Gare de Lyon was an impressive attraction in itself, this grand old terminus built originally for the 1900 World Exposition boasting a striking (in more ways than one) clock tower that looked suspiciously to me like a maladroit copy of London's Big Ben.

The bonus of my short métro trip across town was the opportunity to get reacquainted with a unique and pungent aspect of Parisian life – the peculiar sweet smell that wafts through the tunnels under the city's teeming streets, as characteristic of the city as the Eiffel Tower or the Louvre. Blighted by the mixed odours of sewage, sweat – and before the smoking ban, Gauloises and Gitanes – over time the Paris Métro lost popularity on the understandable grounds that *ça pue!* (it stinks). In an early 1990s response, the city transport authorities commissioned a leading French perfumery to come up with a suitable fragrance to obliterate the pong. The original product put into service to tackle the problem was called *Francine* – a mint, lavender and eucalyptus concoction that was soon withdrawn after offending the nostrils of a deluge of complaining Parisians. Its sweet-smelling successor was *Madeleine*, the winning entry of 500 to a competition ran by métro authorities to select a suitable alternative. Rather beautifully its name is taken from Madeleine, a métro station notorious for its particularly nasty niffs. Consisting supposedly of the aromas of oranges, lemons and lavender mixed with chemical cleaning agents, the heady

Madeleine blend is used daily to cleanse the platforms, corridors and stairwells of the system's 300 stations. As I changed lines at Bastille, I wasn't entirely convinced that the scented experiment had worked. There was no doubting the aroma of fragrant disinfectant hanging in the air like an overpowering toilet cleaner, but it couldn't detract from the reassuring, overriding waft of a Parisian sewer. Recently the London and Berlin transport authorities have looked to Paris for a lead on tackling the odour issues blighting the subterranean platforms and stairwells of their own underground systems. But surely, sometimes in life things are best left just as they are.

I grabbed a take-away from the elegant *Le Train Bleu,* Gare de Lyon's buffet restaurant, experiencing the unique thrill that comes from taking breakfast in London and lunch in Paris on the same day. I paid the perfectly-attired *garçon* a surprisingly modest sum for a lavishly-filled crusty baguette, inviting an unfavourable image to flash through my mind of *Le Train Bleu's* less illustrious catering cousin at Crewe – another fine historic railway station I had passed through recently, but one seemingly incapable of serving up for the peckish traveller a cheese and tomato sandwich that doesn't look and taste as if it has been through a washing machine. I took my seat on the upper deck of the Duplex *Train à Grande Vitesse* – a high speed TGV – opposite an elderly and rather lugubrious couple who spent the early stages of the journey south towards Lyon unwrapping boiled eggs from white handkerchiefs, then demolishing them in a manner so anti-social that had the train not been so crowded, I would have moved along the carriage and changed seats. The eggy

atmosphere was no deterrent to a prepossessing chocolate Labrador puppy called Bruno though, who emerged
from under his owner's seat to steal the hearts of the
train with his beguilingly floppy ears and winning glint
in his eye. An uncomplicated creature whose dual purposes in life seemed to be sleep and the pursuit of food,
Bruno earned a dinner's-worth of tit-bits from the carriage – only the boiled eggs met his disapproval. Sitting
on the upper deck of the immaculate Duplex train as
it raced through the southern *banlieues* of Paris (those
insalubrious districts largely populated by disadvantaged immigrant communities, sometimes featured on
the TV news showing burning cars during periods
of civil unrest), and then on through the Burgundy
vineyards felt a little like flying, without of course all of
flying's mountain of drawbacks. So in what seemed
like no time at all I arrived at Lyon's Part-Dieu station,
where I stood disoriented for a while at its front entrance
in the centre of a bleak and windswept public square,
before following my nose towards the 2nd arrondissement hotel I had booked into on the touristy city
peninsula of Presqu'île.

I had just over twenty-four hours in Lyon en route
to the sunny deep-south, so after a quick check-in
I headed for the one outstanding Lyon attraction I was
set on seeing: the quirk of the city's *Les Traboules*. A
mazy network of three hundred dimly-lit (or in some
cases not lit at all) passageways that wind their way
between the city's oldest streets through apartment
blocks and into hidden courtyards, *Les Traboules* really
are an historical oddity. The earliest Lyon traboules
were built as far back as the fourth-century to allow
quick access from crowded areas of poor housing to the

nearest source of water on the banks of the River Saône. Most of the mysterious pedestrian thoroughfares accessible to today's visitors to the city are the much later traboules built for silk weavers and other craftsmen as a means of moving their valuable wares swiftly around the city in wet weather, doubling up as short cuts to the river through the densely housed streets. The traboules later took on an intriguing role as clandestine routes for French Resistance fighters during the Nazi occupation of the city between 1940 and 1944, helping to make control of the older parts of Lyon as awkward as possible for the German administration.

And there was every reason for Lyon to be a determined cradle of resistance. During the German occupation at least 4,000 *Lyonnais* were killed, with another 7,500 deported to Nazi death camps under the orders of the city's least favourite former resident, the infamous Gestapo chief Nickolaus 'Klaus' Barbie. Specialising in sadism, among Barbie's most infamous acts in Lyon was the torture of a prominent resistance leader who was beaten and skinned alive before having his head submerged in a bucket of ammonia acid. Unsurprisingly, the wretched man died soon afterwards. Shocking stuff maybe, but all in a day's work for Barbie. So it is no great surprise to learn that the man was also personally responsible for the 1944 deportation of over forty Jewish children to Auschwitz from an orphanage close to Lyon. As for the role of the traboules during this violent period of Lyon's history, it is impossible to say how many souls were saved from torture at the hands of the 'Butcher of Lyon' by the city's intricate network of hidden back alleys and passageways. It can only be hoped it was many.

Immediately after the war Barbie escaped the noose by his recruitment into the U.S. Army Counter Intelligence Corps (CIC), with a brief to aid its anti-communist activities in Europe. Eventually the CIC helped Barbie flee the French death sentence placed on his head by ensuring his safe passage to Bolivia. The American intelligence services continued to make use of Barbie, most notoriously in 1967 when he allegedly supported the CIA in its capture of Cuban Revolution champion Che Guevera as he set about overthrowing the Bolivian government and install a communist replacement. Possibly thinking he had got away with his wartime barbarism after four decades of U.S.-aided scot-free living in South America, events finally caught up with Barbie in 1983 when he was extradited from Bolivia, tried for crimes against humanity and sentenced to life imprisonment. Barbie died in custody in Lyon three years later in a warm and comfortable bed aged 77, having shown not a shred of remorse throughout his trial.

I picked up some handy traboule tips from the tourist office on the breezy expanse of Place Bellecour before setting out on the trail in the city's oldest quarter, Vieux Lyon. Following closely my 'traboule map' I began by pushing an intercom button to enter the traboule at 54 Rue Saint-Jean and passed through a long dank tunnel linking it with house number 27 of the parallel Rue du Boeuf. Facilitating undetectable movements like this around the old city, how smart a tool of resistance and espionage these alleyways must have been during the wartime occupation, helping to keep the local police, the army and the dreaded Gestapo at bay. Disappointingly for the curious modern visitor, amid safety and maintenance concerns many of the oldest of the Vieux Lyon traboules are now filled in or used only as storage facilities. Fortunately though, the architectural jewel in the traboule crown remains accessible. So to seek out the elegant *Tour Rose* – Pink Tower – I walked through an arched wooden door at 22 Rue de Boeuf that led me towards the tower along a typically dark, cramped passageway. Built in warm pinkish stone, the *Tour Rose* was intended initially as a sort of multistorey traboule to convey the residents from floor to floor of what was once an adjoining apartment block. The ensemble of sixteenth and seventeenth-century housing and its emblematic pink tower has in recent years been opportunistically converted into a boutique hotel and quirky Michelin-starred restaurant of the same name, creating a must-do dining experience for foodies visiting the city.

As far as I could tell, residents of the historic quarter of Lyon have a pretty high level of tolerance for the constant traffic of nosey tourists intruding on their very public pedestrianised byways. The cooperation of the traboule community is largely down to money. As a payback for agreeing to keep their traboules open to the public each day between 8.00am and 7.00pm, residents enjoy the benefits of low rents in their attractively located old town apartments. For their part, visitors are expected to keep their snooping as unobtrusive as possible. Try as I might to maintain a suitable decorum as I crept stealthily around the traboules, I couldn't help getting a little carried away by the novelty of it all, and on one occasion overstepped the mark. The longer I spent walking the cobbled alleys of Vieux Lyon, the more apparent it became that quite apart from those that were marked on my map, dozens of the wooden doors built into the little houses led into traboules. In one particularly dank back-alley I investigated off Rue St-Jean, I came across an anonymous-looking unmarked door that I hoped might open into a separate, little known passageway allowing me to emerge triumphantly through a similarly anonymous door on Rue du Boeuf. Such adventure! Anyway, whatever lay behind the door, it looked ripe for some firm pushing. As planned the door swung open assuredly as I leaned against it, but revealed not some long-forgotten medieval rat-run, but a plump lady in a pinny rolling out pastry at a large wooden table. I turned the colour of the nearby *Tour Rose* as I realised that I had inadvertently stumbled through the door of a private residence and into someone's kitchen. For a second, the woman held out the rolling pin she was using to create her French culinary masterpiece as if to strike me with it. But as I spluttered my apologies and turned to run, the jovial *ménagère* beamed a huge rosy-cheeked smile and offered a sympathetic wink as if to say, '*ne vous inquiétez pas*' – don't worry m'dear, you're the third camera-wielding idiot I've had through the door today already.

I was so wrapped up in pushing open doors and scrambling through narrow passageways, that in the time I had in Lyon I saw little else beyond its thoroughly engaging network of traboules. That is apart from climbing to the summit of Fourvière – the site of the Roman city of Lugdunum, crowned since 1884 by the over-iced wedding cake of the Basilique de Fourvière. The panoramic views from the basilica were superb (far better than the views of the building itself) – down the slope towards the Presqu'île peninsular, across to the confluence of the Rivers Saône and Rhône and further still to the distant commercial centre and the rather brutal, modern focal point of the Crédit Lyonnais tower. The gaudy basilica didn't look to me much like a building meant to be taken too seriously. In fact, its four towers stick up into the air with such inelegance they have earned the building the unflattering local nickname of 'the upside-down elephant'. Yet despite its clumsy appearance, somehow the basilica has become the symbol of modern Lyon – the city's resident Dumbo of a thousand postcards.

Britain hasn't been at war with France, its nearest continental neighbour, since the Napoleonic period – unless of course you count 'Operation Catapult', the Royal Navy's contentious bombardment of the French fleet in July 1940 at what was then the French Algerian port of Mers-el-Kebir. Amid fears of an imminent invasion, the British government could not risk Hitler getting his hands on added naval power following France's armistice with Germany, so took the unorthodox step of attacking her ally – albeit an ally now collaborating with the occupation through the pro-Nazi French government administered from the Auvergne town of Vichy under Marshal Philippe Pétain. Given that this violent episode led to the deaths of 1,300 sailors, if you are French you might well wish to count it as an act of war. Nevertheless, a non-belligerent Brit like me can these days expect a decently warm welcome when he crosses the narrow channel of water that separates the erstwhile sparring partners. Perhaps my lack of inclination thus far for visiting France had been down to it being located just a little too close to home to rate as a genuine travel adventure. But then again, the enormity of France makes its most southerly regions of

Languedoc-Roussillon and Midi-Pyrénées a considerably longer trek than other parts of western Europe that I often return to.

Whatever the reason, it was high time to plug those Gallic gaps, and so to keep up the southerly momentum I jumped back on a TGV service, this time on a direct route *du soleil*. A quick dash south from Lyon through Avignon, Toulon and Cannes brought me to the Riviera capital, Nice, where I hoped to be in time for some sunny afternoon mingling among the monied – a perfect antidote in fact to David Kynaston's *Austerity Britain*, which I trawled through en route. In the event, on arrival in Nice there wasn't so much as a whiff of the moolah as I checked-in to my modest digs on a litter-strewn side street behind the Gare de Nice-Ville. After dumping my bag (it was *that* sort of hotel), I walked down Avenue Jean Médecin and away from the grime of the station area towards the Mediterranean in the hope of finding the essence of *Nissa la Bella* ('Nice the Beautiful' from the local Occitan language). Sitting in consultation with my map next to a small palm tree close to the steps of the mid-nineteenth-century Neo-Gothic Basilique Notre-Dame de Nice, I was alerted to a powerful odour that would get nostrils curling even on the Paris Métro. Evidently still someway short of encountering the full-on niceties of Nice, I looked around with surprise to find the offending whiff emanating from an open-air toilet improvised in close proximity to the east front entrance of the church, directly below the vibrantly decorative rose window. So much for any lingering notion of Nice being the exclusive preserve of the prim and proper. Thank goodness, here was a city for real.

Having tickled the Nice underbelly I pressed on, at last finding signs of the unrestrained opulence the city is synonymous with on the celebrated Promenade des Anglais – a slick parade laid out in front of Nice's surprisingly un-sandy beach by wealthy, nineteenth-century aristocratic sun-seekers from England. Enjoying their ritual jaunt on the Côte d'Azur to avoid the worst of the English weather, we can thank those privileged few for introducing to the English language that most resonant of travel verbs – 'to winter'. However, I doubt that many of those *haut monde* – who could count among them in the immediate pre-war years the transient Duke and Duchess of Windsor – would approve of the wide strip of stationary traffic their former playground and favourite spot for a pre-dinner stroll has become today. Yet as I stood outside the eccentric exterior of the promenade's famous Hôtel Negresco (a building looking for all the world like Veruca Salt's birthday cake topped lavishly with pink icing), I guessed that little had changed in this part of town in the 'I Want it Now' stakes since that Edwardian heyday of warm-wintering. Hardly dressed for the occasion myself in a ragged tie-dye t-shirt and jeans both some way past their own heydays, I more than likely cut an incongruous figure as I stood just inside the hotel under the huge glass dome of the ostentatious Royal Lounge. A jazz quartet was warming up in the corner in preparation for some cocktail-soaked extravaganza to which I wasn't invited. Feeling decidedly out of place as a result, I walked through to the hotel's walnut wood and tapestry-clad Le Relais bar. With its distinct air of raffishness, this could have made an inviting spot to take refreshment had it not been for the comedy bar prices and the discernible sneer of the waiter implying my money would be better squandered elsewhere.

As is the wont of the budget-restrained visitor in this city of gross monetary disparity, I made the short promenade to Vieux Nice, relieved to find there among the designer chic and smart restaurants an air of pronounced shabbiness in the recesses of its warren of tiny streets. After some fairly aimless wandering – an enjoyable pursuit I was fast becoming a dab hand at – I pitched up under a striped parasol on a café terrace on Place Rossetti, trying to make the best of my obscured view of the long-winded Basilique-Cathédrale Sainte-Marie et Sainte-Réparate. While I agonised over the lengthy dessert menu, it occurred to me that one knock-on-effect of abandoning the previous order of my nine-to-five lifestyle had been a marked lapse in food discipline. I would still eat starters (in places I could afford to, so not too often in Nice), main courses and desserts, but no longer necessarily in that order. So once I was done with my main course *crème glacée sundae*, I wandered through the Cours Saleya market square and past the Italianate former home of Henri Matisse on Place Charles-Félix. My destination was an enthusiastically-reviewed Turkish caféteria on Rue du Marché, where I ate a decidedly un-French plateful of moussaka, which worked perfectly well as a dessert. Or perhaps it was a starter. Perhaps I no longer really cared.

Like much of Nice, the lively Avenue Jean Médecin was full of surprises. I didn't stop at the al-fresco lavatory to check if it was still being put to good use, but noticed that by night the area had transformed into a thriving red-light district. And wouldn't you know it, the closer I got to my digs the seamier and thus more intriguing the scene became. As I walked along Rue d'Alsace-Lorraine towards the hotel, wondering if I might have booked into the sort of establishment that offers the option of hiring its rooms by the hour, I was approached by two individuals of unwholesome appearance – an unfair assessment to make, I admit, in such a dim light. With less in my pocket than the price of a Daiquiri cocktail in the bar of the Hôtel Negresco, I was tempted to launch a pre-emptive strike by announcing that I wasn't worth the effort of mugging, adding that I wouldn't be interested either in any type of proposition involving violence, legal or illegal highs, or indeed any kind of exchange of DNA. As it turned out, their interest in me lay only in their guess that I was *Anglais*, and so would naturally be on for a chat about football. A few minutes after a rushed appraisal of the prospects for the coming season of the Sky TV 'Big Four' (about which I cared little), I was back in my hotel room with mixed feelings of relief and disappointment that all I had been confronted with on my nocturnal walk through the back streets of old Nice, were questions about the money-soaked state of my country's national game.

The following day, after a night spent with my head on a concrete hotel pillow, I made my way back towards the Mediterranean and the Quai des États-Unis – a wide and sunny promenade named in gratitude for President Woodrow Wilson's game-changing decision in April 1917 to enter World War One. I rounded a headland to meet the colossal Monument aux Morts, Nice's outstanding war memorial carved thirty-two metres high into an outcrop of rock to mark the city's dead of two world wars, as well as the sacrifice of its wartime resistance fighters. Unmissable from the approach road to

Nice from the east, I was surprised to find myself alone at the memorial. In fact, I had been studying its multitude of intricate carvings and inscriptions for almost an hour before I was joined by other sightseers. Even then the young Japanese couple – cheek-to-cheek under a tiny polka-dotted brolly to protect them from the fierce sun – couldn't be bothered to cross the busy road to get a closer look, choosing instead to admire the memorial through an extraordinarily long camera lens. I left the shrine to take the scenic stairway that climbs a sheer cliff in an inviting zigzag up to the Parc du Châteaux – the best vantage point for that famed postcard view of the Baie des Anges. After a much needed half-hour rest sprawled in the shade of the park, I followed an alternative set of steps back down to sea level and walked eastwards around the bay to take a look at the lines of expensive yachts moored exclusively in the Bassin des Amiraux harbour. I inhaled deeply, partly to benefit from the sea air, but also to sample the scent of money that hangs over much of Nice. Looking closely at the shining collection of cruisers in front of me bobbing in the water of this particularly gilded corner of the Côte d'Azur, that scent of wealth had suddenly become a heady, quite overpowering stench.

Like in many other wealthy enclaves of Europe, much of the new money doing the rounds of the South of France has been exchanged from the rouble. In fact, the new generation of Russian billionaires currently soaking up the sun along the Côte d'Azur, certainly know a thing or two about flinging their money around. In a recent prime example, one particularly deep-pocketed Russian speculator – the owner of a substantial property in the nearby resort of Beaulieu-sur-Mer – was apparently aggrieved by the intrusion on his expensive comfort of local train noise. In a response that possibly demonstrates the man's understanding of the price of everything but the value of very little, he sent a sheepish representative to lobby the local authorities to *move the railway line* out of earshot of his property. His offer, which I am happy to report was rejected out of hand, was to finance the relocation of the line from his personal contribution of €100 million. In another warning of the inherent dangers to the soul of having just a little too much money, an oligarch owner of a well-known villa in Sant-Jean-Cap-Ferrat had improvement works of his own in mind. Deciding one day to increase further the already considerable square-footage of his property, he submitted plans to raise the building's height. His money-no-object plans were dismissed – and let's hope derided too – by the local planning committee on the grounds that no structure in the area was allowed to exceed the height of the local highly prized Napoleonic lighthouse. Unable to respect the integrity of this decision and the preservation reasons behind it, as the rouble signs flashed before him the monied resident offered to put up a further sum of €15 million to fund a baffling plan to simultaneously raise the height of the lighthouse, thus avoiding any inconvenient planning infringement – and while he was at it telling us all we need to know about his character. The committee remained gloriously unmoved, and the town lighthouse continues to stand proudly above all else around it.

Once I lost interest in the floating ostentation of the Bassin des Amiraux (this did not take long), I made my way towards the more earthy attractions of the area north of Place Masséna. I waited several minutes to cross the wide boulevard of Avenue Félix Faure, watching the gleaming Ferrari and Lamborghini playthings of the sons of local oligarchs pass by among the heavy traffic. Of all the places I had visited recently, none could match Nice for such blatant disparity of haves and have-nots. Only steps away from the monied hotel lobbies of the Promenade des Anglais and the billionaire yachts of the Bassin des Amiraux, exists an underclass reduced to open air sanitation on the steps of a church. According to the slogan of a well-known homeless charity – and here is a sobering thought – *'all of us are but two bad decisions away from a life on the pavement'*. In fact, when you stop to think about it, many of life's impulsive everyday decisions could be deemed 'bad', particularly if they set off an unlucky chain of events leading eventually to al fresco bathrooming. The possibilities for this seem endless. There's always the easy oversight of failing to include a pre-nup when planning to tie-the-knot with a money-grubbing partner. Not to mention the understandable folly of stomping out of a fraught team meeting dismayed by an infuriating agenda, leading to resignation from a promising career and complete loss of income. In the most luckless of circumstances, this could end up proving to be a ruinously 'bad' decision. Then there's that oligarch's investment of sheer avarice to increase the height of a lighthouse although in his case, even if the deal had gone through but then somehow gone horribly wrong, I doubt he would then have been on the wrong end of a snarling letter from a bailiff. As for old friends Candy and Cooper, the two fellow 'career absconders' I had bumped into in Granada and Dubrovnik respectively, as I considered the perils of penury, I began to wonder what might now have become of them.

Having recently exited the comfort zone of paid employment, perhaps I was only one or two bad decisions shy of financial meltdown myself. But I felt no such anxiety as I sat cross-legged among a group of chatty Erasmus students on the chequer-board surface of Nice's elegant Place Masséna, enjoying the spectacle of the square's seven illuminated Buddha-like resin statues sitting atop tall poles – the colourful signature work of Catalan artist, Jaume Plensa. As the light faded, I watched as the seven figures calmly changed colour from pale blue to orange and green to violet. Each of the figures, I was assured by a similarly crossed-leg onlooker from Turin, represents one of the seven continents engaged in a peaceful, creative discourse with another. Goodness knows how much this flashy, rather idealistic installation had cost the taxpayers of Nice. Perhaps the artist had been commissioned by a local Russian billionaire from his harbour yacht. But even if the steps of a cathedral were doubling up as a public convenience only metres away, as my last tourist sighting in Nice this unique and vibrant attraction felt a whole lot more meaningful than any fairytale hotel or collection of billionaires' yachts.

In search of a gritty contrast to Nice within a short travelling distance, I set off the following day on a scenic Côte d'Azur TGV service to Marseille through Antibes, Cannes and Toulon. Arriving at Marseille's Gare St-Charles terminus was a surprisingly verdant experience. I left the train astonished to find myself walking through a wooded area of trees in full leaf on the gleaming station concourse, flourishing only a few feet away from the usual station paraphernalia of newspaper stands, cafés and Tie Rack kiosks. This was certainly an appealing distraction from the less welcoming group of heavily armed *Gendarmerie* watching my every move as I made swiftly for the exit. And so onwards to my hotel. Now, I have stayed in some gems that would test the resolve of the most hardened traveller: the pensión in Ronda devoid of a flushing WC, the itinerant guest house in downtown San Francisco where pushing furniture against the back of the unlockable door was the only night-time security option, and that little wooden shack-come-hotel in New Orleans that looked so cute in the photographs, but was actually the violent epicentre of a theatre of war for local drugs gangs. At this last place, leaving and arriving could only be done safely by taxi – a tiresome and expensive blight on the trip. So the apocalyptic reviews I had read of my chosen and quite probably soon-to-be-out-of-business, *pied-à-terre* in Marseille fazed me not a jot. In fact, one early advantage of the hotel of which I dare not speak its name – let's just call it *Hotel Quelle Surprise* and leave it at that – was its ease of location directly opposite the station above a dingy bar on Boulevard Charles Nédelec. Notwithstanding its many and very considerable drawbacks, the establishment was marginally redeemed by the Gallic charm of its receptionist Étienne, who in all fairness made a pretty good fist of being the jovial public-face of what might well rank as one of France's worst hotels. At any rate, I have yet to stay in one worse.

With a knowing wink and beaming smile, Étienne handed me the key to my room, directing me back out to the street and through a side door leading to an unlit communal stairwell littered with the detritus of recent drug use. Not a great start it has to be said, with the sight of a used needle setting off an exceedingly loud alarm bell about the possibly damaging effects to my well-being of spending forty-eight hours of my life in such a place. Yet hope always springs eternal, and there was still time for redemption in the form of a luxuriant bed with a featherdown duvet perhaps, or a deep tub in an en suite bathroom with brass taps yielding lashings of piping hot water, made fragrant and foamy by complimentary toiletries of the quality worth slipping into your suitcase. I opened my door to find that yes, I did indeed have my own en suite facilities, but in an open plan arrangement that I had never before experienced. To my great and lasting surprise, not to mention dismay, the entire bathroom was unpartitioned from the room, with the toilet plumbed-in somewhat unappealingly next to the headboard of the bed, a few inches from where I might later, if I got really lucky, sleep. I decided long ago not to bother writing bad hotel reviews. Unless I was punched in the face by a receptionist for requesting a room change or deliberately poisoned by a breakfast chef, then I consider life to be way too short to be putting livelihoods at risk. Anyway, I was in Marseille to enjoy the city for what it was and the fact that the hotel I had chosen would work perfectly well as the set for any remake of *Midnight Express,* was neither here nor there. *Hotel Quelle Surprise* was unutterably dreadful, but I reasoned that if I could cope with an open-plan office (although in truth, I hardly could), an open-plan lavatory arrangement would be a breeze.

Happy anyway just to be in this live-wire, sun-drenched seaside metropolis, I made a beeline towards the Vieux Port area, walking south to the *La Marseillaise* monument at Place Jules-Guesde. The square is best known as the place where the jaunty French national anthem was born, and also as the starting point in 1792 of the march of revolutionaries who, legend has it, hummed, sang and whistled the *Hymn of the Army of the Rhine* all the way up to Paris. Proving to be a popular tune with the comrades in arms, the hymn was renamed *La Marseillaise* en route. For a few moments as I stood near the monument, I even had a go at humming the tune myself. To begin with I just couldn't get the melody into my head, so as I do now when I feel the need to show some comradeship with the French, I thought instead of the opening bars of *All You Need Is Love,* the Beatles' rousing anthem to a 1967 doped-up world as they set out on their own '*Magical Mystery Tour'*. Try it for yourself – it always works.

In recent years France's second largest city has under-gone quite a renaissance, culminating in its stint as European Capital of Culture in 2013. Incidentally, it now seems that almost every sizeable continental city has had its turn at this – quite soon, as the organisers run out of cities, to have *not* at some point been Capital of Culture, or at least been a contender, will be a badge of dishonour. Anyway, the gleaming new tram that wooshed past me on Rue de la République was the first evidence I saw of this gigantic clean-up act in Marseille, ringing its bell with an upbeat tone that momentarily took me back to the shining tramlines of another great sun-kissed city of the south, Seville. I eventually hit Vieux Port, the focal point of Marseille from which its fifteen *arrondissements* radiate. I sat for a while on the sun-drenched terrace of a small café on Quai des Belges, close to the seventeenth-century Hôtel de Ville. If I had been searching here for a defining substitute for Nice's scent of money, Marseille delivered with its own signature whiff of seafood, right at that moment rising pungently from huge crates of wriggling, freshly caught fish piled high and wide around the thriving harbour market.

Keen to see the city's oldest *arrondissement*, I moved on to Le Panier. Sitting just to the north of the port, this ancient area of steep stone staircases linking narrow lanes and tiny squares is nowadays home to an enticing collection of artsy cafés, smart studios and gift shops. Yet despite their cuteness and present day tourist charms, those same quaint alleyways were once the scene of danger and despair. With Marseille under Nazi occupation, Le Panier became an unofficial 'ghetto' and dumping ground for those considered by the occupiers to be *untermenschen* – a predictable roll call of Jews, communists, resistance fighters and others of a liberal bent or otherwise non-Aryan disposition. Not surprisingly, the Nazis considered Le Panier to be a hive of resistance, partly due to the layout of its narrow streets and alleyways aiding clandestine activities. In January 1943, the wretched 30,000 ghetto residents were given a mere twenty-four hours of notice to leave the area – to go goodness knows where. Predictably, many of them ended up being deported east to the death camps, with the added stain on this Marseille history being the co-operation of the local French police with the Nazis during the roundups. Not content with destroying the human community, in a further act of unfathomable spite the occupiers blew to oblivion great swathes of Le Panier's medieval streetscape, as well as many less impressive residential tenement blocks rendered obsolete by the liquidation of the ghetto. Fortunately, the destructive urges of the Nazis stopped short of bringing down the Roman-Byzantine Cathédrale de la Major, which I approached as I left Le Panier by way of one of the area's remaining steep narrow streets that tumble down so invitingly towards the old port.

I continued my walking tour of Marseille along its historic high street, La Canabière. When I turned off the busy thoroughfare at the Noailles Métro station, I found by a lucky accident the bohemian quarter of Cours Julien – an area that immediately put me in mind of Barcelona's scuzzy district of Gracia and any number of public spaces in Naples. In the heat of the mid-afternoon, groups of grungy, heavily-tattooed locals with braided hair lounged on randomly scattered deck-chairs and bean-bags, drinking from bottles of super-market plonk as their kids and dogs ran amok around them. Pleasantly at ease in this laid-back corner of the city – and very much inclined to put off for as long as possible returning to the hotel – I made the area my base for the remainder of the day. To escape the excesses of the heat, I sat on the rammed, shady terrace of a café where I picked up a menu so much influenced by fresh vegetables, garlic, tomatoes and olive oil, I could have been back in Italy. So I ate a Venetian salad, not minding at all in this most laid back of locations that the waitress completely overlooked my request to leave out of the preparation my old culinary nemesis the hard-boiled egg, an accoutrement to any dish that I tend to avoid at all cost. Several hours later, I was still rooted in that same spot, the uneaten egg long since cleared away, the book I was reading all but finished and me staring in the face the approaching reality of returning to *that* hotel.

All too soon I was back at the gates of hell. As I made a cautious approach to the reception desk to pick up my room key, a respectable-looking German couple were mid-argument with the ever-sanguine Étienne about the lack of hot water from their shower. When I had checked my own shower earlier, it had deigned to work enabling me to cling all day to the consolatory thought that if all else failed, I might at least be able to spend some quality time standing under a jet of warm cleanish water, well out of range of the open toilet arrangement. Predictably, my raised hopes for the room were dashed by two sleep-depriving obstacles. The first was the WC that was not only positioned inches from my face, but dripped continuously. The second was the persistent buzzing around my ears of the room's infestation of mosquitoes basking in the room's hot foetid air, each one of them determined to make the most of the blood-sucking opportunities presented by my prostrate body. I got up several times (this had to be done in one ungainly movement of leaving the bed and vaulting the toilet), in a hopelessly vain attempt to obliterate the infuriating swarm of critters. Under the mean glow of the naked bulb, I was alerted to an array of bloody smears adorning the walls – the dried-up remains of generations of mosquitoes vanquished in previous battles that had doubtless been played out in the decrepit theatre of the room. The degradation pervading my surroundings put me in mind of that chilling scene from *The Silence of the Lambs*, where the young woman imprisoned at the bottom of a well by serial-killer Buffalo Bill is shown looking in terror at the ripped-off fingernails of his victims, who had tried but failed to escape before her. Back to my own rather smaller

Marseille trauma, after a desperate chase around the bed I managed to splatter one of the bloated pests against the wall with a yellowing, year-old copy of *Le Monde* I found discarded behind the toilet waste pipe. I stood back to check on the bloody aftermath staining the wall, my rather shameful triumph at slaying the little beast tempered by the appalling thought that the freshly drawn blood in the dead creature that now decorated the wall like an exhibit of wayward modern art, was more than likely my own.

I had spent years of my working life helping others devise 'action plans' to improve their lives and prospects. Hardly ever had I felt in such dire need of a plan of my own as I did at that moment. A few short steps across the road from 'Mosquito Towers' lay an alternative I had spotted earlier with raw envy – an attractive, fit for habitation (and doubtless far more expensive) chain hotel. What the new hotel lacked in character (which was a fair bit) and used syringes (totally), it more than made up for in my room's bug-free king size memory foam mattress (incidentally a NASA invention from the 1960s that has done more for the night-time comfort of humanity than pretty much anything), a WC area elegantly (and conventionally) concealed behind a bathroom partition wall and an extravagant stock of complimentary toiletries. As for the infested dive I had just left behind, I wasn't about to write the damning review it deserved, partly because I couldn't help but like Étienne and guessed that the dire condition of the place had little to do with him. I just wish he would take the trouble one day to don a pair of protective gloves, get hold of a strong bin liner, and then dispose for good of the used syringes. His business really could survive without them.

I spent much of my final day in Marseille visiting the Neo-Byzantine Basilica, Notre Dame de la Garde – a landmark that dominates the city from its lofty position on a hill south of the Vieux Port. I reached the summit by walking the steep incline of Boulevard Notre Dame, an incline so steep it reminded me of the hands-and-knees technique I once deployed to reach the top-end of San Francisco's vertiginous Filbert Street. Like its Lyon counterpart I had visited a week or so before, it's fair to say that Marseille's Catholic Basilica isn't the prettiest of buildings. With its monumental crowning glory of a golden virgin astride the bell tower glowing in the sunlight like the tip of a lighthouse, the overall effect is a touch gauche. Yet since the basilica's consecration in 1864, the glowing virgin has also served the life-saving purpose of guiding generations of seafarers and their craft safely into the city's harbour. Inside the basilica, I skim-viewed an exhibition of kitsch paintings depicting a succession of shipwrecks that the golden virgin had evidently failed to prevent. I was far keener on the views from the summit, the highest point of Marseille that fifty-odd years ago I could have reached by a funicular railway.

Built in 1892 by Gustave Eiffel (of 'Tower' fame), at its peak the now disappeared funicular carried an impressive 15,000 daily passengers up the sheer cliff to the basilica. Despite remaining popular locally over its seventy-five year lifetime, thanks to the even greater popularity of the motor car the funicular became unprofitable and in 1967 met an ignominious end. Not content with mere closure of the historic line, the powers-that-be went for complete demolition. Nowadays, visitors not feeling up to the stiff climb under their own steam are offered the less-than thrilling option of a frivolous Disney-esque road train. By foot, funicular or novelty train, whichever way you reach the summit the reward of the view is immense – a magnificent sweep of Marseille's terracotta rooftops, a flotilla of miniature boats in the Vieux Port harbour and a great expanse of glistening Mediterranean sea stretching out to the horizon to meet a perfect afternoon sky. But my progress was relentless and it was time to move on once more. Enticing me a little further west was my next destination, the sophisticated Languedoc Roussillion capital, Montpellier.

Just shy of two hours from Marseille – most of which I spent looking out of the window for last glimpses of the Côte d'Azur from the picture window of my TGV train – I crossed the eastern Languedoc border and pulled into Gare de Montpellier-Saint-Roch. Clutching a rough back-of-a-beer-mat set of directions to the Abbéliss Polygone hotel, and unable to connect to any mobile map device, I was pointed in what turned out to be vaguely the right direction by a brusque taxi driver, whose interest in my progress receded considerably when I told him I preferred to walk. As it turned out, the walking route to the hotel was as interesting as it seemed unlikely, involving clambering back across the main railway line via a footbridge, before a risky dash across more platforms and tracks of the elevated Du Guesclin tram station. While not altogether the safest of routes for the disoriented visitor, it did at least offer a small sense of the intrepid, especially once I had managed to dislodge the wheels of my case from a tram line – a small mishap that occurred a little too close for comfort to a tram accelerating towards me. I returned to the safety of street level down an unstable wrought-iron spiral staircase taking me into an anonymous side street where I found my hotel – a touch dilapidated from the outside maybe, but not without a peeling southern charm. In the event, and just to prove that occasionally in life it is possible to get a fair bit more than you might think you have paid for, the Abbéliss Polygone turned out to be just about everything its budget counterpart in Marseille was not – despite providing me once again with digs sited very firmly on the wrong side of the station.

I arrived in Montpellier at the same moment some crisis or other was crashing into the beleaguered presidency of the wretched François Hollande. As I attempted to check-in, the hotel receptionist was distracted by the enormous TV screen behind her desk flashing images of the glum-faced president. Looking for all the world like a man in the wrong job, from what I could tell from his gloomy expression, Monsieur Hollande was either informing his news-hungry nation of his management of some or other national security crisis, or squirming his way through an explanation of what he was up to when photographed by the paparazzi on the back of a moped, rocking up at the Parisian apartment of a well-known actress half his age. Having quite recently been alerted to the very real risks to health and well-being of cheap French hotels, when I was finally given a key I was astonished to find that my room featured not only a conventional bathroom arrangement, but brightly painted walls without a trace of dried blood, two recently-made beds and a wall-mounted TV, enabling me to keep up to speed with any salacious goings-on 750 kilometres north at the Élysée Palace.

I had no prior knowledge of the Languedoc-Roussillon capital to speak of, and had done no real research before I arrived. So why was I here? Well, a friend of a friend had intrigued me with the revelation that she owned a house in nearby Aigues-Mortes, a location I had also seen featured recently on a blue-skied episode of one of those 'escape to the sun' TV shows. What's more, before consulting my dog-eared *Thomas Cook Rail Map of Europe*, I hadn't realised just how tantalisingly close to the Spanish border Montpellier actually sits. If recent experience has taught me anything, it is that you can never know when the urge to dash south in search of *la buena vida* might grab you. So if ever there was a city of open options, Montpellier was it. To find my bearings in this fortu-itously located city, I walked along the traffic-choked Rue Boussairolles to the main focal point at Place de la Comédie, a large oval-shaped public space known locally as 'l'Oeuf' (the egg), where I stood for a while to admire the ornate Opera Comédie. *Liberté, Egalité, Fraternité* proclaims the implacable slogan of the French Republic, carved boldly into the stone beneath the three great arched windows of Montpellier's most-photographed building. Brief homage to the nation done with, I contin-ued along the Haussmann-esque Rue Foch, the street that bears the name of the much revered figurehead of Second World War French Resistance, Jean Moulin, where he once lived at number 21. Interestingly, Moulin's resistance activities eventually took him to Lyon, where even the city's clandestine warren of traboules could not prevent him from falling into the unforgiving hands of the Gestapo tormentor, Klaus Barbie. Moulin died in July 1943 after a brutal period of interrogation by the 'Butcher of Lyon', his reputation as unchallenged hero of the struggle cemented by the widespread belief that he revealed not one resistance secret to his captor.

Mood-compatibly wandering Montpellier's elegant avenues, I came upon the city's very own Arc de Triomphe, standing quite splendidly on the edge of the gargantuan Place Royale du Peyrou. As I stood very tourist-like under the giant arch wrestling with my three-sheets-to-the-wind (literally) city map, I was approached by a young North African man with a distinct limp who introduced himself as David. Cheerful and charismatic, in faltering English David proceeded to detail the various physical and mental disabilities he told me had blighted his life since an orphaned childhood – disabilities he told me that had restricted his earnings potential and consigned him now to near destitution. Inevitably, David ended his story with a request for money. Although not entirely convinced by much of what he told me, I emptied my pocket of paltry change into his hand anyway, grateful to him for landing two-footed on my map to prevent it disappearing across the square in the stiff breeze. I was glad of course to still have use of the map, but given the nature of the ailments that David had just listed, I was a little surprised by the athleticism of the lunge that rescued it. I thought nothing more of this innocuous encounter until thirty or so minutes later. As I stood on the Promenade du Peyrou taking photographs of the eighteenth-century aqueduct (a small scale replica of its more authentic Roman counterpart, the nearby Pont du Gard), I looked down to see David trotting nimbly to join a line of people at a soup kitchen set up under the graceful sweep of the aqueduct's arches. Putting on a show of great *bonhomie* with his friends as he jostled in the hunger queue (and now minus the pronounced limp he had shown off only minutes before), David no longer seemed quite the sorry soul he had pretended earlier. As for me, I remained a sucker for a sob-story.

During the short time I was in Montpellier, I was struck by the large numbers of North African immigrants just like David in this smallish city of around 250,000 people. Hungry, begging, disaffected and gathered around on street corners in small and sometimes intimidating groups, this was Montpellier's firmly established underclass – a hard-up group of people desperate enough to fake disability for money. The city of Montpellier is in fact a microcosm of the often intractable problems facing *les sans domicile fixe* – homeless French immigrants – and also of the markedly low-levels of assimilation of minority groups in French society in general, who in the case of Montpellier gather in the district of Mosson – the city's very own *banlieue*. Some distance from the prosperous centre of Montpellier at the terminus of one of the city's tramlines, since 1962 this area has been an easy dumping ground for French nationals who fled Algeria after the war of independence. In an attempt to accommodate them all, the city built vast housing estates with a vision to create a harmonious and contented suburb, a heady optimism that has proved to be spectacularly misplaced. Nowadays Mosson is a virtual no-go zone, an overcrowded urban hell of semi-derelict apartment blocks, roaming dogs and precious little hope for the large numbers of firmly unassimilated North Africans who live there. For those few fortunates who do manage to escape the city's ghettos in a bid to forge a meaningful life and career, just having an ethnic-sounding name is enough of a barrier to real advancement. In a sad reality, in Montpellier and other French cities, doctors, lawyers and other highly trained professionals with immigrant backgrounds are often forced to change their names, simply because many French people will refuse to put their trust in them if they don't. Just having the name, let's say Mohammed, could on its own be well more than enough in Montpellier to bar you from meaningful employment. So here in this surface-beautiful city, you might arrive as a foreigner with every good intention of embracing the French way of life to the full. The problem is, with the fear of extremism so rife in France after its recent bloody encounters with terror, these days it simply isn't a country that is likely to go out of its way to love you back.

Happily, none of this detracts from Montpellier's other indisputable charms. By taking an entirely random route, I found my way to l'Écusson, a lovely old quarter of buildings of biscuit-coloured stone and tranquil squares. I sat for a while in the fragrant Place St-Pierre, surrounded by the contrasting sights of rose bushes in full bloom and groups of itinerant young men with their inevitable dogs in tow, having a very merry time strumming on beaten-up guitars, smoking fat roll-ups and drinking fiery-coloured liquids from plastic litre bottles. Ready for some sustenance of my own, I made my way through a warren of narrow streets into Place des Martyrs-de-la-Résistance, where I sat at a windy table to set about tackling an extraordinarily long baguette that offered the chewability of kitchen lino. Wondering if I might unknowingly be sporting a bright tattoo bearing the legend *'easily duped tourist'* on my forehead, I fielded the attentions of a succession of local storytellers who approached me with their inventive tales of woe and imaginative schemes to lighten my pocket. Never before in my life having felt so popular, I was asked to sign spurious petitions on behalf of disabled groups (while 'donating' €5 to the cause) in return for the reward of 'discount' vouchers for local Moroccan restaurants. Really taking the proverbial though was one young man on a getaway pushbike, who politely requested the 'loan' of my mobile phone to call 'a friend who had his house keys'. For once I was uncooperative, moving on instead to take a closer look at a more appealing feature of the Montpellier streetscape – the city's generously funded multi-coloured tram system.

Montpellier's tram network has approximately 282,000 daily journeys made on it, telling us something about the system's popularity in a city of just a quarter-of-a-million people. Opened in 2000, the colourful design-conscious labyrinth of four thematic tramlines that criss-cross the city is both innovative and eye-catching. Line 1 features cars presented in a tranquil blue design adorned with white swallows. The carriages of Line 2 are a canvas of extravagant floral blooms. Line 3 (my personal favourite) follows a watery maritime theme, while Line 4 comes in bold paintwork of gold and black. In clear and imminent danger of developing anorak tendencies since the day I turned my back on the confinement of 'the office', I stood for a while at the tram stop on Place de la Comédie, engrossed in watching the artistic carriages of Lines 1 and 2 slinking quietly and cleanly in and out of the platforms. I was joined in this utopia of transport-spotting by a lifelong aficionado (so he told me) of urban métro systems from north London called Kevin. We agreed that Montpellier's tram service was probably the most stylish public transport network that either of us had ever seen, and that our home city was all the poorer for not being in the process right now of building something exactly like it. So captivated was Kevin by his trams, it was to my great surprise when suddenly he announced that he was married and needed to be on his way to rescue both his wife and credit card from the chip and pin machines of the boutiques on Rue de la Loge, a pricey retail paradise I had swerved around earlier on my walk through the old city.

Once Kevin had gone and I was left with only trams for company (and in Montpellier you could do far worse), I hopped aboard one of the blue-sky-and-swallow creations of Line 1 which for the benefit of any reading transport buffs, with 120,000 daily journeys is the busiest tram line in France. I didn't know the city well enough to have a real destination in mind as I boarded my tram, but decided to get off at Antigone for no better reason than it having an appealing name lifted from Greek mythology (Antigone was the sister of Oedipus). After the smooth but disappointingly short journey, I left the tram to discover one of Montpellier's best but lesser visited attractions. Evidently skipped by other tourists and largely ignored by residents (Antigone was all but deserted when I arrived), this outstanding project of new town planning built between 1979 and 1994 is the work of Spanish architect, Ricardo Bofill. Beauty of course is always firmly in the discretionary eye of the beholder, but the word masterful sprang easily to mind as I looked down Antigone's west-east axis of landscaped public boulevards and squares, framed each side by imposing residential blocks. Named inauspiciously after a fifth-century Greek tragedy (none of it ended well), the Antigone project came about in response to Montpellier's rapid population growth and immigration spurt after 1962. Bofill's monumental buildings are made up of pre-fab panels, each one faced with a dominant veneer of classical details including plinths, friezes, balustrades and pediments. Surely no starker material contrast in Montpellier can exist than between Antigone – this architectural gem of classical influences in the east of the city – and Mosson, its far poorer neighbour of neglected tenements way out of the centre to the north-west.

As a visitor to Montpellier, it was easy to love Antigone. But I wasn't altogether surprised to learn from the hotel receptionist that its radical design has attracted as much criticism as it has plaudits. Much of the vitriol thrown the way of the ambitious project is based on a perception that it was conceived on an inhuman scale, and in turn for its grandiose architectural pretension. Some criticism has even gone as far as likening it to Nazi architect Albert Speer's megalomaniac 1930s plans for Berlin. That I could see, but as I stood wide-eyed at its strikingly uniform sweep of stone blocks, it was a slightly later politically-motivated Berlin building style that came to mind. Before I reached Antigone, I had spent the better part of the day exploring Montpellier's medieval warren of alleyways and byways, finding pretty squares of warm-coloured stone and traversing elegant Haussmann avenues. Quirky as I found much of Montpellier's oldest quarters to be, I was unprepared for a reminder in the same city of that great Soviet boulevard in Berlin – the mighty Karl-Marx-Allee. I stood in the cooling spray of Bofill's fountain in the centre of Place Zeus (the Greek allusions continue in Antigone throughout), and looked across the sunlit square at two giant granite-faced blocks. Or, just as easily I might have been facing the thundering water of the GDR fountain at Berlin's Strausberger Platz as I looked along Karl-Marx-Allee to the twin towers of Frankfurter Tor. I walked away from Antigone feeling like a first year architecture student might, tasked with writing up a comparative study of a modernist French social housing project and a monolith of the East German Politburo. Personally, I could barely separate the two.

The end of this French leg of my journey was fast approaching, but I had one last place to see. The following morning I caught a bus to the walled town of Aigues-Mortes (in Occitan meaning literally, 'deadwaters' – a reference in part to the town's long-standing lack of a supply of drinking water), located twenty kilometres south-east of Montpellier through the gentle Languedoc-Roussillon countryside. Architecturally at least, Aigues-Mortes was something to behold – every school-kid's fantasy of a secret magical little city hidden behind a forbidding wall of turrets and ramparts. Originally a fortress port (although the sea never actually reached the town, its trade activity taking place via a network of canals with sea access), Aigues-Mortes was built by Louis IX as a starting point for his aborted Egyptian crusade of 1270. Nowadays home to 8,000 people, this perfectly preserved citadel sits in the mysterious topography of a flat salt plain of the Petite Camargue, eight kilometres inland from the

Mediterranean in an area often shrouded in a low-lying, rather disquieting mist reminiscent of fenland.

Apart from the considerable presence of the town of Aigues-Mortes, the area is also notable for its rather lovely feature of Camargue horses, a small grey breed that have roamed wild and flourished in the harsh wetlands for hundreds of years. Although Aigues-Mortes itself has enjoyed a largely peaceful history, it has known belligerent times – most notably in August 1893 with the slaughter of nine Italians following an altercation with the local French authorities over access to the area's lucrative salt reserves. The incident caused such a ruction that it quickly became a source of diplomatic angst between France and Italy, even sparking anti-French riots in Italian cities and gifting Marseille-born playwright Serge Valletti some feisty material for his stage production of *Dirty August*. Yet once I was inside the cocoon of its austere walls, walking its small but perfectly formed grid of cobbled streets lined with colourful cottages, frilly cafés, *tabacs* and gift shops, unlike the bleak topography outside the walls, the town seemed wholly benign – less a dour mystery than a predictable honey pot of tourism. Self-evidently for an enclosed walled city, it is impossible to get lost in Aigues-Mortes, and all roads in the town lead to the focal point at Place Saint Louis, a spot besieged these days by souvenir-hungry tourists rather the salt-seeking adventurers of the past. I moved away from this commercial merry-go-round and left the citadel by the sternly fortified Queens Gate (the subject of a well-known 1867 painting by the impressionist Frédéric Bazille), to take a walk around the fortress's outer circumference. I peered up at the sheer face of the walls for a few moments then climbed onto the ramparts, close enough to take a butcher's into the backyards of houses adorned with parades of clothing hung out to dry by *Aigues Mortais* – the rather ghoulish name given to the town's residents. Drying washing may not reveal a great deal about its owners or the place they live. Yet it does have a certain fluttering urban appeal, even if in the end laundry is laundry, whether it is French, Italian or Cuban.

Of far more interest to me than the laundry of strangers though, was the view I discovered in the opposite direction across the flat 10,000 hectares landscape of salt-marsh. Framed by a neat little mountain range of salt heaps – piles of white gold known locally as *camelles* – the otherworldly marshy landscape raised the moot question of my own recent out-of-office transition to something akin to otherworldliness. Standing alone in that eerie Languedoc-Roussillon landscape, I found myself once more cast somewhat adrift, all part of the pleasing impetus that was guiding me from office don't-wanna-be to a man in control of his destiny. Satisfying as that progress indubitably was, the end of each physical stage of the journey brought with it a noticeable heavy-heartedness. I shielded my eyes against the dipping sun and peered to the right beyond the dunes of salt, far out towards the Mediterranean and the Golfe du Lion. I imagined at that moment how wonderful it might be, possessed of extraordinary visionary powers, to be able to see across that stretch of sea towards Perpignan, and then further south to the northern Costa Brava *sur-mer* resorts of Argelès and Banyuls. How close I would then be to a seductive glimpse of the north-eastern extremity of Spain.

A midriff tremor of intuition alerted me that it was time once more to confront the bitter-sweet dilemma of choice. Would I head north, back towards the cloudier skies of dear old Blighty, or south towards the Iberian Peninsula that tugged at me to return? And with all due apologies to those Catalans of an independent spirit, the pull of their autonomous region (to me as an outsider still very much a part of Spain) was too strong to resist. Enjoying the head rush of this continuing riot of mood-driven decision making (and I really do recommend this as a way forward in life), I settled on a joyous return path to Spain, my rationale resting on the laughable basis of needing to practise rolling my tongue around those troublesome '...*rrrrrrrs'*, and of finally making some sense of that decidedly lengthy list of irregular verb forms – even if Spanish grammar could hardly be a priority in a region where the purist *Castellano* language plays a poor second fiddle to proud Catalan. But as much as I enjoyed dreaming up high-minded excuses to return to Spain, I didn't really need them. My gut feeling was guiding me back there, and how enticing it felt to have as my gateway to the country, that passionate and sometime hotbed of rabid anti-Spanish sentiment – Barcelona.

Madrid's underbelly at Plaza Chueca – down
and gritty where anything goes

'*I travel a lot; I hate having my life disrupted by routine*'.

Caskie Stinnett, travel writer.

– 7 –

El Clásico: Barcelona and Madrid

I can't tell you how glad I was that the TGV train that carried me out of Montpellier was heading neither in a northerly direction or anywhere near an airport. I was bound for Barcelona but after passing through Narbonne, I decided to delay gratification by breaking the journey briefly at the small city of Perpignan, right at the heart of the Roussillon plain. These days very far from the 'villainous ugly town' of traveller Henry Swinburne's damning review of 1775, Perpignan lies only a short and tempting eighteen-mile hop from the Spanish border, and given its proximity to Spain the city's Iberian influences are no surprise. As I made my way towards the centre every street sign I passed was marked in both French and Catalan, and at its tourist heart there seemed to be a tapas bar on every corner. To get into the spirit of this charming little city, I found a sunny corner of the lively Place de la République where I sat to read that the city's distinct Spanish flavour is a legacy of the *retirada* – the sorry exodus of more than half-a-million refugees from Spain to southern areas of France during the Spanish Civil War. As Barcelona fell to Franco's Nationalist forces during the war's latter stages in January 1939, this influx charged across the eastern Pyrénées in the hope of finding a bit of French respite and hospitality. The reality was somewhat different.

Although an uncomfortable truth largely overlooked by modern European history, the welcome awaiting the influx of war-weary Spaniards has remained a stain on the image of France ever since. Having signed a European non-intervention agreement, the French government was content to herd the refugees into a miserable collection of long-forgotten concentration camps, the biggest of which was built as a virtually open-air facility along the sand dunes at nearby Argelès. Many of the 100,000 refugees with the misfortune to end their bleak odyssey from Barcelona at the camp were reduced to burrowing makeshift homes in the sand in an effort to repel the bitter winter weather. Known locally as 'camps of scorn', these internment complexes quickly and predictably became sandy hell-holes of death, disease and downright despair. Those that didn't perish from exposure often ended their days instead in the overcrowded hospitals of Perpignan. I was planning to delve into the impact of the Civil War on Barcelona when I reached the city, but hadn't imagined that my lunchtime stopover in this most genteel of southern French towns would present such a vivid introduction to the catastrophe the war visited on the Catalan capital. And all of this before I had even reached the border.

Rejoining the rail route south to Barcelona, I marvelled at an extraordinary achievement of rail technology. Thanks to a new high-speed link between

Perpignan and Figueras – part of the appealingly-named 'Mediterranean Corridor' – fifteen minutes and twenty-five kilometres after leaving Roussillon, I crossed the border into Spain via the twin-bore eight-kilometre Perthus Tunnel. A border crossing made in a pitch-dark tunnel through the middle of a mountain without a single armed guard to enliven the experience by barking at you for your passport was in some ways a tad under-whelming. Not even a sharp rap on the ankles with a wooden baton to report, as I was once treated to as a souvenir of my crossing by sleeper service of the border between Turkey and Bulgaria. Inarguably though, the €1 billion rail connection linking the two countries is impressive, particularly given that the project faced two major logistical hurdles. The first was the incom-patibility of the wider track gauge used on the Iberian side of the border. This inconvenience made smooth links with the French rail system impossible without the use of gauge-changing installations at the border. The second barrier was the decidedly tricky issue of France's rail system running on the left (as in the UK), while Spanish trains run on the right. How the eigh-teenth and nineteenth-century French and Spanish rail engineers failed to spot the future problems stored up by building incompatible systems on the same land mass is a mystery to me. But twenty-first century inge-nuity has circumvented the snag by the construction of a flyover ten kilometres shy of the Spanish border, which enables the lines to switch. I must have passed over the flyover without noticing which in some ways was a pity, but the seamless border crossing it now pro-vides is of course its whole point. Luckily the gauge problem proved less insurmountable than the right-left switch as the new high-speed line runs along a track gauge suited to both the French TGV and Spanish AVE (*Alta Velocidad Española*) high-speed networks. Anyway, the tunnel technology, gauge changes, the right-left flyover and lack of snarling border guards could not entirely flatten the thrill of crossing the border into Spain by rail. Through the other side of the Perthus Tunnel and into a dazzling light, suddenly it was the engines and rolling stock of the Spanish national railway – RENFE – that I saw at the trackside, while the otherwise unremarkable buildings of small towns and hamlets I passed were also now decidedly Spanish in style and no longer French – a wonderful reminder of how, with the help of technology and no little imagination, two distinct cultures and traditions can abut in so short a space of track and time.

So in a miraculous dash of less than two hours from Perpignan, I arrived at Barcelona's rather soulless sub-surface Estació de Sants, the city's 1970s main railway hub which suffers so badly from its architect's 'brave new world' attempt to replicate an airport terminal. But just like any other self-respecting major railway station, Barcelona Sants oozes shadiness of the kind that had me tighten the grip on my belongings and sharpen my wits. Such is the complexity of the station's platform configuration, escalator system and disorienting concourse, the first time I arrived in Barcelona by train some years before, it took me a good half-an-hour to find my way out. A little sharper this time, once I had batted-off the attentions of the various chancers in competition for a piece of me, I was on the platform of the Barcelona Metro heading for Plaça de Catalunya where I had a room waiting for me at a fine old establishment called the Pensión Noya. Cheap digs – so long as they offer proper sanitation facilities (preferably behind a lockable door) and a prime location – for me usually offer a more memorable travel experience than staying in more salubrious, four-times-the-price chain hotels. Meeting the budget criteria perfectly, the Noya sits on the fourth floor of a grand mansion block at the north end of Barcelona's main tourist drag, La Rambla, with views of Plaça de Catalunya from its front-facing rooms. This is tourist Barcelona's location bullseye. And if you are a generous enough reviewer to count as adequate sanitation the pensión's sole bathroom shared by the occupants of six rooms – and by the looks of it installed when General Franco was a boy – then at the equivalent nightly cost of a bottle of al-fresco *cava* out there on La Rambla, this place is less a find than a revelation. As indeed is the Noya's proprietor, the delectable Feli, a petite *mujer* of a certain age who I admire greatly for having made not the slightest effort to learn a single word of English in her forty-odd years running a guest house at the heart of one of the world's foremost tourist cities – a clever ploy no doubt to avoid any confrontations with demanding visitors over the state of the bathroom. But I won't spoil the positive image I feel I am struggling to portray of casa-Feli with stories of the erratic and intermittent flush action in the solitary WC. Just keep pulling that rusty old chain and eventually you might see water.

I dropped my bag and left Feli's place to join the perpetual motion of human traffic filing up and down La Rambla – a ceaseless conveyor belt of sightseers where spotting the Brit is made easy by the widest array of football shirts pulled over beer bellies you're ever likely to see. But La Rambla does have a certain charm, and once I was beyond the off-putting cages of squawking exotic birds, wide-eyed please-take-me-home puppies, mewing kittens and any number of cuddly (and not so cuddly) rodents for sale at the Plaça de Catalunya end of the tree-lined boulevard, I adjusted quickly to its crowded spirit. One of the principal attributes of La Rambla is that it is entirely given over to pedestrians. Here, for once, the car is not the star. Cutting a 1.2 kilometre swathe between the atmospheric quarters of El Raval to the west and the Barri Gòtic to the east, La Rambla is a gaudy paradise of entertainment, petty crime and – especially by night – vice. Having said all of that, La Rambla is also rather beautiful. Once a sewage-filled stream (the Spanish word *Rambla* translates roughly as 'stream bed'), by the 1400s the boulevard had been transformed into Barcelona's vibrant focal point of markets, festivals, outdoor drinking and general merry-making. Six hundred years later, and not a great deal has changed. La Rambla's canopy of signature plane trees were added in the early eighteenth-century, which as I walked south towards the port I thought gave the boulevard a surprisingly wooded feel, right at the heart of a teeming metropolis.

The poet Federico García Lorca, no less, once described La Rambla as *'the only street in the world I wish would never end'*. Not that Lorca would have faced the daily hassle of negotiating scrums of tourists crowded around mime artists, or the obstacle course of pavement entrepreneurs demonstrating the art of trans-forming vinyl LP records into wall clocks. Nevertheless, the 1930s La Rambla would have had its own period tackiness, and if a walk down to the promenade's end to take a look at the statue of Christopher Columbus was good enough for Granada's great lyricist, then I wasn't about to turn back. Columbus of course was another man with a keen eye for an auspicious location. In fact, when the maverick traveller returned to Spain in March 1493 from his first odyssey to the Americas, he chose Barcelona as his port of re-entry. Fortuitously for the great explorer, the Royal Court was in situ as he arrived and he was greeted with great enthusiasm by the King and Queen, Ferdinand and Isabella, both more than likely licking their lips at the prospect of receiving gifts of an exotic array of new world trinkets. I couldn't find a record of their reaction to being presented by Columbus with an ensemble of souvenirs that included varieties of plants that they wouldn't have had names for, several extravagantly coloured parrots and six very much alive, kidnapped 'Indians' that had taken his fancy as he explored the island of Hispaniola. More treasured gifts for the lucky monarchs perhaps, than a printed t-shirt or souvenir ash tray.

When I reached the southern end of La Rambla, I paused for a while under Columbus's statue – a tribute to the national hero unveiled somewhat belatedly in 1888 during the Universal Exhibition. The statue has Columbus clutching route maps in his left hand, while marking his navigational exploits by his finger pointing in the general direction of the sea, although I was disappointed to learn not specifically in the direction of his New World discovery. A little less intrepid for the moment at least, my own immediate direction was easterly towards La Barceloneta and the city's long stretch of sandy beach. A popular spot for party-animals, sun-worshippers and pick-pockets, I walked

along the wide expensively-paved promenade and followed Columbus's lead by looking out to sea, thinking
it a little greedy of Barcelona to have a beach of its own
at all. What a blessed city it is that can boast more
natural and man-made beauty, more forms of culture
and entertainment, and more diversity and historical
interest than you could shake a stick at. And if all
of that wasn't enough, there's the city's hedonistic lure
of a flamboyant Mediterranean resort. With its highly
favourable climate of mild winters (when December days
on the beach are quite possible), long warm summers,
little rain and 2,500 annual hours of sunshine, when
all's said and done you might agree that Barcelona is
a city well worth hanging around in.

Stepping a few metres into the narrow streets either
side of La Rambla takes you, more or less, into a different world. On one side lies the atmospheric – albeit still
very touristy – Barri Gòtic, while on the other the entertainingly edgy El Raval. Formerly notorious as an area
of vice and petty crime, El Raval has pulled off its transformation to a partially gentrified place-to-be-seen
apparently without losing any of its earthy charm in the
process. The area may be high on the buzz of its gentri-
fication, but luckily for the curious visitor in search of
some unadulterated urban grit, El Raval's position adjacent to the city's port ensures that it will likely remain
for some time to come a magnet for immigrants, prostitution, crime and their attendant social problems.
Throw into the mix its meandering medieval street plan
hosting a grungy itinerant population and eclectic
collection of weird and wonderful bars and restaurants,
then El Raval was well worth dodging La Rambla for.
Having said that, I hadn't the slightest appetite to mark

my visit with a cash snatch at knifepoint, so to avert such an outcome, before entering Carrer de Sant Pau – a popular rat-run into El Raval off La Rambla – I placed my small roll of euros inside my sock under the arch of my foot. Who needs a money belt? Fifty metres or so down the narrow dimly-lit street, I came to a doorway where a drugs deal was in full flow – incidentally the first I had witnessed since I was in Berlin's über-cool Kreuzberg – but not the last I would see in just that one evening in El Raval.

I was pondering the audacity of dealing in such a public place when I was approached by a large female of dubious attraction who offered me thirty minutes of her charming company for a sum roughly equivalent to the amount currently residing inside my left sock. This was not a lot. Strangely, this moment of Barcelona disrepute took me back to an 'assertiveness in the work-place' training course I once attended. Even though I was now out of the office environment, I found that I could still put to good use something I remembered seeing written up on training room flip-chart paper in untidy letters of green marker pen. Among the many and varied workplace attributes practised on that cor-porate away-day, one in particular that I would often pull out of my 'tool kit' when faced with some or other office-based drama came to mind – the ability to think on my feet. So on my feet and thinking fast, I warded the lady off with the perfectly reasonable excuse that I couldn't accept her proposition because 'my wife wouldn't like it', which I thought might do the trick even if in reality I didn't actually have a wife, which anyway wasn't the point. Not to be out manoeuvred, the smart lady came back at me with some quick on-her-feet thinking of her own and the equally feasible suggestion that 'your wife won't ever know'. This gifted me my follow-up response that, 'yes, maybe my wife wouldn't know…but *I would know*'. Seeing the chances of a deal with me fast receding, the lady switched her attentions instead to a tall blonde man of Scandinavian appearance and smart clothing who also looked like he just might have a banknote or two tucked inside his shoe, not to mention a wife waiting inside a hotel room wondering where on earth he had got to.

Virtue still firmly intact, I spent the rest of the evening innocently bar-hopping on the Rambla de Raval, a wide strip of restaurants and diverse drinking dens spilling over with colourful grungy locals and curious tourists. I sat for a while on the fag-butt-strewn terrace of a no-frills Turkish bar, improvising some Spanish conversation practice by eavesdropping on a group of students sitting on the next table. Frustrated by my inability to make much sense of what was being said, I somehow managed to deposit a substantial part of my falafel wrap down the front of the worn-out old work shirt I was wearing, a garment already clinging to life by its threads following the countless rough hand washes it had suffered as I travelled. Anyway, a sober shirt with a stiff collar that I once wore around 'the office' just didn't seem *de moda* in El Raval, so the sorry rag was awarded an undignified send off in the foetid depths of an El Raval municipal bin. It probably deserved better.

Once I was re-attired with a cheap replacement in multi-coloured stripes that I bought from a man with an open suitcase, I looked around the narrow lanes for an inviting venue for a late drink. I was tempted by a review I read of the Sala Apolo Bar, which ran eye-catching weekly speciality bashes nattily named 'Nasty Mondays' and 'Crappy Tuesdays'. That Tuesday session might have been the one to go for, but inconveniently my day in El Raval happened to be a Thursday so I settled instead for the less innovative London Bar. I wasn't attracted to the London Bar by its name – in all fairness I would have preferred it to be called something entirely different – but more for its impressive roll-call of alumni, and given the state of my clothing its complete lack of dress code. Opened in 1910 and still wrapped in what looked to be its original décor, this thumping old-school bar has been at various times a favourite Barcelona haunt of an illustrious clientele including Salvador Dalí, Picasso and that veteran of Havana's La Floridita Bar, Ernest Hemingway – a man who on his sojourns around the globe seemed to have no difficulty at all in finding his way to an atmospheric drink.

I too had a bit of history with the London Bar. Ten years previously it had been the scene of a celebratory evening to mark the end of my teacher training at the International House academy in Barcelona. Tired of the routines of nine-to-five even back then, I absconded from a perfectly good, reasonably well-paid position at yet another central London college to join a disparate band of similarly un-career-focused adventurers on a tortuous, at times masochistic, four-week intensive course. If you haven't had the pleasure, the CELTA course (a branch of TEFL – Teaching English as a Foreign Language) is something approaching a reality TV show set deep in an Australian jungle. Nobody asked me to drink a glass of a rodent's urine or chew on a handful of maggots to pass the course, but the rigorous training consumed four weeks of my life like nothing else ever has. Each morning began with the purgatory of an English grammar session (the course taught us the formal structures of our own language, giving us a fighting chance of being able later to impart the knowledge to paying foreigners) followed in the afternoon by teaching practice on real live students (don't try this at home), an ordeal made more onerous still by the ritual humiliation of being observed through every slip and stumble by the trainers and your fellow-students. Then there was the nightly sitting up into the early hours to prepare teaching materials for the next day, not to mention the weekend candle-burning spent writing long missives on the less than enthralling theories of language learning. And if that wasn't enough to have you rushing for the next plane home, there were the hand-wringing one-to-one 'feedback' sessions with a zealot of a teacher-trainer, whose greatest pleasure in life evidently came from grinding her trainees into the ground as if they were dog ends. After a month of that, you may appreciate why we all went a little overboard on that final Friday knees-up.

My big mistake in the London Bar that evening a decade before had been to imbibe one shot too many of the house absinthe – a popular ritual for the foolhardy bar-hopper in Barcelona. Being of a low alcohol tolerance level, within seconds of swallowing my third shot I was reduced to a helpless wreck with my head between my knees on the pavement outside the bar, desperate to avoid the fate of the young man close by. Lying in his own vomit (or even worse, perhaps someone else's), his lack of movement wasn't an altogether promising sign, a developing emergency that at least sobered me up a little. I remember approaching the drunken figure to pull him clear of the nasty yellow pool he was lying in, realising as I did so that it was drink-intolerant Phillip, a fellow TEFL masochist from my course. Phillip, me, and the rest of the group certainly garnered a thing or two about teaching English as a foreign language during that intensive month in Barcelona, but very few of us seemed to know anything at all about holding our drink. Ten years on, as I ordered an altogether less risky brand of refreshment in that same El Raval bar, I felt an odd pang of nostalgia for that character-building, liver-twisting teaching course. But I wouldn't touch absinthe again if you paid me.

The morning after my evening in El Raval (followed by a peaceful night in casa-Feli), I walked up to the 200-metre summit of Montjuïc – 'Jewish mountain' from medieval Catalan – a verdant outcrop of sandstone rock blessed with a lucky vista over Barcelona's opulent harbour. As well as offering a brush with nature in the heart of the city, Montjuïc boasts a number of outstanding buildings including the landmark eighteenth-century Castell de Montjuïc, now serving as a military museum but once notorious as a torture centre used by both sides during Barcelona's bitter internecine struggle during the Spanish Civil War. Montjuïc's identity as a modern attraction though, lies in its legacy of hosting two seminal events in Barcelona's twentieth-century cultural and sporting history – the 1929 Universal Exposition and the dazzling 1992 Olympic Games. Not many of us were around for the Exposition, but if you remember those sun-blessed Olympics I would bet that one of the images that has stayed with you is of the acrobatics of divers as they leaped from their ten-metre diving board. What wonderful camera work it was that suggested to the watching world through clever angles that the diver was on a trajectory, not towards the pool, but down the sheer face of Montjuïc into the sprawl of the city below. But when I stood now behind that same Montjuïc diving board and looked down at that same city view, it was with a heavier heart. Possibly an effect of Spain's recent economic woes, or even of public indifference in the near quarter-century since the games ended, the area around the pool has shamefully been allowed to decline to the point of shabbiness.

A couple of hundred metres further on, I reached the far better maintained Olympic Stadium. Constructed originally for Barcelona's earlier 1929 extravaganza, in 1936 the stadium was intended to host an alternative anti-fascist Olympics to Hitler's games taking place at the same time in Berlin – a laudable plan unfortunately put paid to by the Spanish Civil War. The stadium did of course eventually get its Olympic-moment, serving as the iconic focal point of the 1992 sporting extravaganza and home of the Olympic flame. More recently the stadium has found its purpose as a major concert venue and was also the home ground of *La Liga* football club Espanyol until it moved to a purpose built stadium elsewhere in the city. I walked down one of Montjuïc's wooded slopes back towards the city and passed the monumental Palau Nacional, also built for the 1929 World Exposition and now the site of a major art gallery. Carrying on through the exquisite 1920s Jardin de Larabal, I stopped for a while to admire the botanical gardens that showcase the various regions of the world that can boast a 'Mediterranean' climate – areas of southern Europe and California, parts of western and South Australia, south-western South Africa, sections of central Asia and parts of Chile. It seemed incredible that this area of lush shaded pathways and serene little squares of trickling fountains lay at the heart of a pulsating city. With the hum of the metropolis below in one ear and the gentle sound of birdsong in the other, I felt closer to a natural paradise in a major urban area than I had thought was possible.

Back in the alluring chaos of the city centre, I spent much of the rest of the day seeking out the outlandish impression made on Barcelona by two of its maestros, Antoni Gaudí and Joan Miró, who between them almost managed to turn Barcelona into a gigantic open-air art gallery. To find examples of Gaudí's modernism (and in Barcelona you don't have very far to look), I began on the elegant shopping boulevard Passeig de Gràcia, reputedly Spain's most expensive street and home to two of Gaudí's seminal works. The best known of these is Casa Mila (popularly known as La Pedrera – the stone quarry) – an eccentric bulk of twisted, undulating stone completed in 1912 that does indeed resemble a quarry. Reckoned by fans of Gaudí to be among the most imaginative residential buildings in the entire history of architecture – so quite a claim – La Pedrera looks more like a giant sculpture than a house, a quality recognised by UNESCO when granting it World Heritage status in 1984. Carried a short distance along the stylish Passeig de Gràcia on the crest of a wave of other hot tourists, I reached Gaudí's Art Nouveau experiment at Casa Batlló, a project on which he was let loose in 1904 by the planning authorities with a brief to restore what had originally been a fairly ordinary and conventional house. Gaudí of course entertained nothing of the conventional in his renovation plans for the building, flouting all local planning and design bye-laws in the process, not least by decorating the roof in a kaleidoscope of colour that looks now like a thousand 'E-numbers' topping a cake. The transformed mansion block also sports a stirring skeletal 'skull and bones' feature – the skulls forming the balconies of the house, with the bones their supporting columns.

In his re-furb of Casa Batlló, Gaudí may have achieved the last word in 'putting your own stamp' on a property, but the pinnacle (quite literally) of his Barcelona portfolio is the flamboyant Basílica de la Sagrada Família (Holy Family) – or at least it will be when it is finished. Gaudí missed seeing his greatest project completed in his lifetime by some distance. Somewhat incredibly, the building is still under construction today with a promise for completion in 2026 – a full 144 years after the first stone was laid in 1882. This lengthy project may well be the ultimate in broken builder's promises, but when completion day finally arrives it will at least be in the nick of time for the centenary of the architect's death, following his unwinnable confrontation with a Barcelona tram in June 1926. Even when Gaudí was still alive, the building work on the Sagrada Família was blighted by incessant delays, leading to Gaudí joking about the longevity of the project, that his client (God) was in no hurry to see it finished – which is probably just as well. But as the construction work on the Sagrada Família approaches its final stages, it is mired in the artistic controversy that the end product will not be quite as Gaudí envisaged.

His original plans for the basilica were destroyed by anti-Catholic anarchists during the Civil War, so much of what has taken shape since has been based largely on guesswork and financial expedience. Concerns about the integrity of the ongoing building work at the Sagrada Família have also grown amid recent plans laid down by the Spanish and French rail companies to build a tunnel underneath it to accommodate improvements to the high speed rail link between Barcelona and the South of France. Yet even incomplete and engulfed by towering cranes, Gaudí's basilica cuts a miraculous sight. I strained my eyes upwards to meet the summit of its towers, reaching up to the heavens like great stone tentacles (to eventually total eighteen) – the crowning glories of a building so astonishing as to warrant an ongoing campaign by Gaudí aficionados to have the necessary paperwork drawn up and sent to the Vatican in the expectation of making its architect a saint. Through the lens of my camera, I took a closer look at the work being done by today's builders, and spotted a recently completed Gothic window next to a weathered Gaudí-designed original. Just as the man would have wanted it, at least to my untrained eye, the two windows are identical.

On a previous visit to Barcelona, I remember looking in bemusement at a painting in the Joan Miró Foundation gallery entitled, *Man and Woman in Front of a Pile of Excrement*. Showcasing Miró's off-centre talent, at the time I hadn't the foggiest idea what message I was supposed to read in the startling work. What I saw were two chicken-like figures endowed with stylised genitalia, dancing alongside a similarly animated shape suggestive of the waste matter in the painting's title. The real clue to the meaning behind Miró's creation lies in its completion date (1936), suggesting the anti-fascist artist's despair at his fellow Spaniards as they set out on the violent path towards civil war – a war of annihilation that did indeed reduce their nation to something resembling a pile of excrement. More accessible than the messengers of Miró's grim metaphor is his very public, almost childlike, multi-coloured pavement mosaic on La Rambla. Most people, including me until I read about it in my guidebook, are oblivious to its presence and trample over it as if it were a rough work in chalk by a street artist touting for a bit of small change. I stood for as long as I could bear in La Rambla's crowds in the hope of getting a closer look at Miró's free exhibit, but gave up amid the ceaseless tourist footfall blocking my view. Eventually I sought a kind of sanctuary from the melee in the nearby labyrinthine Mercat de Sant Josep de la Boqueria, a purveyor of fresh produce to the good people of Barcelona since 1840, and in itself an art gallery of sorts with its permanent organic installation of the most colourful combination of fruits, vegetables, nuts, chorizo and seafood you could wish to see. The only problem I could detect with this crowded market was that the majority of the people in there (including me) were treating it as a tourist attraction and photo opportunity, rather than as a working market where livelihoods were on the line. This, I guessed, must drive the stallholders mad, although there was a healthy queue building to buy rainbow assortments of fresh fruits sold in plastic tumblers that the trader was letting go for the price of a cup of tea – an irresistibly artsy, one-hit ingestion of three of your five-a-day if ever there was one.

Surrounded by all the gaiety and attendant frippery of a mecca of tourism, as I walked around the modern city it was a little difficult to imagine that in Spain's Civil War nadir, Barcelona had been a cesspit of violence and hatred. To find out more of the city's relatively recent darkest hour, I booked onto a walking tour of some its principal Civil War sites. The tour was expertly led by a Mancunian called Nick Lloyd, who in his twenties had the good sense to dodge the entrapment of a conventional career by moving to Barcelona – and then the exceedingly good fortune to fall in love with a local girl who became his wife. Thirty years on, Nick is fluent in both Spanish and Catalan (but retains his Mancunian drawl), is perfectly content to continue living in the sunshine, and unsurprisingly has no plans at all to either apply for a job in an office or to move back to his native, rainy 'cottonopolis'. With a political conscience somewhere to the left of Chairman Mao and possessed of a passion for all things Barcelona, there was no-one better to lead a defence of the Republican's Civil War plight in his adopted city – a dire plight indeed in the years prior to Barcelona's desperate capitulation to Franco's Nationalist forces in January 1939.

The Civil War tour began in Plaça de Catalunya on the sun-baked terrace of the popular tourist hangout, Café Zurich. In the manner of one of those toe-curling ice-breakers popular at corporate training events, as we introduced ourselves we were each invited to reveal to the rest of the group what we hoped to gain from the tour. This was not a moment, of course, for any ice-breakers along the lines of, '*I'm fascinated by the history of the Civil War in Barcelona, but by the way, I'm a massive Kylie fan'*. Instead, to a man, our objective was the same – to learn how, why and when this stunning Mediterranean city had fallen into such a pit of despair. Nick obliged in his own introduction by holding forth for several minutes on Barcelona's characteristically feisty response to the Franco-led army uprising against the Republic in July 1936. Never a shrinking violet of a city, while Franco was busy kick-starting the Civil War in the south of Spain, Barcelona was even busier setting about its own violent transformation into a Marxist-propelled basket case. As we walked away from Plaça de Catalunya to begin the three-hour foot slog in the sun around some of the murderous city sites, our guide set about demystifying the alphabet spaghetti of acronyms that made up the various disparate groups struggling for ascendancy at the time. To cut a long story short – and believe me, this was a very long story – Franco's army garrison in Barcelona failed in its initial attempt to take the city for the Nationalists. This was obviously something of a setback for *El Generalissimo,* who had met with far less resistance in many other parts of Spain, including in the southern cities of Seville and Granada. Far from finding relief from conflict, once it had repelled Franco, Barcelona was placed in the volatile hands of anarchists and the Partido Obrero de Unificación Marxista (POUM), a revolutionary party formed in 1935 in opposition to the brand of communism espoused by the Soviet Union. POUM (the one acronym among many really worth remembering on the tour) prevailed in Barcelona following what was, in effect, a libertarian revolution. The unions ran the factories and public services, while many of the large hotels – previously the preserve of the wealthy – were turned into makeshift hospitals. People went about their daily business in the city in the heroic garb of workers' overalls and caps, their solidarity also expressed by the outlawing of polite, deferential forms of conversational Spanish such as *Señor, Don* and *Usted*. All said and done, the Barcelona of 1936 may not have been the ideal pick as a destination for a Spanish language course.

In Franco's terms, the Civil War was a kind of 'Holy War', in which conservatism and rigid Catholicism were pitched in a bloody battle against liberal-leaning lefties. Nowhere more so than in Barcelona was this bitter struggle crystallised. In this Mediterranean Marxist utopia, restaurants and bars were collectivised, tipping forbidden and in a mischievous anti-old-order spirit, even one-way streets were widely ignored. On La Rambla, where today it is impossible to walk more than a few steps without encountering some entrepreneurial cash-hungry scheme or other, revolutionary music blared out from loudspeakers hung from trees as comrades took their evening stroll. Unless they were completely mad or possessed a death wish, factory owners and anyone else with a political bent to the right fled the city. Almost inevitably though, with POUM being just one of a number of groups intent on wielding power in this socialist city state, what began as petty internal squabbling soon developed into an acrimonious fight, transforming Barcelona into what Leon Trotsky described pithily as a city '...*like Nice in a hell of factories with smoke and flames on the one hand; flowers and fruit on the other*'. In fact, once Trotsky's nemesis, Stalin, and his Russian communist forces intervened and gate-crashed Barcelona's revolutionary party in May 1937, all hell was let loose – ensuring an emphatic victory of smoke and flames over flowers and fruit. So for five grisly days between the 3rd and 8th of May, the city was locked in a short but bloody struggle for control of the Revolution, resulting in the deaths of 1,500 people. As we walked away from Plaça de Catalunya, we were pointed towards a grand building on the corner of Av. Portal de l'Angel where the May fighting began. Once the home of the Barcelona telephone exchange, the building survived the war and retains its links with the communications industry, serving today as the head-quarters of the Spanish mobile phone giant *Movistar*.

Enter stage left George Orwell, whose part in the struggle for Barcelona is the stuff of legend. Despairing of the plight of Spain, the writer left the comfort of his middle-class Dorset enclave to join the Republican cause, arriving in Barcelona in December 1936 to find what he described in *Homage to Catalonia* as, '*a town where the working class appear to be in the saddle*'. I had finished reading Orwell's book just in time for the tour, but our guide knew the book like the back of his hand. As we stood transfixed outside number 128 La Rambla (the former anarchist headquarters where Orwell was based and what is now the home of the stylish Hotel Rivoli Ramblas), without notes and with evident emotion, he quoted this passage:

'*In outward appearance Barcelona was a town in which the wealthy classes had practically ceased to exist. Except for a small number of women and foreign-ers there were no 'well-dressed' people at all. Practically everyone wore rough working-class clothes, or blue overalls or some variant of militia uniform. All this was queer and moving. There was much in this that*

I did not understand, in some ways I did not even like it, but I recognized it immediately as a state of affairs worth fighting for...so far as one could judge the people were contented and hopeful. There was no unemployment, and the price of living was still extremely low; you saw very few conspicuously destitute people, and no beggars except the gypsies. Above all, there was a belief in the Revolution and the future, a feeling of having suddenly emerged into an era of equality and freedom. Human beings were trying to behave as human beings and not as cogs in the capitalist machine."

Phew!

Next door to Orwell's old billet stands the Café Moka, the base used by Republican fighters to fire at Orwell and his fellow anarchists stationed on the roof of the Poliorama Theatre opposite. Pockmarks from heavy gunfire on the exterior wall testify to the café's involvement in the fighting – scars of war that could well have been put there by Orwell himself. Our tour party moved on through a knot of Barri Gòtic passageways to find a well-concealed gem of the old city, Plaça Sant Felip Neri. The first thing that struck me as we walked reverentially into the square through an archway close to Barcelona's old cathedral was the silence. The sobriety of the square is apt, as it was here that one of the worst instances of civilian bombing was visited on the city. As our guide's leftist monologue was building into a bit of a rant, I took a short break and moved slightly away from the group to read a plaque that recalls the devastating bomb that fell on the square on 30th January 1938 causing the collapse of the crypt of the Church of Sant Felip Neri – an annexe of the Convent of the Felipons, the followers of Sant Felip who made the square their home in 1673. Especially poignant on the plaque is the detail of the forty-two civilians who died in the blast as they sheltered in the church – twenty-two of them were children.

In a sort of *El Clásico*-from-hell, aerial bombardment of Barcelona was adopted as a Nationalist tactic at the behest of Benito Mussolini, who decided to use the Spanish Civil War to play out a deadly game of Fascists versus Reds. Believing that the war could be won for the Nationalists by the use of terror bombing, between the 16th and 18th of March 1938 the Italian Air Force unleashed waves of bombardments on Barcelona that killed around 1,300 people – an especially cynical tactic given that the bombers flew over the city from Nationalist held Mallorca bearing the insignia of the Spanish Air Force. During the raids the aerial defence forces of the Republic were conspicuous by their absence, although had they stuck around they may anyway have been impotent against the Fascists' superior technology. This was a level of weaponry to unleash a terror beyond anything seen before. With or without a defence, Barcelona was a sitting duck, an unfortunate victim of an experiment to carpet bomb civilians during the tense pre-Second World War period when a wider European confrontation seemed certain.

Our Civil War tour ended with a bit of light relief and a welcome drink in Bar Libertária, a workers' co-operative that still thrives as a meeting point for the city's remaining anarchists and leftist thinkers – and according to our guide, Barcelona still has plenty of them. As we entered the bar we filed past walls plastered with posters and newspaper cuttings from the days of Barcelona's Revolution, and more recent propaganda demonstrating the bar's pride at being today's focal point of the National Confederation of Labour. Known better by its Spanish acronym CNT, the movement survived the Revolution and continues a modest comradely operation in the capitalist frenzy of modern Barcelona. I walked away from the bar to rejoin the twenty-first century tourist nonsense of La Rambla, and was stopped almost immediately by a one-legged man sat on the pavement holding out a battered paper cup, only feet away from a crowd of visitors armed with selfie-sticks attempting to capture themselves and Miró's street mosaic in the same image. The seeds already planted, who knows, of a future revolution.

I spent my final evening in Barcelona hanging around the back streets of El Raval in a low-key finale that saw me neither mugged, propositioned or offered any kind of high, legal or otherwise. At some particularly ungodly hour the following morning, as I walked towards the metro station at Liceu I was entertained by the harmless antics of drunken kids on La Rambla fresh from depositing the small pools of rainbow-coloured vomit that I picked my way carefully around. More lively still on the short journey from Liceu to Estació de Sants, was the high-spirited scene I witnessed involving a group of English revellers, one of whom was attempting to broker peace between two female members of the rabble engaged in some drunken handbag scrapping. '*At the end of the day, we're all fackin human innitt...?*' the more vocal of the two ladies rasped as she stood drawing on her illicit cigarette underneath a sign advising passengers *¡No Fumar!* Shamed momentarily by my nationality, I moved along a couple of sections of the snake train only to then find myself sitting opposite a bearded young man of indeterminate national origin spitting voluminously onto the floor of the carriage, apparently oblivious to my incredulous stare. He left the train at Poble Sec, swaying dangerously along the platform as he headed for the exit. Abruptly he turned back and attempted to re-board the train, but as the doors were closing he once more changed his mind and slipped, falling face-forwards towards the unforgiving platform surface. Meanwhile, two carriages back one of those same two English girls had somehow got herself tangled in the door, and amid much panicked shrieking required the efforts of three of her similarly intoxicated pals to free her. Clearly, a good night had been had by all...

I was on the move this early as I was heading for Madrid to complete the double act that made up this personal *El Clásico*. Even among non-fans of the beautiful game, my guess would be that many might still know that *El Clásico* is the name given to games played between the two great clubs of Spanish football – Real Madrid and Barcelona – both of which enjoy a huge and loyal global fan base. Second only to the Champions League in terms of its worldwide draw, *El Clásico* is probably the greatest fixture in world club football. Forget the enmity of Milan derbies, the blue-red passion of the Merseyside clashes and the sectarian-driven battles in Glasgow, football-wise at least *El Clásico* is absolutely where it's at. But it is not simply a case of Real Madrid and 'El Barça' being the two biggest clubs in Spain, or even that they are Spain's two best teams. *El Clásico* is about so much more than a game of football. This is bitter politics played out as a sort of sporting civil war for ninety-odd minutes a couple of times a year on a 120 metre-long strip of turf. Fortunately, thus far in these high intensity games, points have been scored and reputations made and broken for latex rubber balls hitting their targets rather than bullets. Nevertheless, when the implacable dictator General Franco launched his rebellion against the Spanish Republic in 1936, the President of FC Barcelona Josep Sunyol was arrested and executed without trial. Some penalty for supporting the wrong team! Mind you, the fact that Barcelona's football club ranked alongside communist and anarchist groups as organisations seen by Nationalists as ripe for purging, tells us something about its importance as a symbol of Catalan national-ism. Merely a football team El Barça most certainly is not. In fact, Barcelona's famous club motto, *Més que un club* – more than a club – was dreamed up initially as a two-fingered Catalan up-yours to *El Generalissimo,* to be waved antagonistically on countless banners in the post-Civil War years of dictatorship. As Phil Ball in *Morbo: The Story of Spanish Football* says of the rivalry between Barcelona and Madrid '...*they hate each other with an intensity that can truly shock the outsider*'. During the dictatorship, links between Real Madrid and the Franco regime were undeniable – but the association remains. '*Ugh....Franco's team*' was the reaction I got (and wholly deserved) on the mention of the arch enemy Real Madrid from a young Barça fan I got talking to one evening in a bar on Barcelona's tiny Plaça del Pi – a remarkable response I thought from someone who in the year Franco died (1975) hadn't yet been born.

The popular image of *El Clásico* is of a fierce rivalry played out on grass between Real Madrid's conserva-tism and the rebellious Catalans of Barcelona. As an

outsider, I cannot claim to feel any of the raw mutual
hatred that exists between fans of the two clubs.
Nevertheless, of the two I have always had a softer spot
for El Barça, partly for having spent more time in the
Catalan capital than in Madrid, but also for the rather
shallow reason of not being too keen on all white kits
like the one worn by Real Madrid (even if the washed-
out strip has gifted the club the enviable nickname *Los
Merengues* – the meringues). But for a more robust
reason to favour El Barça, we need look no further than
this. In an astonishing act of partiality following the
Nationalist victory in 1939, Spain's main cup competition – and let's enjoy the pomposity of its full name –
*Campeonato de España-Copa de Su Majestad el Rey de
Fútbol* (the *Copa del Rey*) – was renamed *El Copa del
Generalissimo* (the General Franco Cup – incredible).
And if one *El Clásico* clash sticks out above all others
in showing the world just what a football victory over
the city of Barcelona meant to Franco, then it was the
1943 *El Copa del Generalissimo* two-legged semi-
final. Despite Barcelona's healthy 3-0 lead from the first
leg (and we can only wonder how many heads rolled
in the Madrid dressing room after the game), in the
return leg in Madrid Real prevailed by the barely
feasible scoreline of 11-1 – wouldn't you just know it!

These days of course the performance of the referee
officiating at an *El Clásico* clash is scrutinised in the
minutest detail by cameras and pundits zooming-in
from every conceivable angle. For that suspect 1943
semi-final second leg, I couldn't find any record of the
performance of the referee, or what he may have got
up to during the Civil War. But for such a politically
loaded fixture, it is not stretching the imagination too

far to believe that a bent referee may have helped the mass of goals to fly in. Better might have been expected of the performance of the Madrid police though, who before the match kicked-off had a good go at intimidating Barcelona's players, and shamefully stood aside as Barça's unfortunate president Enric Piñeyro took a bit of a hiding outside Madrid's Santiago Bernabéu stadium from a group from Real's less enlightened fan base. Given that Piñeyro had fought for Franco during the Civil War and was awarded the Barcelona presidency for his services to the Nationalist cause (despite never once in his life having attended a football match), the poor man may have felt a little hard done by after his treatment by Real's supporters. Regarding the game itself, despite the various and futile Barcelona protests the 11-1 (11-4 on aggregate) trouncing stands in the record books as a permanent humiliation by Nationalist Madrid, not only of Barcelona's football team, but of the entire Catalan region.

Rising above the animosity, it is gratifying to know that there has been the odd occasion when in the name of sporting decency football hostilities have been suspended. One of these was an extraordinary moment during the 1983 *El Clásico* played in Madrid. Showing sublime ball control and a penchant for the old-fashioned dribble, Barça's then star player and talisman, one Diego Maradona, was bearing down on an empty Madrid goal. The only thing standing in his way was a hapless Madrid defender, who in a desperate lunge to stop the Argentinian maestro succeeded only in missing both the ball and player. Instead of thwarting the attack, the highly embarrassed defender slid painfully into one of the goalposts, allowing the imperious Maradona to slot the ball home unchallenged. But far from this tremendous goal precipitating the outbreak of a new Civil War in the Bernabéu stands, or even just a bit of a ruction, to a man the huge Madrid-supporting crowd stood and applauded Diego's brilliance. However, such generosity of spirit has rarely accompanied the transfer of players between the two clubs. Perhaps the most high profile of recent inter-club transfers was that of Luís Figo, who astonished the football world and insulted the entire Catalan region when he dared to move from Barcelona to Real Madrid in 2000. On his return to Barcelona's colossal Camp Nou stadium in the white shirt of Madrid, the tricky Portuguese winger got a very hot Catalan reception, with derisory howls from the stands of 'judas', 'scum' and 'mercenary' being among the more welcoming greetings aimed his way. Throughout the game Figo was bombarded with missiles thrown from the crowd, an indignity possibly cushioned by the thought of his mind-boggling salary. After the match (which ended in a 2-0 triumph of partial revenge for El Barça), when the clear-up operation of missiles began the debris included a pig's head. How the miffed Barcelona fan who launched the severed animal head at Figo managed to smuggle it into the ground in the first place is a bit of a mystery. Tucking it discreetly inside his match programme might have proved tricky. But given Figo's widespread unpopularity, it wouldn't be such a surprise to learn that the pig's head had been handed to the fan by one of Barça's own club stewards.

There is of course rather more to the city of Madrid than its bitter sporting rivalry with Barcelona. A little under three hours after leaving Estació de Sants on a high-speed AVE service via Zaragoza-Delicias – a station name I thought almost too good not to get off the train for – I arrived at Madrid's gargantuan Atocha terminus. Before I left the station to find my accommodation, I paused for a while in Atocha's extraordinary 4,000 square-metre botanical garden, planted in the oldest section of the station after it was taken out of service in the 1990s – a rather less evocative concrete terminal of tracks and platforms now serves the train services. This converted commuter pleasure ground retains all the usual retail paraphernalia and coffee shops associated with major transport hubs. Yet how innovative to give travellers the benefit before their journey begins (or ends) of a mini-trek through a jungle of 7,000 plants, a stroll around a pond containing more than twenty species of fish, and the photogenic allure of a family of resident turtles. Such was my unexpected welcome to the Spanish capital.

I left the natural wonders of Atocha behind to find my Madrid homestay in the district of Lavapiés. The area was within easy walking distance of Atocha, but I made the short journey by the city's metro as I wanted to see for myself whether it lived up to its claim to be Europe's 'cleanest and most efficient' underground railway system. As I made my way into the bowels of Atocha towards the metro platform of Line 1, I didn't meet any of the aromas of drainage or unwashed bodies you might expect to find on the underground systems of, say, Paris, London or New York. In fact, wholly justifying the cleanliness hype, the Madrid Metro positively gleams. Opened in 1919 as only the second (after Buenos Aires) on the Spanish speaking map, the

Madrid underground is the eighth longest in the world, but serves a population that ranks as only the world's fiftieth largest, making overcrowding a rarity and explaining in part the exceptional spruceness. With ninety-two per-cent of the track serving the metro's 231 stations running sub-surface, Madrid's is a genuinely underground railway and its 1,656 escalators are the most of any similar-sized system worldwide. Cheap and efficient and with numerous expansion projects pending, the reputation of the Madrid Metro looks set to grow further still.

'*Living Lavapiés*' headlined the advert that grabbed my attention when I was trawling the sites for the flat I was to spend the next couple of weeks living in. Living up to its billing, the area was very much alive as I emerged from the metro blinking into the sunlit Plaza Lavapiés. Tugging a case on wheels and with an unwieldy backpack hanging lopsidedly from my shoulder, I doubt at that moment whether I looked on for entering into any variety of illicit deal. But sure enough, as I stood at the top of the metro station stairs catching my breath from the steep climb – not to mention cursing my luck for choosing what I suspected was the only station on the network not fitted with one of that multitude of escalators – I was made an offer of the health-wrecking kind I was delighted to refuse. Welcome all to Lavapiés – once the centre of Jewish life in Madrid, now better known for its grungy, hippy decadence and multi-culturalism. With my Spanish level on the up thanks in part to the practice I got in Barcelona warding off street hawkers, I translated Lavapiés roughly as 'washfeet', a nod to the historic ritual of foot-washing that was required before entering the area's synagogues during its Jewish heyday. But Lavapiés was always somewhat neglected by the Madrid authorities, and by the 1980s the city's problem-child barrio had become a vertical slum of high-rise apartment blocks popular with squatters. Happily though, a high level of immigration has restored some of Lavapiés colour, vim and vigour, lending it an edgy bohemian charm that nowadays draws in crowds of tourists and *Madrileños* in search of a good time. I stood in the centre of Plaza Lavapiés for a few moments to acclimatise and get my bearings. My eye was drawn to a shabby block of flats adorned with old bed sheets hanging from rusty wrought iron balconies, daubed with protest messages such as *'Justicia para Lavapiés...dejar las drogas'* – 'justice for Lavapiés...stop the drugs'. But there was no stopping the Lavapiés pushers, and as I made my way from the plaza along Calle Lavapiés towards my digs I was offered dodgy deals no less than *six* times in a stretch of road less than a hundred metres long, reminding me of evenings out in Brixton. As for being offered drugs, there's nothing novel or even especially interesting about that in a gritty inner-city suburb, but the trade was in full flourish only feet away from what I soon gathered was a permanent police presence, most of whom looked wholly disinterested in what was going on around them. Noisy, dirty and possibly a little dangerous, in the free-spirited mood I was in, Lavapiés was most definitely for me.

Approaching my temporary home on the litter-strewn Calle Ministriles, I had another street obstacle to overcome in the shape of a small gang of *guiri*-baiting youths (*guiri* being the street term for a foreigner), energetically re-enacting *El Clásico* clashes with an empty beer can and screwed up shirts for goalposts. Amid cries of '*Ronaldoooooooo…*', and '*gooooooool…*' (imitating those crazy Hispanic football commentators), I watched a couple of well-taken goals fly in as I waited at the front door of the flat. I was eventually met there by my host Raúl, a bouncy *Madrileño* in his early forties possessed of a glint in his eye suggesting he would be hanging on to his youth for a while longer yet. Once I was inside, it struck me that if ever an apartment was in the image of its owner, it was Raúl's – neat and compact, no-nonsense and adorned with boyish trinkets. Everywhere I looked, each surface and shelf was filled with vintage boys-toys – cameras, replica sports cars made from recycled beer and coke cans, small piles of *Tintin* magazines and Lego and Meccano diggers scattered around each room like ornaments. Raúl and I gelled immediately, partly I think because I too was hanging on for dear life to the youthful-me, a process I had given a timely fillip to by walking away from the drudgery of 'the office'. But that's another story entirely, with which you may now be familiar…

Before I made this trip, the seductive barrio of Lavapiés had grabbed my attention as the setting for a book called *Errant in Iberia,* a true and uplifting tale I had read recently about an Englishman who flees a failed romance and the London rat race to pitch up in Madrid knowing barely a word of Spanish. They say you make your own luck in life, and by taking his chances this adventurer from middle-England was rewarded by one of his Spanish-English *intercambio* contacts becoming his wife, enabling him in rapid time to become a fluent Spanish speaker and adopted *Madrileño*. What's more, in a canny move this can-do nine-to-five escapee bought, renovated and sold on for a tidy profit a dilapidated apartment on a previously insalubrious Lavapiés street when the going eventually got good. Life, as somebody once said, is indeed either 'an adventure or it is nothing at all'. As for my own objectives in Madrid, they were a tad less ambitious for now, at least in as much as I wasn't expecting to leave the city as a Spanish property owner with a marriage certificate tucked inside my bag. The focus for me was on the rather lower commitment of improving my Spanish and simply walking (and biking) the city's cacophonous streets. But apart from a brief chat with Raúl about his Lego collection, the first meaningful conversation I had in the city wasn't with a Spaniard at all, but with two brassy Bulgarian women called Elena and Tonka.

I bumped into them in Café Libreria, an artsy, bohemian Lavapiés hangout dedicated in equal measure to strong coffee and the workers' struggle. Madrid's answer to Barcelona's Bar Libertária where I had been a few days earlier, the walls of the Libreria were plastered with posters of anti-establishment figures and leading lights of the left including Bob Marley and, a little too predictably, *that* Alberto Korda image of Che Guevara. With its book stacks given over to heavy volumes of leftist writing, Café Libreria felt just the sort of place for a bit of intrigue, a clandestine meeting or simply for scheming-up a plan – precisely, in fact, what Elena and Tonka were up to when I met them. As she knocked back her luminous alcopop, Elena (who had the better English of the two) told me of the drudge of their former lives in a dull dormitory town outside Sofia, and of their excitement that an opportunity had come their way to work as chamber maids in a Marbella hotel. Seeing this as very much the start of a new life of sun-kissed partying rather than a serious career move, their enthusiasm was infectious. I stopped short of accepting their offer to join them – my bed-making days were probably behind me. But just like that English 'errant in Iberia' who sought adventure away from his previous routines of the nine-to-five, there was inspiration to be drawn from these two high-spirited risk takers, and I very much hoped that in the sunshine of the Costa del Sol they would find exactly what they were looking for.

Part of the deal that saw me speed through the exit door of my former employment was a modest allowance for vocational training, intended to give me a leg up in my search for alternative work (should that be part of the plan, which patently thus far it wasn't). My request for Spanish classes in Spain just scraped through the eligibility check, unlike the application of another former colleague leaving the organisation at the same time who was knocked back in her attempt to win funding for flamenco guitar classes on the highly debatable grounds of flamenco 'not qualifying as a vocation'. The injustice of it! With the credit I had remaining after my Spanish dabbles at the Don Quijote schools in Seville and Granada, I signed up for another week of grammatical torture in Madrid. As was the custom, I turned up at the school early on a Monday morning to take the 'level test', but made a complete dog's breakfast of the oral section by misunderstanding an interrogation of my knowledge of the dreaded *pluscuamperfecto del subjuntivo,* a baffling item of Spanish grammar every bit as awful as it sounds. So without even trying, I had managed to slide from 'advanced' level in Granada to 'intermediate' in Madrid – some progress!

For my sins in Spanish, I was taken on a walk of shame down a stuffy corridor to join other middling-level students, who fortunately for the entertainment value of the class, would have fitted perfectly as a cast of that gloriously politically incorrect 1970s sitcom, *Mind Your Language*. Set in an 'English as a Foreign Language' classroom in a London Adult Education College, featuring the fairisle-sweater-wearing teacher, Jeremy Brown, *Mind Your Language* could not possibly be made today – it was too funny by half. The show depicted with an uncanny accuracy the travails of an English teacher attempting to control a diverse group of foreign students, with all the attendant linguistic and cultural misunderstandings that make an EFL class-room no place for the faint-hearted – that's teacher or pupil. Key to the show's side-splitting hilarity was that each student was dressed in their national costume. Think a Mexican student in a broad-rimmed sombrero sat next to an Indian woman in a sari, next to a Japanese girl in a geisha costume sat behind a Frenchman resplendent in a beret – quite possibly also sporting a string of onions around his neck – and you'll get the picture. Come back 1978, all is truly forgiven.

My twenty-first century language classroom in Madrid was all the poorer for its lack of national costumes, but was enlivened by an Italian student named Paolo who spoke little Spanish but made up for it with fluent jazz hands, an American priest in his mid-fifties called Chris, who as a bored eleven-year-old might do, passed me notes during the classes remarking unflatteringly about the decidedly iffy performance of the teachers. Next to Chris sat a Chinese girl called Marie, who barely spoke a word in any language (including her own) for the entire week, who in turn was sat beside a partially cross-dressed Frenchman named Henri. Finally there was Veronica, a Nigerian nun dressed for the classes in full habit, who as the week wore on revealed some eyebrow-raising intolerance about any number of minority groups – an intolerance far more befitting of Jeremy Brown's fictitious 1970s class than the one she was actually in. One exercise in particular brought her prejudices to light, given to us by our young teacher Clara, to tackle amongst ourselves in her absence – a ruse I think for her to leave the room for a few sanity-sparing minutes, and perhaps for a crafty ciggy. She tasked us with deciding which passengers deserved saving from certain death from an over-populated hot-air balloon plunging fatally towards the ground. Would it be the young mother of two, the elderly couple in their seventies, the four-year old twins or the single man of thirty? Making sweeping value judgments as she set about the task, Veronica was happy to share her gut-feeling that the single man's hitherto failure to marry and reproduce suggested a deviant sexual preference warranting his expulsion from the balloon and ultimate oblivion. Favouring the septuagenarian couple for pro-longed life ahead of him, she impressed the class still further by managing to get her entire prejudiced argument out in a more than decent level of Spanish, even slipping in the odd bit of 'subjunctive' as she went. Having said that, the more I got to know Veronica, the less convinced I was that Madrid had been a sensible choice of city for her to make.

Surprising as it sounds, grammar classes are no certain way of learning how to *speak* a language, so I answered an online advert from a *Madrileño* called Tony who was seeking English speakers for *intercambio* language swaps. When we met under the landmark *Tío Pepe* sign at the vast open space of Puerta del Sol, I hadn't imagined facing a man comfortably north of fifty. Reminding me of the type of language used by my old fascist buddy in Seville, José Miguel, Tony's advert was peppered with youthful vernacular like 'cool' and 'hook-up', so I fully expected the appearance of a young dude. I only spent one long afternoon with Tony, but in that very short time he doubled-up brilliantly as both language mentor and tour guide. Intent on showing me some of the lesser known corners of his home city, Tony took me first through the Plaza Mayor, bringing on the pleasing thought that as this vast square sits at the heart of Madrid, and that Madrid sits at the dead centre of Spain, then here I was myself slap-bang at the very heart of the country. More intrepidly we reached the edge of the trendy district of La Latina, where we ducked in and out of empty side streets off Calle de Segovia. Although we were never more than a few steps away from the polluted drag of Calle Mayor (a traffic-blighted street that draws tourists along it towards the Royal Palace like iron filings to a magnet), this elegant barrio of silent squares and narrow passageways really wouldn't look out of place in medieval Segovia or Toledo.

During our walk we stopped for a while under one of the giant arches of the Segovia Viaduct, a towering construction that takes Calle Bailén past the Royal Palace and the Almudena Cathedral. Always ready to share a cheery anecdote, Tony pointed up towards the panels of thick acrylic 'glass' installed on the viaduct by the local authority in the 1990s as suicide-prevention barriers. This, my *Madrileño* friend explained, was in response to fatalities from the bridge reaching as many as one a week – a statistic that not surprisingly the authorities feared would blight Madrid's reputation as a desirable place to visit. Since 1874 when the first viaduct was built on the site, it has become infamous as the city's favourite suicide spot, with around 500 poor souls feeling desperate enough to throw themselves from it. By the time the decision was taken to install the barriers, as well as wanting to deter the would-be suicides and save lives, the authorities had also grown tired of the inconvenience of bodies falling from the viaduct in front of, or onto, traffic and pedestrians going about their own business twenty-five metres below on Calle de Segovia. Standing under the death-bridge prompted Tony into a morbid commentary on suicide rates in Spain in general. Since the start of the country's financial meltdown in 2008 (known generically in Spain as *La Crisis*), suicides have risen from six per 100,000 to eight per 100,000. Much of this increase is attributed to the hopelessness of economic hardship, and in many cases eviction after mortgage defaults. Tragically, many of these suicides have been of young people, a reflection of the socially-destructive unemployment rate among 18 to 25 year olds currently running in Spain at over fifty percent.

To counter this terrifying national blight, the Spanish banks – generally loathed institutions these days – are offering repayment moratoriums to families with a combined income of less than €1,500 per month. This, along with a recent marginal economic improvement suggests that better times may lie ahead, although Tony and plenty of his compatriots remain unconvinced. However, this recent economic upturn is of no use to the many British Spanish property owners who have already been forced to sell their villas on the sunny costas at a fraction of the prices they paid. Understandably Tony had little sympathy with this, although one such case I came across of a British couple who had been hit hard by the double whammy of plummeting Spanish property values and surging prices in Britain, seemed particularly harsh. Having been the envy of their neighbours in suburban Devon back in 1999 after paying €250,000 for their 'place in the sun', they soon found their Spanish dream to be not all it was cracked up to be. Amid concerns about lack of access to the NHS as they grew older, in 2012 the sun-weary couple decided to sell up and return to Blighty. Unfortunately for them, the value of their whitewashed villa with a pool and mountain views had dropped by a ruinous 65% to a modest €87,500, giving them the purchasing power (with the help of some savings) on their return home to pricey Devon of no more than a small ex-Local Authority house in Plymouth.

To avoid being dragged down by the dual gloom of suicide and financial ruin, Tony and I pitched up in a café on an elevated terrace above Calle de Segovia. Cheered by chilled bottles of Mahou, we sat back and gazed up at the flawless blue sky, a little detail of Spain that no economic woe could ever take away. Tony clearly enjoyed candid conversation and had a real talent for self-disclosure, helped along no end by the beer. Given that I was a total stranger, I was surprised that within an hour of shaking his hand under the

Tío Pepe sign, I had been made privy to an intimate rundown of failed relationships, marital near misses and career mishaps. As we relaxed into the late afternoon on that rarefied terrace, this refreshingly open *Madrileño* then set about detailing the nitty-gritty of a delicate health issue that had brought him to a complete re-evaluation of his life. The outcome of this period of navel-gazing was his impending resignation from a steady – if rather dull-sounding – job in a firm of accountants, the sale of his property (triple glazed he told me to counter its location next to Madrid's Barajas Airport), and an early retirement to the enticing-sounding Costa del Azahar – orange blossom coast – a much sought after location close to the wonderfully clement city of Valencia. Tony had mapped out an impressive plan for a stress-free life of self-determination, and fully intended to see out his days enjoying a sea view, far away from the micro-management of 'the office'. As we parted company on the banks of the Rio Manzanares at the main entrance to Atlético Madrid's Vicente Calderón stadium, my sense was that we were unlikely to meet again, so I thanked him for what had been one of the more productive *intercambio* sessions I had thus far experienced. With who else other than *Madrileño* Tony would I have encountered, in a single sentence, the Spanish words for holiday home, gallstones and resignation?

When my course at Don Quijote ended I found myself youngish, free and single in Madrid. This felt like a pleasing state indeed, and high time to take to two wheels and try out Madrid's public cycle sharing scheme, *BiciMAD*. And MAD is the word. If not quite guaranteeing 'Mutually Assured Destruction' as in the

Cold War acronym, cycling in Madrid is an endeavour most definitely not for the enjoyment of the risk averse. Even as a pedestrian on the glam, architecturally rich city thoroughfare, the Gran Via, I had noticed a complete disregard from drivers for the welfare of cyclists – the polar opposite of, say, in Berlin where the cyclist is nigh-on revered on the city's equally busy streets. Cycling through green spaces is especially exhilarating in city centres, and paradoxically for such a traffic-heavy city, Madrid is reputed to have more trees growing in its congested centre per inhabitant than any other European capital. The overwhelming majority of these flourish in the city's two great green lungs, Casa de Campo and El Parque del Buen Retiro. Funnily enough though, the best known and most recognisable of Madrid's abundance of trees plays no part at all in improving the city's air quality. Instead, the strawberry tree that has featured as half of the city's coat of arms since the thirteenth-century, along with a bear on its hind legs apparently eating the fruit – *El Oso y El Madroño* – can be found in twenty tonnes of statue on a plinth in the middle of Puerta del Sol. The precise origins of this unique *Madrileño* motif are uncertain, but it seems likely that the symbol was adopted by the city's medieval authorities in honour of the large number of bears that centuries ago roamed the fields beyond the city's borders. If Madrid is a twenty-first century city of trees, it most certainly was also such in the thirteenth-century long before concrete was king, and the strawberry tree in the motif nods to the abundance of fruit bushes that grew in and around the city environs when this design for the coat of arms was first adopted. This endearing emblem was redesigned in 1967, retaining both the bear and the tree. As a mark of its popularity, the Puerta del Sol statue incorporating the modern design is now surrounded permanently by hordes of camera-wielding tourists admiring Madrid's furry pin-up, a feature that adds a level of charm to the city that is perhaps otherwise lacking in much of its gritty, rather polluted, layout of frenetic streets and plazas.

As a freer alternative to joining the crowds in the Puerta del Sol to ogle *El Oso y El Madroño,* I picked up a hire bike half-way along the traffic-choked Gran Via. After a couple of near misses with buses on Plaza de España, I began my exploration of the more verdant areas of Madrid to the west of the centre in Casa de Campo. Overwhelming in scale for an urban park at nearly seven square miles of open country, Casa de Campo (country house) was originally laid out as a royal hunting estate. The giant space is now multi-functional, containing a lake which I cycled around, a 'teleférico' cable car that I cycled under, the city's zoo which I cycled past and a thriving outdoor sex industry that operates at full tilt in the middle of the day, which I pedalled hurriedly through. The latter of Casa de Campo's wide range of facilities interested me for an extraordinary piece of liberal thinking I read about on the part of the Madrid police. Besieged by complaints from certain *Madrileños* about the revealing outfits on display in the shadier corners of the park often befitting of some racy scene in a Pedro Almodóvar movie, the Madrid police department flatly refused to intervene. Not wanting to undermine the earnings potential of the girls (and indeed of the boys-dressed-as-girls) the police argued that the skimpy clothing was an essential requirement of the job. Good for them, but for just a moment I did wonder whether in this particular case there might be another motivation for their leniency, besides the welfare of the girls. Just a thought...

Both Casa de Campo and Buen Retiro Park were laid out on prime central Madrid real estate, and in both cases were annexed for the relaxation purposes of the Spanish monarchy. So in a green, eco-argument that could be used against Republicanism, Spain's retention of its monarchy has helped ensure the continued immunity of these great parks from any money-grubbing development schemes. Nevertheless, there was little that the monarchy could do about Casa de Campo's bloody three-year Civil War episode. In an exhaustive effort to resist the Nationalist offensive on Madrid – led from the vanquished city of Seville by 20,000 troops aided by Franco's German and Italian friends – Casa de Campo was used by Republican fighters as the scenic frontline of the Siege of Madrid. Although the Republican cause was bolstered by the arrival of an International Brigade of 2,000 comrades who marched to Casa de Campo along the Gran Vía on November 8th 1936, their efforts to enforce the anti-fascist rallying cry of ¡No pasarán! – 'they will not pass!' – eventually came to naught. Despite repelling Franco's superior Nationalist forces for nearly three years, Madrid finally fell in March 1939.

Back in the present, I left Casa de Campo to make the white-knuckle ride I had been relishing the prospect of (honestly) along the Gran Vía to the Buen Retiro entrance at Puerta de Alcalá. Unlike its bigger sister Casa de Campo, the Buen Retiro (pleasant retreat) feels far more like an accessible public park, albeit a spectacularly grand one. Rather more than a space to merely take a stroll, feed the ducks or walk the dog, the tree-lined avenues of Buen Retiro are peppered with sculptures, monuments, fountains, small galleries and the remains of a royal palace. Although set out by Phillip IV in the 1620s as a place of recreation and his second home, in the nineteenth-century the sacred green space was handed over to *Madrileños* to enjoy as a public facility. The park is also of course a haven for cyclists, and a short pedal from the northern entrance brought me to the striking feature of the Buen Retiro lake, a little boating paradise dominated by the huge monument to Alfonso XII – an iconic Madrid landmark consisting of a semi-circular colonnade mounted by the king on horseback. As I cycled away from the lake the rather stunning Palacio de Cristal came into glistening view, reminding me that if there was one building lost to Britain that given the option I would bring back, it would be London's Crystal Palace. There are schemes currently doing the planning rounds to do just that, but in the meantime I was more than happy to make do with Madrid's very own crystal equivalent, albeit on a far smaller scale. Modelled on both London's ill-fated cathedral of glass and the palm house at Kew Gardens, Madrid's Palacio de Cristal and adjoining pond were built for the 1887 Phillipine Islands Exhibition by Ricardo Velázquez Bosco. Like its Hyde Park prototype, the Palacio de Crystal was designed with an eye on easy removal to an alternative site should the need arise. Given that London's Crystal Palace burnt to the ground in 1936 at its new location in Sydenham after an ill-judged move from Hyde Park, *Madrileños* might prefer that the Buen Retiro management leave their own palace of crystal well alone.

As for me, I could hardly imagine a more relaxing spot at the heart of a heaving metropolis than the interior of the Buen Retiro glass house. From a collection of rocking chairs placed randomly around the wide and airy space, I selected a pitch under the crowning glory of the building's cupola where I sat for a while to consider my lot, shielding my eyes from shafts of sunlight streaming through the glass panels like lasers. In an utterly charming touch, each chair had a book attached to its arm by a small chain. My good fortune was to find on mine a copy of *Azul* (Blue), written in 1888 by twenty-one year old Rubén Darío, the Nicaraguan poet whose works inspired the late nineteenth-century Spanish-American literary movement, *Modernismo*. In his forward, the young writer describes his colour of choice – blue, naturally – as the colour of his dreams, the colour of art, the colour of the ocean and ultimately the colour of '*la formación espritual de mi primavera*' – 'the spiritual formation of my spring'. After half-an-hour in the calm of that sunlit palatial space and feeling, well frankly somewhere up in the clouds from the sentiments of *Azul,* I left the Palacio de Cristal and cycled away from the park to return my *biciMAD* to a bike station just off the Gran Vía.

There's nothing quite like a bit of variety in life. And to prove just that, after abandoning my hired bike I walked along the rubbish-strewn Calle de Valverde to experience, in the short distance from Buen Retiro, a total transformation. Whereas only minutes earlier I had been reclining on a rocking chair absorbed in the dreamy words of a young poet, here I was now immersed in the grubby, entertainingly ridiculous, anything-goes back streets of Chueca, the heart of Madrid's alternative bar scene and famed nightlife – *la marcha*. What a pity it was still only the middle of the afternoon. But Chueca is never dull at any hour, so in anticipation of things warming up as the day progressed I sat outside a café facing the barrio's main square, the rough-and-tumble Plaza Chueca, soon wishing I hadn't bothered to pay so business-savvy a price for my drink. From where I sat I enjoyed a fine view of the great open-air beano building up a head of steam in the plaza – a mixed gathering of *Madrileños* taking a rest from their urban dog-walking, LGBT couples or groups of friends working up a drinking pace for the evening ahead, and curious tourists happy to dip in briefly to Chueca's boozy eclectic charms. Those with any sense had found perches on pavements and street furniture to drink carry-outs bought from the nearby *Dia* supermarket. As for me, I had been nursing my beer through an hour of crowd watching when I was approached by a forty-something English woman called Kate. She was looking for donations towards a charity biking pilgrimage she was planning across northern Spain to Santiago de Compostela – the legendary *El Camino de Santiago*. After I had donated to her cause, Kate and I swapped mutually compatible 'nine-to-five escape' stories before parting with a vow to both complete the ride to Santiago before the year was out (a promise I would have fulfilled had it not been for the bike I hired for the purpose giving up the ghost on the outskirts of León, a city some 300 kilometres short of the finish line in Santiago). For the record, my 'pilgrimage' was completed by train – something that eventually must be put right.

Once the glower of the waitress eager for another order became too much to bear, I left my terrace table to wander idly through Chueca's narrow streets of high-spirited nonsense. Straying unintentionally beyond its borders, I soon found myself back at Puerta del Sol and in the midst of a huge crowd gathered under the *Tío Pepe* sign – a crowd so dense to be reminiscent of VE Day. I soon realised that I had entered the fray of a demonstration led by Spain's rising left-wing anti-austerity party *Podemos* (meaning 'we can' – now that the party has made electoral advances in Spain, time will tell if indeed it can), that judging by the heavy police presence looked like it might soon get a little feisty. I pushed my way through the crowds away from the square, past the now engulfed statue of *El Oso y El Madroño,* and made my way along Calle del Príncipe, a fortuitous choice that led me to a smart area imaginatively named Barrio de las Letras. I had reached Madrid's literary quarter. To feel the literary vibe, I stood for a while on Calle Cervantes looking up at an inscription on the façade of an elegant apartment block that reads, '*Here lived and died Miguel de Cervantes Saavedra, whose genius the world admires*'. In 1605, the first print run of the Cervantes classic about his 'Ingenious Gentleman', *Don Quijote de la Mancha,* was also produced nearby at a printing house on Calle Atocha. Some 400 years after his death, fragments of Cervantes' remains were discovered in a Madrid convent in 2015, leading to a formal, very high profile re-burial. However, in an unhappy irony, literary precision has been found wanting. In an error that may have landed the stone engraver responsible in hot water, the vowels *i* and *e* were confused in the title of Cervantes' final novel, *Los trabajos de Persiles y Sigismunds,* a quotation from which marks his tombstone. The author of the 'Ingenious Gentleman' story may not have been best pleased.

Cervantes was in fact just one of many literary lumi-
naries who made this area their home during a prolific
period of Spain's scholastic history spanning much of
the sixteenth and seventeenth-centuries. This high-brow,
so-called *siglo de oro* – golden age – saw an abundance
of talent move into the Barrio de Letras, including Luis
de Góngora, Francisco de Quevedo and Lope de Vega.
Nowadays, the area is an attractive mishmash of literary tributes, eclectic stores of all varieties, über trendy
bars and cool student hang-outs. With no effort at all
I found just what I was looking for in the barrio –
namely good music and a buzzy atmosphere – in the
Cuban-themed Bar El Hecho on Calle Huertas, which
caught my eye for its improvised art installation of an
old bicycle taking up virtually an entire wall. I ordered
a Mojito and as I chewed on the sprig of mint dunked
in the intoxicating mix, mused that had it not been for
the eminently European bar prices and the tempting
menu, I could have been hanging out once more in the
back streets of old Havana.

Having settled nicely into casa-Raúl (although I had
barely seen my host – I sensed he was out enjoying his
city's *marcha*), the following morning I joined a multitude heading along Calle Duque de Alba towards La
Latina and its famous Sunday morning flea market,
El Rastro. Dating from the fifteenth-century, El Rastro
– meaning 'the trail' – is the most popular flea market
in Madrid, and therefore quite possibly in the whole of
Spain. This 'Portobello Road in the sun' has a pretty
bloody history itself, but not for once because of war.
The market's name is a neat derivation from the trails
of blood left by the bodies of cattle as their carcasses,
fresh from slaughter at a nearby abattoir, were dragged

through the streets for skinning and treating at local tanneries. I arrived at the market just before eleven planning to spend a couple of pleasant hours digging around its countless stalls of clothing, antiques, books, CDs, vinyl and assorted trinkets. This proved a vain hope, even though I followed the exact walking route through the market recommended by Raúl, which took me through the narrow La Latina streets from Plaza de Cascorro to Puerta de Toledo. So dense was the crowd, outnumbering anything I had seen even at Puerta del Sol, not only was it impossible to get near enough to any of the stalls to buy anything, it was a feat just to see beyond the swarm of bodies what was actually for sale on any of them. I hadn't the patience to wait for the crowd to thin out, so settled instead for an indulgence of that morning-after-the-night-before Madrid staple, *churros y chocolate* – a sumptuous combination of deep-fried pastry (worked into the shape of a Cumberland sausage) dipped in thick dark chocolate, a deliverance from food heaven so rewarding as to be reason alone for booking a city break in Madrid. I chewed and slurped my way through this sugary pleasure in the wonderfully rowdy Chocolatería Muñoz, wondering if by some nutritional miracle we might one day be advised to count this cholesterol-packed paradise as one of our five-a-day. As I sat contemplating the risks to my health and waist measurement of a second helping, a street organist piped up with an up-beat rendition of the Madrid classic, *The Chotis* – a jaunty country dance tune with Scottish and French roots that had the entire café terrace foot-tapping along in the morning sun. *I Love Madrid* screamed the logo of the tight t-shirt worn by a large lady who swayed past my table in time with the music. By the looks of things, she looked like she might have put away the odd helping of *churros y chocolate* herself in her time. As for loving Madrid, I knew exactly how the lady felt.

I got away with the *churros y chocolate* without the immediate need of defibrillation, so picked my way through the Rastro crowds back towards Lavapiés and the next destination on my Madrid bucket-list, the Museo Reina Sofía. I was headed there to pick up the Civil War theme I had left behind in Barcelona a couple of weeks earlier by visiting Picasso's *Guernica*. The iconic mural hanging proudly in Madrid was Picasso's dismayed response to Hitler's and Mussolini's deadly bombing raid carried out on the small Basque town of Guernica on 26th April 1937. In one respect, the bombing of Guernica was an artistic deliverance for Picasso. At the beginning of 1937 he had agreed to paint a mural as the centrepiece of the Spanish Pavilion at the World's Fair in Paris. Struggling for inspiration and ideas following problems in his personal life, the bombing of the small Basque town gave Picasso the artistic impetus to produce a strong anti-fascist work. Three months after the indiscriminate attack that killed around 1,600 and injured another 900 hopelessly exposed and defenceless people, Picasso delivered his finished article to the Paris Exposition. Painted in black, white and grey, *Guernica* provides a high-profile, much-vaunted example of how pre-Second World War horrors can often seem magnified when presented in mono-chrome. Yet when it was finally unveiled, Picasso's masterpiece unleashed a fierce storm of criticism. Predictably, much of the ire came from German critics, one of whom dismissed *Guernica* as 'the work of a madman', adding insult to his injurious review by describing it as 'a hodgepodge of body parts that any four-year could have painted'. Way too harsh, surely. As I stood in a silent line of similarly awestruck visitors trying to make sense of Picasso's jumble of tortured figures splayed under an explosion of a symbolic light bulb, I settled for the uncomplicated analysis that the chaos, confusion and ambiguity of the painting was ultimately its entire point – an ambiguity that *forces* the viewer to consider the futility of war and its violent impact on the innocent. Even the Soviets – who naturally sided with the Republicans during the Spanish Civil War (although not unequivocally) – gave *Guernica* a cool reception, venturing that a more realist work would have had more impact on anti-fascist public opinion. Responding to criticism of *Guernica* and requests to demystify the painting's abstract imagery, a clearly irked Picasso opined, '...*it isn't up to the painter to define the symbols. Otherwise it would be better if he wrote them out in so many words! The public who look at the picture must interpret the symbols as they understand them*'. So I took his advice and studied the stylised image of a bull standing over a woman grieving for the dead child in her arms, and then at the painting's central image of a horse falling in agony from a spear thrown clean through its torso, the animal's torn innards seen through a gaping hole in its side. Picasso may have given us permission to interpret his mural as we wish, yet as an anti-war symbol and emblem of Spain's post-Franco democratic recovery, *Guernica* could hardly be clearer.

Once the Civil War was over, Picasso intended his masterpiece to be exhibited in Spain, but only on the proviso that liberty and democracy had not only been restored to his native country, but was seen to be flourishing. In the immediate aftermath of the war it was clear that this wasn't about to happen in Spain any time soon. Instead *Guernica* went on tour, serving the important purpose of bringing to the attention of the world some of the suffering the Civil War had inflicted on civilians. Following its worldwide odyssey, the painting finally came to rest in a temporary home at New York's Museum of Modern Art. That *Guernica* didn't make its way to Spain until as late as 1981, tells us far more about the oppressive state of Picasso's homeland than the demand of the Spanish people for possession of their celebrity painting. But when *Guernica* did at last go on show in Madrid, disappointingly for all those champing at the bit to see it, the painting was placed behind a bomb and bullet-proof glass screen at the Casón del Buen Retiro, an annexe of the Museo del Prado. In 1992 *Guernica* was finally granted the prominence its creator intended when it was moved to its permanent, purpose-built home where I viewed it at the Museo Reina Sofia. In an ironic and sad twist to the tale, unlike his masterpiece Picasso himself never once returned to Spain after the Civil War, choosing instead to live out his life in the South of France where he died in April 1973, aged 91.

I have no idea whether Picasso had even a passing interest in the 'beautiful game'. Nevertheless, as a sporting symbol of the intense rivalry between Spain's two biggest cities, the Real Madrid versus Barcelona clash remains highly charged. And it was my good luck to be in Madrid as Lionel Messi and his El Barça teammates rolled into town to do battle in the latest instalment of *El Clásico* at Real's Santiago Bernabéu stadium. Buying a match ticket from a tout for a price that wouldn't jeopardise my entire financial future was impossible, so I figured that watching the clash of the Spanish titans in a bar full of partisan fans was the next best thing. From the pick of literally thousands of bars (there are so many bars in Madrid that the local authority has been forced to impose restrictions on the opening of new ones), I opted for a buzzing hostelry on Plaza del Ángel which boasted a TV screen as wide as the wall it was hanging from, and just enough room left inside it to push past the English beer bellies squeezed into Arsenal and Chelsea shirts to get to the bar for a drink. Unsurprisingly, most people in the bar for the early evening kick-off were supporting Madrid, so I kept my preference for a Barcelona victory quiet – an effort challenged as early as the fourth minute of the game as Barça's great Brazilian hope, Neymar, put the Catalans ahead. Judging by the groans around me, the assist for the goal from the universally unpopular Luis Suárez (in his first competitive action for Barça since his dental indiscretions at the World Cup finals) really rubbed salt into the Madrid wound. However, I can report that the air of gloom hanging over proceedings was lifted, in equal measure by the abundant on-tap *jarras* of Mahou, and then by the home team's rousing comeback. On thirty-five minutes Cristiano Ronaldo, irrepressible and petulant throughout, equalised from the penalty spot. Then, in a tumultuous second half that had the bar in a joyful and drunken uproar, goals from Pepe and Benzema completed the turnaround and secured an emphatic 3-1 victory for General Franco's old favourites – yet more

Spanish-inflicted grief for the region of Catalonia. So that was the result of this latest *El Clásico*, battled out by twenty-two men in shirts of white, red and blue chasing a latex rubber ball around a wide field of grass.

But what had I made of my own, personal *El Clásico*? My time in Barcelona and Madrid had been, to use the football vernacular, a game of two halves – the first kicking-off in rebellious Catalonia, the second in Madrid at the seat of the Spanish government and home of the Royal Family and Iberian Establishment. For the record, the outcome of this latest leg of my odyssey, played out in Spain's two greatest cities as part of my fast-evolving, out-of-office plan for life, was a hugely entertaining high-scoring draw, offering the very high likelihood of an extended period of extra time. And as far as that was concerned, the clock had already started to tick.

Straw parasol pointing the 'Blue Sky' way

*'Twenty years from now you'll be more disappointed with
the things you didn't do than the ones you did do. So sail
away from the safe harbour...explore, dream, discover...'*

Mark Twain.

AFTERWORD

Blue Sky Thinking

And that, for now at least, was that. Looking back over
the events of the past months, it may not be necessary to
select one location or single moment from my post-
work travels that presented me with, in the starkest
relief, the absolute antithesis of that drab meeting room
where this story began. Any one of those intoxicating,
inspiring afternoons spent grappling with the Spanish
language in the company of new friends on sunny terraces would fit the bill, as would any number of laid-
back hours on Caribbean beaches, or the thrill of every
kilometre of track covered on continental rail journeys.
Or how about simply exploring Berlin's verdant city
parks on two wheels, entertained by the Teutonic passion
for lunchtime nudity? And for virtually any experience
that came my way in Havana, Nice, Naples or Sarajevo,
then take your pick. But I am writing this in Madrid, so
for the sake of choosing a moment and place of near-
perfect resonance I will settle on that precious afternoon

a few days earlier in the city's El Parque del Buen Retiro, where I had sat on a gently rocking armchair savouring the warmth of shafts of sunlight piercing the glass cupola of the Palacio de Cristal, inspired by youthful, uplifting verse. On this final day in the Spanish capital, I returned to that serene space to mark no less than 'the end of a beginning', where this opening phase of my excited dash from the rhythm and obedience of the workplace faded to a perfect close. If anywhere, this was perhaps the place where I felt my transition from reluctant office politician to man of suitcase and dirty laundry to be complete.

It all began under a deluge of corporate claptrap in an airless meeting room on that long-gone 'Transformational Tuesday'. It couldn't be so neat that my last day in Madrid happened to fall on the second day of the conventional working week. Yet as I reviewed the months of travel and the pursuit of passions that had passed by since, my thoughts swivelled back to the dull monotony of that team meeting agenda fifty-odd Tuesdays before. I had entered that room with its low ceiling of expectation, a little short on inspiration. An hour or so later I walked out of there emboldened, not by the empty assertions of the team discussion, but by the realisation that unless I acted on my instincts I could look forward to many more Tuesdays ploughing the same tired furrow. With my refresh button firmly hit, and risk-aversion cast decisively aside, I emerged into a new and fresher reality of post-work reinvention.

So after indulging in the heated ambience of Spain, the vibrant communist relic of Cuba, self-confident, nature-loving Germany, super-cool-and-don't-we-know-it Italy, the monied (and at times sullied) French Riviera and the war-recovering Balkans, what have I learnt? And unstrapped from the faux-straitjacket of my old workplace routines, how have I progressed? In the end, perhaps it doesn't matter a great deal precisely where geographically my post-work travels have so far taken me, or even very much what I did when I got there. The most important thing as I embraced my freedom and moved from place to place at will, was the invigorating sense that I had finally shaken the tiresome nine-to-five monkey from my back. This release had enabled me to do *something else* with my time, at my own behest, while in the process proving to myself, and who knows to others too, that it can be done without your own world – or indeed the world around you – grinding to a halt. Consider Fatboy Slim's *Eat, Sleep, Rave, Repeat – Eat, Sleep, Rave, Repeat* (for *Rave* read *Work*) and there in the 'master' of the big beat's incessant, repetitive rhythm, you will find the soundtrack for my own take on the corporate world: a scratchy needle stuck in a dusty old groove, the mood music of predictable, agenda-driven living. Yet how different – and how much lighter – I felt once I had added to the mix my own melody, verse and rousing chorus.

That's not to say that from the moment I put an end to my salaried security with a four-line letter of resignation, I was a wholly changed man. I wasn't. That was never intended as part of the plan. Nor can I claim to have walked away from the workplace without feeling at least some trepidation in anticipation of the P45 winging its certain way to my door. Nevertheless, the new me felt a lot more like the *real* me, at last freed from the cellophane-wrap conventions and hierarchies so typical of 'the office' and its limitations of plodding, formulaic thinking. By and large, mood-compatibility had triumphed. And how energising it was to have bumped into so many like-minded souls as my journey unfolded: those impulsive, open-armed Spaniards with their insatiable appetites for conversation and late nights, the admirably uncomplaining Cubans (in a country where there is much about which to complain), intrepid Argentinians on continental trains, errant Americans enjoying a second flush of youth in the energising environs of Granada or Berlin, voluminous Italians in any sunlit corner of their blessed country, the embattled, hospitable Bosnians, and more. In fact, with barely an exception (and the exceptions I quickly forgot about), my journey had been a lesson in some of the more uplifting aspects of human nature. Each one of those great and good folk I had met in railway carriages, bars and on sultry terraces – enthusiastically and in their own fascinating ways – were all joined with me in attempting to buck the nine-to-five trend. Alone in my quest, I most certainly was not.

To rewind for a moment, many years before, in a somewhat surprising (albeit, you might guess, short-lived) incarnation as office keen-bean, my drive to work took me past the factory of a best-selling producer of thickly-sliced, doughy white bread. Ever punctual, at some time between 8.45 and 8.50am each day I would look to my left from my place in the slow-moving queue towards the factory windows, through which I was privy to the curiously captivating sight of lines of freshly-baked loaves moving soldier-like along a con-veyor belt to meet their non-negotiable end in a plastic air-tight packet. You might wonder – because I do wonder myself – why the fate of that uniformly-sliced, carb-laden product should spring to mind as I kicked-back amid the soothing greenery of Madrid. The answer lies in the reminder it serves of the perils of destiny-without-control. And following my long period of disquiet when I operated amid the interminable agendas and invasive appraisal systems of 'office-land', I had finally managed, if nothing else, to wrench back my own life's control. A slice of that pre-destined bread, ultimately I could never have been...

Back to my post-work odyssey, I had one final physical journey to make to complete its opening phase – an overnight sleeper berth on a train from Madrid to London St Pancras, taking me back through Barcelona and northern Spain, across the Pyrenees and then on through central France and Paris to Blighty. A perfect setting, then, for any intrigue that may come my way, and plenty of time to dig out a back-of-an-envelope on which to plot a new path, further away still from the yawning inertia of office politics. I couldn't say at that moment exactly where that path would take me: to the exotic climes of south-east Asia perhaps, a prolonged spell living the Parisian dream in a central arrondissement, making an extended west-to-east traverse of the Continent by rail, or a stint combining work with adventure teaching English in the sun. Anything now seemed possible, with most things more than probable – my self-driven agenda for free-spirited living from which there could be no turning back.

For now, though, I was content in those final few hours in Madrid. As I looked up through the soaring roof of that mesmerising *Madrileño* Palace of Glass, shielding my eyes once more from the fading rays of the late afternoon sun, I wondered momentarily about the place where I had once heard some well-meaning soul utter that catchy corporate cliché, '*Blue Sky Thinking*'. Now, at long last, I had found its true meaning.

Lightning Source UK Ltd.
Milton Keynes UK
UKOW02f1900130416

272198UK00003B/113/P